THEME 1

Business objectives and the business environment

THEME 2

Marketing

Contents

THEME 5

People in organisations

INTRODUCTION

This book aims to:

- encourage you to view business from the points of view of consumers, shareholders, employees and managers

- allow you to develop knowledge and understanding of key business activities and the dynamics of business

- develop your ability to apply business terms, ideas and methods to a wide range of contexts and to recognise the strengths and limitations of the ideas and methods used

- encourage you to analyse business problems and cases, distinguish between fact and opinion, and make informed judgements and conclusions

- provide you with business contexts which allow you to develop the key skills of communication, application of number and information and communication technology.

The content of the book is divided into five themes:

THEME 1
Business objectives and the business environment

deals with the nature of business activity and the stakeholders involved in it, government influence over business and the links between business and the community and the world.

THEME 2
Marketing

looks at the way businesses market their products, from the research and planning they carry out to the marketing mix used in selling a product.

THEME 3
Production

focuses upon the production process: how production is organised and resourced, the way businesses grow, and how production is made more efficient, especially through the use of new technology.

THEME 4
Accounting and finance

examines the way businesses are financed and the accounting and financial records that they keep. It looks at how a business measures its success, and what happens when a business fails.

THEME 5
People in organisations

concentrates on the Human Resource side of business: how the workforce is recruited, trained and organised, what good communication involves, the way the workforce is rewarded and the way changes are negotiated, and how work itself is changing with the development of the "networked" workplace.

The tasks provide opportunities for you to gain first hand experience of a business situation, take part in a practical activity and respond to some real business data. They encourage you to research other resources from the real world of business. The questions set will develop your skills in applying ideas and methods, analysing and interpreting data and making conclusions.

The same skills will be developed in the end of unit assessment, but these also encourage you to pull together or "synthesise" ideas from across the unit and sometimes from other units. They are based on real, up to date business case studies.

The authors would like to thank all the staff at Pearson Education for their support and "endurance" in working with us on this book.

I would like to dedicate this book to Georgina who will always be with me.

Ian Chambers, Stockport, May 2001

THEME 1

Business objectives and the business environment

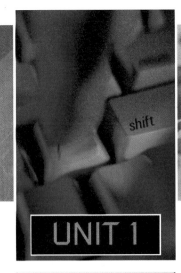

What is business?

This unit is about why business exists, the different types of business activity and how businesses are divided into sectors.

At the end of the unit, students should be able to:

- understand why businesses exist
- explain the difference between needs and wants
- explain the concept of opportunity cost using relevant examples
- explain and give examples of goods and services
- understand the sectors that make up business activity and describe recent trends in these sectors in the UK
- define and give examples of the factors of production
- describe the role of the private, public and voluntary sectors in the UK.

Satisfying needs and wants

We all have needs and wants. Ask people around you 'What would you like to have?' and you will get a range of answers from 'the next meal' to 'a trip to Disneyland'. This is because our needs and wants depend on what we already have and what we would like in the future. Some people may see their needs as being food, shelter and drink. Others, who already have their basic needs met, may want luxury items such as cars, holidays and meals out. This example helps to show the difference between a need and a want. A need is for basic goods and services such as food and drink, a want is for a non-essential item such as a DVD player or microwave.

Businesses exist to meet these needs and wants by producing goods and services. They will be able to sell the good or service to a person or firm only if they have the right product at the right price. This has introduced the idea of money. We all have wants and needs but we have to recognise that we cannot always have what we want or need because our income may not be enough to pay for it. This leads us to make choices which will be covered in more detail in the next section.

TASK 1

In small groups, use newspapers and magazine cuttings to create a poster that explains what business is/does. Present your findings to the class.

From your presentation you should be able to produce a list of keywords that represent business. (You may wish to compare this list to the subject specifications you are going to be studying.)

Opportunity cost

Unless you are very lucky or very undemanding, you will not be able to have all the goods and services you would like. We could all produce a long list of needs and wants, but the resources needed to buy these items are limited. Because we cannot have everything we might need or want we are forced to make a choice.

In the same way that individuals are forced to make choices due to scarce resources, businesses and governments also have to make decisions. A business, for example, may wish to recruit skilled staff but find that there is a shortage of people trained to do the work it requires. The business has then to decide whether or not to employ the staff, and whether it can offer high salaries to attract the right staff.

Government also has to make decisions. For example, the government has a budget that it can spend each year, that is, the money it raises through taxation (see Unit 7). This may be a limited budget and the government may have to decide where to spend that money and what may have to be cut.

Example 1
Mr and Mrs Jones have saved £1,000 since Christmas. They hoped to use the money to go on holiday but the roof of their house has now started to leak. They cannot afford both to go on holiday and to repair the roof … a choice has to be made.

Example 2
A builders' firm has gradually expanded its order books over the last few years and the yard can no longer take the amount of stock that it needs to hold. The firm needs to expand the yard but the land surrounding it is all taken up by houses and offices … a choice has to be made.

Example 3
The local council has £55 million to spend on education and roads. It needs to build a new secondary school and a motorway link to attract new business but cannot afford to do both … a choice has to be made.

You will have seen in the above examples that individuals, businesses and government cannot satisfy all their wants and needs, They have to make choices. In order to have the thing that they want most, they have to give something else up. This is known by economists as **opportunity cost** and is clearly shown by the following example.

Sue has £10 pocket money every week which her parents give her on a Monday morning. On Friday at school her friends discuss going to the cinema on Friday night and going ice skating on Saturday, both of which Sue wants to do. When she gets home Sue realises that she has only £3.50 of her pocket money left. She does not like to borrow money as she has learned that it only has to be paid back the next week. She rings her friends and decides to go to the cinema as the film finishes that week.

Sue's wants are to go to the cinema and ice skating, the limiting factor is money and the choice is to go to the cinema as this is what she wants most. The opportunity cost of her choice is that she will not go ice skating, a lost customer to the owner of the ice rink.

Classification of goods and services

The way in which businesses meet needs and wants is to produce goods and services. By satisfying our wants, we are consuming the goods and services. (This does not mean consumption in the way that you may have previously understood – it means the satisfying of a need or want, e.g. you can consume a car!)

A **good** is a physical object which can be purchased, e.g. flour, a CD system, oil, a computer, etc.

A **service** is a non-physical item that can be purchased, e.g. education, tourism, banking, a concert, etc.

Goods and services are organised into different categories according to certain characteristics that they may have.

Consumer goods and services

These are goods and services that we consume (that satisfy a need or want). They can be either:

- *single use*, e.g. a chocolate bar
- *durable*, e.g. a chair.

Producer goods and services

These are goods and services which allow businesses to produce, that is, make something to satisfy a want. The good or service can again be:

- *single use*, where it is used up in the production process such as a raw material, or
- *durable*, where it is used for a longer period, e.g. a piece of machinery.

Some goods and services are very difficult to put into one particular category as their use may vary, e.g. coffee may be a consumer good when it is used to make a cup of coffee at home but is a producer good if it is used to make a coffee cake in a factory.

TASK 2

Here are pictures of 15 items. Copy the grid below and put each item into the correct category by placing a tick in the appropriate box.

In class, discuss whether people have entered the same item under the same category and also any items that were difficult to classify.

Classification of goods and services						
Item	Good	Service	Consumer	Producer	Single use	Durable
1 Personal CD player						
2 Haircut						
3 Recipe book						
4 Chair						
5 Kettle						
6 Bar of chocolate						
7 Lorry						
8 Pair of jeans						
9 Nut and bolt						
10 Car						
11 Money						
12 Spade						
13 Personal computer						
14 Pair of trainers						
15 Cash dispenser						

Types of business activity

Businesses produce goods and services to satisfy the wants and needs of consumers. Just as we have been able to classify goods and services we are also able to classify the different types of business. One way to do this is to look at what it is that individual businesses are actually producing and at what stage of the production process the activity is taking place. With this in mind, a business may fall into one of three sectors.

The primary sector

The **primary sector** is often seen as the first stage of the production process where raw materials and natural resources are extracted. This may involve extraction from both land and sea and includes mining, fishing and agricultural industries. We have seen recently the importance of ensuring that these resources will be there for future generations to use. The difference between renewable items, e.g. nuclear fuel, and non-renewable items, e.g. coal, has become a vital one. The importance of maintaining renewable items such as food crops has become greater as world population pressures have increased.

The secondary sector

The **secondary sector** is the second stage of the production process where the products of the primary stage are processed and turned into manufactured goods. The items may be a consumer good, e.g. food, TV, or a producer good, e.g. a component, a piece of machinery etc.

The tertiary sector

The **tertiary sector** involves the production of services rather than goods. The services may help the first two stages of production or they may help the public or the state. In this way, three types of service facilities can be described:

- services to industry, e.g. banking, insurance
- services to the public, e.g. hairdressing, leisure facilities
- services to the state, e.g. education, health.

TASK 3

Produce a report for others in your class or group describing the changes in employment over the 16 years from 1984 to 2000. Within your report try to include the following:

a Examples of jobs you would expect to find in each sector (primary, secondary and tertiary).

b Appropriate graphs to show the changes in some of the employment sectors. (You may wish to group the activities together and produce graphs for each of the primary, secondary and tertiary sectors.)

c A description of the changes you have observed from the figures. For example, the percentage employed in the manufacturing sector has fallen drastically from 27% in 1984 to 14% in 2000.

d Any consequences you think this has for the future of the UK economy.

You may wish to word process your report, importing the graphs to illustrate your arguments.

Employees in employment in the UK (%)			
	1984	1994	2000
Agriculture, forestry and fishing	1.6	1.2	1.3
Energy and water supply	2.9	1.5	0.8
Metals, minerals and chemicals	3.8	2.7	3.0
Metal goods, engineering and vehicles	11.6	8.6	2.6
Other manufacturing industry	10.1	8.8	6.6
Construction	4.9	3.7	5.2
Distribution, hotels and catering, repairs	20.0	21.8	23.5
Transport and communications	6.3	5.7	6.1
Banking, finance, insurance etc.	9.3	12.6	19.6
Public admin and other services	29.6	33.4	31.0

(Source: Department for Education and Employment)

The factors of production

In order for businesses to produce goods and services they need the basic tools of production. These are known as the **factors of production** and are land, labour, capital and enterprise.

Land: tree felling on forestry commission land in Scotland

Land is defined as all the natural resources and therefore includes not only the land that we stand on, grow crops on and build upon but also fisheries, mines and forests. The payment given to the owners of land is rent.

Labour includes not only the physical effort that we may put into production but also the mental effort. The payment for labour is a wage/salary.

Non-manual labour

An industrial machine: capital

Capital is the manufactured resource that is used in the production process to make goods and services for the future. Capital is not wanted for itself but for what it can go on to produce. The payment to capital is interest.

Enterprise is similar to labour but it is separated because enterprise is the unique ability that certain people have to organise the factors of production to produce goods and services and make a profit or loss.

Richard Branson: entrepreneur

Private, public and voluntary sectors

We have already looked at one way of categorising business – according to the stage of production (primary, secondary or tertiary). Another way is to look at the sector of the economy that the business is in.

Britain is a **mixed economy**. That means that we have some resources that are owned by the state and some that are owned by private individuals. We can therefore categorise business as being part of either the public or private sector.

The **public sector** is the part of the economy that is owned by the state. It includes local government services, the National Health Service, public corporations like the BBC and quangos (quasi autonomous non-governmental organisations). The size of the public sector has been drastically reduced since 1979. This will be covered in more detail in Unit 4.

The **private sector** is the part of the economy that is owned and controlled by private individuals and firms. It includes a whole range of businesses from large to small, e.g. Virgin trains, the local corner shop. The main categories of business in the private sector are sole traders, partnerships and limited companies. It now includes industries that were previously in the public sector but have been privatised, e.g. Powergen, Centrica. Private sector business will be covered in more detail in Units 4 and 5.

Voluntary organisations are part of the private sector but they are unusual in that they do not aim to make profit. They are often ignored when looking at business activities but when you consider that they include charities, playgroups, care for elderly people, clubs, etc. you will see how important they are.

UNIT 2

Business stakeholders

The stakeholders in business

A **stakeholder** is an individual or group who affects and is affected by business activity. There are a great many stakeholders in a business and each may have different reasons for being involved. The relationships between the different stakeholders can be complex, and conflicts can arise. At other times, their roles can be totally separate. The main stakeholders in a business are:

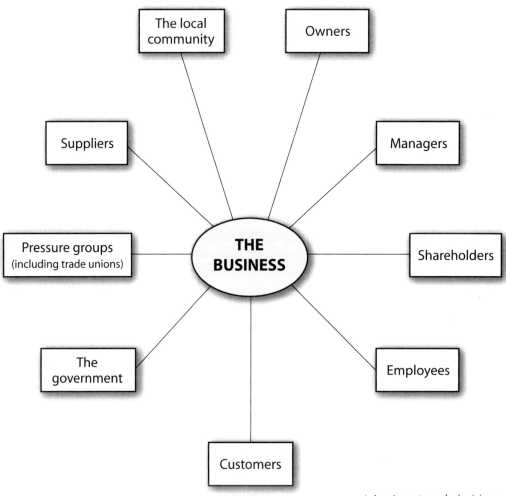

A business's stakeholders

Owners and managers

An **owner** is someone who has contributed his or her own money to developing a business and because of this has a right to participate in decision making.

A **manager** is someone who makes decisions about the way in which a business operates.

A sole trader is the only owner of a business. He or she is also the manager since one of the reasons for starting up a business is to be able to make his or her own decisions. Any business set up by a sole trader is also usually a small one. It may employ workers but they are unlikely to include a manager.

Belinda is a sole trader. She has set up a business called Stepping Out which runs aerobics classes. She employs six part-time instructors who take the classes in different places. Belinda is an owner and a manager.

A partnership has more than one owner. Most often the partners jointly fund and manage the business. It is possible, however, for a partnership to employ a manager. For example, a group of doctors in partnership may employ a practice manager while they concentrate on dealing with patients.

In a private limited company, the owners are those who hold shares. Since only employees, family and friends can hold shares, most shareholdings are likely to be substantial and the controlling interest is likely to be held by the family. Some of the shareholders may or may not be managers. It is usual in a private limited company for some of the family to hold managerial positions.

Similarly, in public limited companies, the owners are the **shareholders**. However, since in public limited companies shares can be sold to members of the public and to institutions such as other companies, owners who have substantial amounts of shares are not likely to be managers. There are also likely to be many owners in public limited companies. The owners employ managers to make decisions about the running of the company on their behalf although the owners can make important decisions at the Annual General Meeting if they choose to attend.

Heaton House is a hotel owned by the Sutcliffe family. It is a private limited company. There are currently two generations of Sutcliffes involved in owning and running the business. Mrs Sutcliffe senior owns 40 per cent of the shares. She is an owner and helps to make important decisions but she does not work for the company. Mrs Sutcliffe's two daughters, Susan and Nancy, both own 20 per cent of the shares. Susan is employed as the managing director of Heaton House whereas Nancy is a part-time receptionist. Susan is therefore an owner and a manager as well as an employee. Nancy is an owner and an employee.

Shareholders

Only companies have shareholders. In private limited companies, shareholders are restricted to members of the family, friends and employees so shareholders can also be employees. In public limited companies, since shares can be bought through the Stock Exchange, shareholders can include the general public and corporate investors, that is, other public limited companies. Shares can be bought on issue, that is when a company is first launched on the Stock Exchange, and second hand. Shares are also used to reward employees. In some companies, employees are allowed to buy shares at preferential rates while in others they may be given the shares as an incentive. Encouraging employees to hold shares in a company is likely to establish a greater sense of responsibility towards the company. Owning shares in the company, however, does not give employees the right to interfere in the decisions which the managers make, except via the Annual General Meeting.

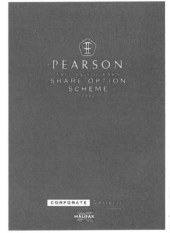

PEARSON
SAVE AS YOU EARN
SHARE OPTION
SCHEME
1992

CORPORATE BUSINESS
HALIFAX

Invitation to Pearson employees to buy shares

Employees

Employees are those who are paid to carry out a specific job of work for a business. Most businesses have employees. Being a sole trader does not mean the owner cannot employ workers. Some employees are also managers, particularly in private and public limited companies where managers are employed to carry out the task of day-to-day management.

Employees perform the basic tasks of the business including production and delivery. In recent years, they have also been encouraged to become involved in decision making and therefore they can play a significant role in any business.

Customers

Without **customers**, the business would not survive. Their purchases provide the revenue that generates the cash flow. Businesses must ensure that they are providing goods and services that meet their customers' needs and in the long run gain their loyalty.

The government

The government can be seen as a stakeholder for a variety of reasons. Firstly, the government collects taxes from business. These can include VAT, corporation tax and business rates. Secondly, businesses are affected by economic policy. Decisions about the interest rate, the euro and grants to relocate all have an impact on business. Thirdly, the government creates legislation that businesses have to take account of. Legislation can include anything from hiring and firing staff through to the level of pollution emitted during the production process.

The Houses of Parliament – where new laws are created

Pressure groups

Pressure groups may take a particular interest in the activities of certain companies. Where they successfully campaign against a company, their actions may cause policy change, e.g. public reaction to the food manufacturer Heinz announcing that it was to stop manufacturing salad cream kept the product on the market.

Suppliers

Businesses need raw materials in order to manufacture and provide their customers with goods and services. The relationship with **suppliers** needs to be a good one and covers prices, delivery dates, quantity and quality of supplies.

A timber yard supplying wood to construction businesses

The local community

Businesses may have contact with the local community for many reasons. The local community is likely to provide the labour force, but businesses may also seek to train staff at local colleges, sponsor local events and provide a social club for employees and their families. Problems usually occur where a business pollutes, causes traffic congestion or closes down, as these actions have adverse effects on the local community.

TASK 1

The AA was founded in 1905 to protect the interest of pioneer motorists and remains a non-profit making mutual benefit organisation, offering a range of products and services. It is a huge business group with 9 million members, more than 12,000 staff and 40 different business activities.

AA patrols attend 4.9 million breakdowns per year and the organisation takes and receives 35 million telephone calls each year.

Source: *The Times 100 Case Studies and Business News,*
MBA Publishing, 1996.

a In a group, identify the different stakeholders in the AA.

b Give one example of where the interests of stakeholders may conflict.

c Why might other stakeholders benefit from there being no shareholders?

Roles and responsibilities

The role of owners and shareholders

In all businesses, the owner's main role is to provide **capital** for the business. The reward which the owner receives for providing the business with capital is profit. Where the capital is provided as shares, for example in private and public limited companies, the part of the profit given to shareholders is called a **dividend**. Sole traders and partners may be able to receive part of the profits as an increased salary or by withdrawing some of the capital.

In sole traders and partnerships, owners are likely to have a role which includes: **strategic management**, that is making important decisions about the future of the business; and **operational management**, that is decisions about what happens on a day-to-day basis.

In private limited companies the owners are likely to maintain close control of the business as most private limited companies are family concerns. In public limited companies, owners or shareholders have the right to attend the Annual General Meeting. This is a meeting held once a year at which the senior managers report on the position of the company and its future prospects. Shareholders are allowed to vote on any decisions taken at this meeting.

The Annual General Meeting of a public limited company

The role of employees and managers

Managers who are employed by the business are paid a salary as a reward for the work which they do. They may also receive other incentives such as company cars, subsidised canteen facilities and private health care.

Other employees will be paid either a wage or a salary for the work that they do. They also may receive incentives such as social facilities and subsidised canteen meals. Employees have a job description which sets out the details of the work which they are required to do.

In a large company, managers are employed at different levels. The managing director is the senior manager and his or her role is concerned with the strategic management of the entire business. A departmental or middle manager may have responsibility including strategic decision making for his or her department. Assistant or line managers have responsibility for operational management, that is, carrying out day-to-day tasks.

The role of customers and suppliers

Customers and suppliers provide the link for production and cash flow.

A business buys raw materials, equipment and semi-processed goods from suppliers in order to sell something on to the customer. During the process, the business will hope to add value. If the supplier is unable to deliver raw materials at the right price, of the right quality or in the right number, the business may find itself unable to satisfy customer needs. Where customers are unhappy with their purchase, or unable to make a purchase because of shortages, they will turn to competitors. Likewise, without customer orders, the business will not need to buy from its supplier.

The responsibilities of owners and shareholders

It has already been explained that owners and shareholders are sometimes the same people. Owners and shareholders often have the same responsibilities. They have a responsibility to:

- their employees
- other shareholders
- the community.

Owners and shareholders have a duty towards their employees in terms of their pay and working conditions. They must ensure that employees are paid a fair rate for the job, that the conditions in which employees are asked to work are adequate and that the business does not engage in any activity which is against the law or which might put their employees at unnecessary risk.

Owners and shareholders have a duty towards themselves and their fellow owners/shareholders where there are some. Most owners/shareholders have objectives for the business. The most usual objective is to make the maximum amount of profit. Large profits mean the business is more likely to share the profits with the shareholders, declaring a large dividend, although most years a business will distribute a proportion of its profits to the shareholders.

Owners and shareholders also have a duty towards the community. They must ensure that the business is legal and that the goods and services offered for sale conform to the requirements of national legislation. This is covered in more detail in Unit 5. Owners and shareholders also have a responsibility to the environment. They should ensure that the business creates as little pollution as possible and that care is taken with regard to the use of scarce resources. The difficulty is that owners and shareholders may prefer to receive a larger dividend than know that the company spends money on protecting the environment.

The responsibilities of managers and employees

Managers are almost always employees and therefore have some responsibilities in common with other workers. All employees have a general responsibility under the *Health and Safety at Work Act 1974* to maintain a healthy and safe working environment. All employees are issued with a contract and they have a responsibility to adhere to the terms of the contract. This includes turning up to work unless prevented by ill health from doing so.

Managers have extra responsibilities over and above those of employees. They are employed by the owners to manage the resources of the business. Managing means using resources to obtain the maximum possible benefit from them. Managers therefore have a duty to motivate the workers so that they contribute their best. They must ensure that waste of any raw materials which the business uses is minimised and that plant and equipment are used to as near full capacity as demand for the business's goods and services requires. Managers are responsible for maintaining and, where possible, improving productivity rates, that is, the amount produced in a given period of time. They are also responsible for selling the final products. Accountants have responsibility for the financial resources of the business. They must set financial targets and monitor spending against those targets.

Managers are responsible not merely for implementing the policies set by the owners but also for advising the owners on how the business should be run and what strategies it should adopt.

Managers are also responsible for ensuring that legislation relating to equal opportunities is upheld in the workplace. The *Sex Discrimination Act 1975* sets out rights for men and women and prevents someone from being discriminated against because of their sex. The *Race Relations Act 1965* makes it illegal to discriminate against someone on the grounds of colour or race.

Woman banker wins £500,000 over sex discrimination case

Breaking the laws against sex and race discrimination can be extremely expensive for companies

The responsibilities of customers and suppliers

Unlike managers, owners, shareholders and employees, customers and suppliers have little responsibility to the business, other than any contract that they may have entered into with the business. Where they have agreed a contract to buy or deliver goods, the contract must be upheld. This may include paying for the goods on time and informing the business if goods are faulty. Outside of the contract, customers and suppliers are free to deal with any business that they feel meets their objectives.

TASK 2

Wickes profits up 20%

Wickes, the UK DIY retail chain which it fought off a hostile bid from Focus Do-it-all two months ago, on Thursday announced half-year results up by 20 per cent on last year.

Pre-tax profits were £13.9 million ($19.81) for the six months to June 30. However, the group's bid defence costs of £6.9 million hit pre-tax profit which was down 42 per cent to £6.57 million against £11.48 million.

In a statement, Bill Grimsey, chief executive said: 'Following the rejection of FDIA's offer, the Wickes team is fully focused on building on the success we have achieved so far. Our performance in the first half confirms that we are on track to meet our expectations for the year and beyond.' Total sales in the first half increased by 7.1 per cent to £308.1 million with like-for-like sales increasing by 3.6 per cent.

Operating profit was £6.4 million compared with £10.55 million while earnings per share were 6.8p against 12.7p. The board has declared an interim dividend of 3p per share.

Source: Adapted from FT.com, *Financial Times*, 3 August 2000.

a What were the responsibilities of the managers of Wickes, at the time of the hostile bid?

b How might Wickes have used the business's other stakeholders to help it fight off the bid?

c What are the rewards for the different stakeholders?

Conflict

In describing the roles and responsibilities of the different groups involved in business, the unit has identified the overlap, e.g. the employee who is also an owner because he or she owns shares in the business. This overlap of roles and responsibilities can cause conflict where the objectives of the groups are different. There may be conflict both within and between groups.

Conflict between groups – DB4 plc

Employee

Oscar Malik works for DB4 plc as an electronic engineer.

Oscar the employee would like to see his salary increased by 10 per cent.

Owner

Oscar Malik has bought shares in DB4 plc.

Oscar the shareholder knows that the company cannot afford to give workers a 10 per cent pay rise.

Owners may disagree about the future direction of the business.

Conflict within groups – FINE FOOD PARTNERSHIP

Alan, Partner

'I think we should expand by opening another sandwich bar in the town centre'

Amy, Partner

'I think we should expand by enlarging and improving our existing sandwich bar'

Where there are many owners there is more likelihood of disagreement. Conflict is particularly likely in private limited companies where small numbers of people own large proportions of the shares. The traditional area of conflict in private limited companies is the family firm which has not moved with the times and owners have two opposing views on how to take the business forward.

Managers may disagree about the role of their particular department in relation to the business as a whole.

Conflict between managers – SURPRISE Ltd

Barbara Murren,
Marketing Manager

'I need about £100,000 within the next three months in order to launch two of our new products on to the Christmas market'

Liz Milne,
Finance Manager

'The company needs to trim its budget by 10 per cent all round if it is to survive'

Managers may also disagree with the shareholders. The shareholders may be intent on receiving a large dividend as their share of the profits whereas the managers may be intent on reinvesting most of the profits in the business in order to purchase new equipment. This is an example of conflict between short-term and long-term objectives.

Conflict between employees and managers and employees and owners is the type of conflict which is most likely to become public. Employees are interested in better pay and conditions of work and in preserving jobs. Employees are often represented in the workplace by trade unions. Conflict can arise, for example, where employees are anxious to receive a pay rise and managers think that the business is not in a position to be able to afford one. Another example of conflict is where managers wish to introduce new machinery which will not only cut jobs but also change the working practices of those employees who remain. Conflict of this type which is not resolved may lead to industrial action.

Suppliers may conflict with business where they feel that they are not receiving prompt payment for goods and services delivered. On the other hand, businesses may complain about poor quality supplies and late delivery.

The local community may suffer where business pollutes, causes traffic congestion or builds on a green area. The community often has to balance these problems against local employment and resulting income that a business may provide.

BP Amoco aims for double-digit earnings growth

BP Amoco said that it expects to increase gross capital spending to an average of $13.5 billion a year for the next three years and aims to grow underlying earnings for the group by at least 10 per cent a year over the same period.

The additional spend-up from a comparable annual average of some $12 billion for the three years to 1999 – for BP Amoco, ARCO and Burmah Castrol combined – will be used to accelerate high-return projects from the group's enlarged portfolio, in particular gas production from Trinidad and oil production from the deep water Gulf of Mexico.

Chief executive Sir John Browne said he and his management team are determined that the extra spend will be accompanied by a continuing focus on unit costs and enhanced productivity from existing assets.

'Let me be clear, there is no question of us taking a pause in earnings growth while we go through an investment phase. We will work our existing assets, as well as the new ones, so that the new level of performance can be achieved without any such pause.'

Browne said the newly-enlarged BP Amoco group now had a superlative asset base from which to grow, with oil reserves of 7.5 billion barrels and 43 trillion cubic feet of gas, a global retail network of 28,000 sites and a world-class petrochemicals business.

'We also have a stronger financial base, a much wider set of opportunities and a superb array of people skills from across the world. We are now ready to move from a phase of retrenchment to a phase of expansion.'

Browne said the group expected to deliver cost-savings of $4.7 billion by year end – 80 per cent of the project total of $5.8 billion, well ahead of schedule. 'This means we can be confident of delivering the target we set out last year – a five to six percentage point underlying improvement in return on capital employed by around the end of this year.'

Source: BP Amoco press release, 11 July 2000.

Greenpeace response to BP Amoco announcement of increased investment in renewable energy and oil exploration

Greenpeace responded with disappointment to Tuesday's announcement that despite an increase in renewable investment, BP's spend on oil and gas exploration and production would be 50 times greater than its investment in green energy technology.

Greenpeace organised this April's shareholder resolution to the BP Amoco AGM calling for the company to cancel its plans for Arctic oil exploration and redirect the expenditure to the company's solar power subsidiary. The resolution received an unprecedented level of support with 13 per cent of votes and £8 billion of stock backing with the resolution.

Source: Greenpeace press release, 13 July 2000.

a In what ways might stakeholders in BP Amoco benefit from the information provided by the company's press release?

b Why is there conflict between Greenpeace and BP Amoco? Are there stakeholders in BP Amoco who might support the view held by Greenpeace?

c What action might be taken by Greenpeace and how could this affect BP Amoco?

KEY TERMS

Capital – the man-made factor of production that involves a present sacrifice in order to make more for the future. It includes machinery, vehicles, money etc.

Customer – the person or organisation that buys from the business.

Dividend – a proportion of the profits paid to shareholders as a reward for contributing capital to the firm.

Employee – a person recruited to a business to carry out a job in return for pay.

Manager – an employee who is responsible for making decisions about the running of a business.

Operational management – making decisions related to the day-to-day running of a business.

Owner – the person or people whose capital is used to finance a business.

Pressure group – an organisation that tries to affect the way another group, usually business or government, operates.

Shareholder – a person who has bought shares in either a private or public limited company.

Stakeholder – an individual or group which affects and is affected by business activity.

Strategic management – making decisions related to the future direction of a business.

Supplier – an organisation that sells to a business.

History of the Broadford Manor Hotel

The Broadford Manor Hotel and Golf Club is located in the heart of the North Cotswolds, in the picturesque village of Broadford-on-the-Wold. Little has changed in the village for the last 200 years. It is now a favourite tourist location and has often been used as a setting for television and film productions. Visitors come from all over the world. The Broadford Manor Hotel was originally built in the 15th century but was first used as a guest house in the early 1900s. After the Second World War it was bought by a family who, realising its potential as a hotel, began to restore it. However, developing the facilities proved to be too expensive for a family business. In 1990 the hotel was sold to Country Hotels (UK) Ltd, a private company which owns five similar hotels. The company has invested heavily in the hotel, adding to and upgrading the facilities.

Along with normal business objectives, the hotel states that its aim is 'to exceed the customer's expectations'.

Facilities available at the hotel

The hotel now has an extensive range of facilities which include the following:

- Accommodation for 120 persons in 60 rooms; 35 of these are in the Manor itself and 25 are in converted cottages attached to the west wing of the Manor. These cottages were originally part of the village.
- 30 acres of gardens and parkland.
- Trout fishing on the River Windbrook.
- A heated outdoor swimming pool, tennis courts, croquet lawn and archery.
- A high class restaurant seating up to 100 persons.
- Conference facilities which are used frequently by major UK companies.
- An 18-hole championship golf course.

Nearby, an additional attraction is the Cotswolds Racing Circuit which plays host to many meetings from Classic Cars to Formula 3000. It also has frequent special attractions for vintage car enthusiasts. There is a test track and skid pan at the circuit. The hotel arranges visits for business groups using its conference facilities who also want to try their hand at go-kart racing or on the skid pan. Publicity is gained through advertising at the track. Visitors to the circuit may stay at the hotel, or use the restaurant.

Future plans and developments

The hotel would like to increase the occupancy rate of its rooms to a minimum of 60%, and is reviewing its current marketing strategy. The hotel is also considering two possible options for long-term expansion. (i) Building additional leisure facilities. The major developments would be to cover the swimming pool and to construct a gymnasium and fitness centre. Such a major development would cost over £1 million and the management is doubtful whether sufficient profit could be earned to justify this investment. However, the two similar hotels closest to the Broadford Manor Hotel have both recently added these facilities. (ii) The purchase and renovation of the five remaining cottages close to the hotel. This would complete the hotel's ownership of all the property around it and would also improve security in the area. Each cottage would cost in the region of £100,000 to purchase and would then need to be renovated. Renovation costs are approximately £10,000 per room and so a further £300,000 would be required, in addition to the purchase price of each cottage.

However, because the hotel is a listed building, the owners have to take great care over changes that are made. Every proposed alteration is carefully controlled by the local council and checked by various pressure groups who are keen to protect the local heritage and maintain the standard of buildings in the area.

Source: SEG GCSE Business Studies Case Study, 1999.

Q Questions

1 Who are the owners of the Broadford Manor Hotel?

2 Country Hotels (UK) Ltd has 'invested heavily in the hotel'. How might this cause conflict between:
   a owners and managers
   b managers and customers
   c managers and suppliers?

3 Write a report, identifying the costs and benefits of the two expansion proposals. Complete your report with a recommendation.

E Extension

Some companies have recently claimed that the legal minimum wage is causing them problems, particularly in keeping costs down. Do some research into the legal minimum wage and decide if you think that managers/owners had a responsibility to pay a minimum of £3.70 from 1 October 2000. Which stakeholders might experience a conflict of interest as a result of the legal minimum wage?

Private and public sector objectives

Objectives will differ across companies and over time. It is clear that **public sector** organisations may have very different objectives to **private sector** organisations. Marks & Spencer may seek to improve profit whereas the National Health Service may want to reduce waiting lists. Likewise, a small company may seek personal satisfaction from growth over maximising efficiency.

Private sector objectives

Generally, companies set objectives which tend to focus on the following:

- **Profit.** Many companies seek to make profit. Profit is what remains after all the costs of running the business have been met. In a small company, the profit may be used as a source of finance, to help the company expand. In larger companies, the profit may be used to pay a **dividend** to **shareholders**. Organisations in the public sector are less likely to use profit as an objective. They will be more likely to seek to break even (a point where neither loss nor profit is made) or measure the financial success/failure of the organisation in a wider sense through cost–benefit analysis (for more information see Unit 8 page 58).

- **Growth.** This is a common business objective and is often measured through **market share**. There are many spin-offs to growth that make it such an important objective. Companies that achieve growth may be able to undertake longer production runs and hence economies of scale. Lowering costs may allow profits to increase or may help the company to lower prices to its customers and so become more competitive. Growth may also indicate that the company has strong customer loyalty and may therefore be in a position to raise prices while retaining sales.

- **Customer satisfaction.** Without customers, the business will not succeed. It is important therefore that companies set objectives with the customer in mind. Measures of customer satisfaction may be achieved through customer complaint rates or customer questionnaires. Most hotels, for example, leave questionnaires in the room for guests to complete, as a means of measuring customer satisfaction.

- **Independence.** Small companies in particular may have been established by their owner so that he or she can be independent and make decisions rather than following someone else's instructions.

- **Satisficing.** In certain companies, ownership is extended to friends, colleagues, relations and employees of the firm. Although it is important for the survival of the business to make a profit, the most important objective might be to provide employment and a comfortable lifestyle for members of the family. The owners may not want to expand because this may require them to work harder, take greater risks and sometimes lose control of the company.

- **Survival.** In the long run, all companies need to ensure that they survive in the market. During economic recession, objectives such as profit maximisation and sales maximisation may be unrealistic; the company may simply set survival as its priority.

In times of recession, businesses' main aim may be just to survive

- **Ethos.** The ethos of the company is the image it presents through the code of conduct by which it operates. Nowadays, many companies are keen to prove that they are environmentally responsible, that they are not involved in testing products on animals, or that they have no business links with countries that have undesirable political systems. Some companies have used the ethos they have developed as part of their advertising strategy.

- Other objectives may include: improved quality, greater productivity, improved efficiency, increased customer awareness and customer loyalty.

TASK 2

Many companies including Marks & Spencer, McDonald's and Sainsbury's have business objectives relating to the environment. They produce a range of literature on policies such as the rainforests, diet and recycling. Two extracts from leaflets produced by Sainsbury's and Marks & Spencer are given here.

We strongly support the principle of recycling and work to maximise the collection of recyclable materials.

Marks & Spencer takes all practical steps to use recycled materials and actively supports new technology for economic recycling schemes in co-operation with the plastics and paper industries.

Recycling

Our purchase of packaging and other materials specifies a recycled content wherever possible. Increasingly, the choice of packaging is

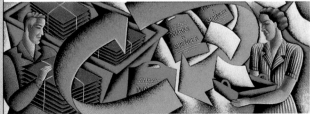

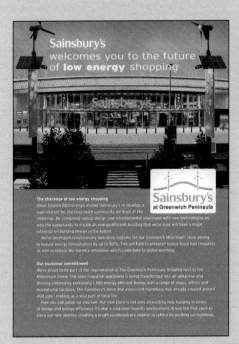

influenced by considerations of how readily it can be recycled. Some 80% of transit packaging materials are now reused or recycled.

We have an on-going programme to encourage staff in our offices and stores to use less paper and to collect waste paper for recycling. This initiative has resulted in a dramatic reduction in the amount of paper used, as well as substantial cost savings.

a Collect as much information as you can about firms which have a business objective relating to the environment. You will find information from adverts placed in magazines and newspapers, displays in retail stores, company annual reports and company profiles on the Internet.

b Does this type of business objective prevent the company from having and achieving other objectives, e.g. maximising profits?

c In your group, use the information you have collected to reach a view about businesses with environmental policies. How far do you consider that they are motivated by a desire to help and protect the environment and how far by a desire to cash in on the Green Revolution?

Public sector objectives

Traditionally, public sector organisations had the objective of providing a public service rather than making a profit. As a result of unclear objectives which tended to relate to commercial, economic and social criteria, many ran at a loss. Governments were willing to subsidise such projects as they were felt to be in the public interest. Since the mid 1960s governments have tried to tighten the objectives of the **nationalised industries**. The introduction of cost-benefit analysis for the public sector encouraged organisations to look at the commercial return from investment and to weigh this against the social costs and benefits which would result.

Since the 1980s, subsidies to nationalised industries have been withdrawn and annual targets are set. Each individual nationalised industry must decide how to meet its targets and be responsible for meeting its objectives.

TASK 3

Below are extracts taken from 'The Patients' Charter and You – a Charter for England'.

The Patients' Charter and You – a Charter for England

The Patients' Charter puts the Citizens' Charter into practice in the National Health Service. It is helping the NHS to:

- listen to and act on people's views and needs;
- set clear standards of service;
- provide services which meet those standards.

This document:

- sets out your rights and the standards of service you can expect to receive;
- tells you what the Charter has helped the NHS to achieve so far;
- introduces a number of new national standards;
- sets out how you can help the NHS to make further improvements to the standards of service it provides.

You have the *right* to:

- receive health care on the basis of your clinical need, not on your ability to pay, your lifestyle or any other factor;
- be registered with a GP and be able to change your GP easily and quickly if you want to;
- get emergency medical treatment at any time through your GP, the emergency ambulance service and hospital accident and emergency departments; and
- be referred to a consultant acceptable to you, when your GP thinks it is necessary, and to be referred for a second opinion if you and your GP agree this is desirable.

You can *expect* the NHS to make it easy for everyone to use its services, including children, elderly people or people with physical or mental disabilities.

Source: Department of Health, 1996.

a How does the information provided in the Charter help patients of the National Health Service?

b In what ways might being a patient in the NHS both differ from and have similarities to being a patient in a private health care scheme?

Conflicting objectives

You have seen in this unit the great variety of objectives that companies set. It is the job of the company managers to ensure that business strategies are devised that allow the company to achieve its objectives, but there may be conflicts between the various stakeholders in the company in both the short and long term. For example, a company may have set an objective of achieving customer satisfaction through improved product quality. In order to achieve the objective, the company may have to buy more expensive raw materials. This might conflict with the objective of maximising profits and, in turn, affect the dividends paid to shareholders.

Many organisations find that they have constantly to evaluate their objectives in order to ensure that conflicts can be minimised. The three main groups involved in organisations – owners, managers and employees – may have different objectives that set up tensions in the organisation. Further examples of conflict are given below.

- Owners. In limited companies, the owners of the company are the shareholders. They will expect a return for their investment, known as a dividend. Some shareholders may want the business to earn a moderate amount of profit in a way which means taking the smallest risk. Other shareholders might be more interested in the price of their shares rather than in the dividends which are paid. This group may be hoping to sell their shares in the near future.

- Managers. They take all the decisions in the running of the company. They may want the company to obtain a larger share of the market, possibly through the takeover of another company. Takeovers are expensive and the company would probably have to use its profits to finance the takeover rather than to pay dividends to the shareholders.

- Employees. They may want to ensure that the company has full order books. Their priority may be for the business to maintain or increase employment prospects. The employees might make it difficult for the business to invest in new technology, and the possibility of employees taking strike action to prevent such decisions cannot be ruled out. They might also not support a merger or takeover because of concerns over job security.

In the spring of 2001, London Underground workers staged a series of strikes in protest against the proposed part-privatisation, which they feared would lead to lowered safety standards and job losses

TASK 4

Below is the mission statement and strategies of the fast-food restaurant chain McDonald's.

McDonald's mission statement

'To be the World's Best Quick Service Restaurant Experience'

We will be the best employer for our people in each community around the world.

We will deliver operational excellence to our customers in each of our restaurants worldwide.

We will achieve enduring profitable growth for our owner/operators, suppliers, and the company.

Source: McDonald's.

a Give three examples of where you think there might be possible conflict between the stakeholders of McDonald's.

b Acting as the managing director of McDonald's, write a letter to all staff, shareholders and managers of the company, assuring them that the objectives stated are achievable without conflict.

Today's Barclays

BARCLAYS

In 1995 Barclays announced the purchase of San Francisco-based fund manager Wells Fargo Nikko Investment Advisers. The business was integrated with BZW Investment Management to form Barclays Global Investors, the world's leading institutional fund manager. The merger brought together investment expertise from the US and Europe to form one of the few truly global investment managers.

In 1998 a new structure for the Group was introduced. Barclays activities were divided into four major global businesses, each focused on the needs of different sets of customers:

- **Retail Financial Services** – meets the needs of personal and small business customers.
- **Corporate Banking** – serves medium-sized and larger businesses.
- **Barclays Capital** – focuses on the international investment banking arena.
- **Barclays Global Investors** – the world's largest institutional fund manager.

Today's Barclays has tremendous global strength and a reputation for being first with innovative products and services. It has almost 80,000 employees, nearly 60,000 of whom work in the UK.

The Barclays Group is committed to the constant evolution of its business, so that it can meet the challenges of the modern financial services industry. It will continue to innovate, identifying ways not just to meet but to exceed customers' expectations.

Source: FT.com, *Financial Times.*

Barclays takes loan risk into account

Matt Barrett, the flamboyant chief executive of Barclays, clearly enjoys controversy. Since he was appointed last year, the bank has hardly been out of the news, with rows over cash machine charges – now abandoned, closure of rural branches, and his pay packet.

The latest furore to hit the bank pits Barclays against consumer groups concerned about the poor, while raising fears of reduced competition.

Barclays plans to discriminate between customers on interest rates for loans, offering better rates to less risky customers for otherwise identical products. It will be the first big bank to move away from one-for-all interest rates but others are expected to follow.

Consumer groups fear 'risk pricing' could lead to widespread social exclusion, with higher charges for the poor. The bank denies it plans to discriminate against certain social groups and argues that the move is about customers' diligence, not their wealth.

Source: FT.com, *Financial Times*, 13 July 2000.

Q Questions

1 What is Barclays' mission statement and why is it important to the company?
2 What policies/tactical objectives might Barclays managers operate to ensure that the mission statement is achieved?
3 What might attract you to become a shareholder or employee of Barclays?
4 Where might Barclays find conflict with its objectives?
5 How do these conflicts affect the company?
6 How might these conflicts be resolved?

E Extension

1 Investigate the mission statements of a range of companies that you are interested in.
2 Do you think they are SMART?
3 Choose one company, and find out how it is measuring its success.
4 Has the company achieved its objectives?
5 How has the success or failure to achieve its objectives been reflected in the salaries of staff and employment levels?

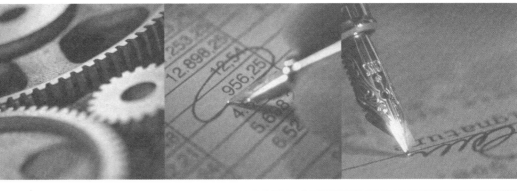

Business ownership

This unit is about the different types of business ownership in the UK.

At the end of the unit, students should be able to:

- explain the difference between private and public sector organisations

- give reasons for people setting up in business

- understand the organisational features of sole traders, partnerships, limited companies, franchises, cooperatives and nationalised industries

- identify the advantages and disadvantages of different forms of organisation

- give examples of different types of ownership in the UK economy.

Private and public sectors

The UK economy is a **mixed economy**, meaning that it has both **private and public sectors** (see Unit 1). In this unit, we will look at the different types of organisations that exist in the private and public sector.

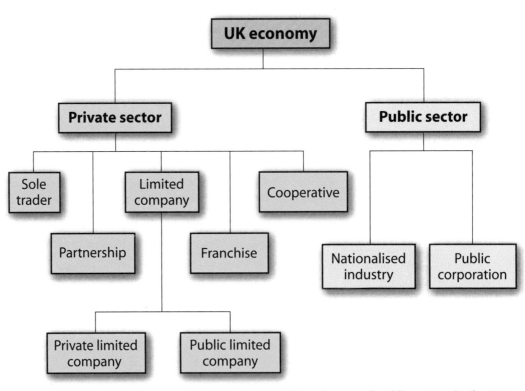

The private and public sectors in the UK

TASK 1

a Using your textbook, the library and the Internet, write a short definition of each of the terms from the chart above.

b Using the same sources plus the phone book and your own knowledge of retailers and manufacturers in the local area, try to name a real business as an example of each type of ownership.

c Why did you choose the businesses you have listed?

Why set up in business?

Most businesses begin in a small way and the people who set them up usually have a variety of important reasons for doing so. Some of these are shown in the results of a survey by Coopers and Lybrand in 1991.

What do you consider are your principal motivations in running your business?

1 Personal satisfaction from success
2 Capital growth
3 Income
4 Ability to do things my own way
5 Freedom to take a longer-term view
6 Personal wealth
7 Security
8 Funds for retirement
9 Something to pass on to the children

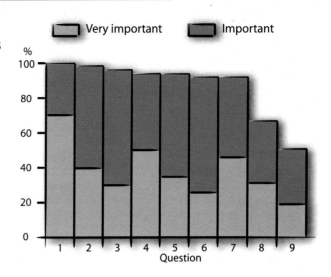

Very important Important

Private sector

The private sector consists of the following types of organisation:

- **sole trader**
- **partnership**
- **private and public limited companies**
- **franchise**
- **cooperative.**

Details of their legal structures will be found in Unit 5.

Features of a sole trader

A sole trader is exactly what it sounds – one person managing his or her own business. This person can employ as many workers as he or she wishes but does not share the finance, control, decision making or profits with anyone else. This form of legal organisation has **unlimited liability**. This means that there is no limit to the business debts for which the owner is responsible. Responsibility extends to the possibility of having to sell private possessions to pay off the business debts. This form of organisation is only suitable for small, simple businesses with few employees and little capital.

This form of business is relatively easy to set up and there are no rules about the records which have to be kept unless the business is VAT registered.

Advantages of a sole trader	Disadvantages of a sole trader
The owner has sole managerial and financial control. Profits are not shared. The owner has complete independence and can run the business how he or she likes.	The owner must make all the decisions. There are no partners with whom to share the decisions.
This form of organisation is simple to set up.	The owner is personally liable for any debts which the business cannot pay (unlimited liability).
There is no requirement to make information about the business public.	This form of business has a low status in the business community.
The owner can introduce new and varied trading activities to the business without having to register the change.	The owner does not get much support as financial institutions see the business as more risky than limited companies.
	The business dies with the owner.

Features of a partnership

A partnership is a way of sharing with others the managerial and financial responsibility for a business. Legally a partnership must consist of between two and 20 partners. Partnerships, like sole traders, usually have unlimited liability, although limited partnerships are possible (this will be discussed in greater detail in Unit 5). Partnerships are generally appropriate for professional businesses such as doctors, dentists, estate agents and solicitors. A partnership allows people to share capital and skills and expertise. If one partner is ill, the business can carry on. Although all the partners are responsible for the business's debts, one partner is not liable for another's private debts. On the other hand, if one partner makes a mistake and signs a contract which has disastrous consequences for the business, the other partners have to honour the contract. The legal regulations which govern a partnership are set out in the 1890 Partnership Act. This is dealt with in more detail in Unit 5.

Advantages of a partnership	Disadvantages of a partnership
Responsibilities and decision making are shared.	Profits are shared.
Continuity and support is possible. Several partners means that the business does not come to a stop if one partner is ill or takes a holiday.	The size of the business is limited by the total number of partners allowed.
	Partners have unlimited liability.
Partners may have expertise in different aspects of the same area of business and this can help the business to be successful.	A friend or partner does not necessarily make a good business partner.
More finance is available because all the partners can contribute.	If your partner runs up debts, you are equally responsible.

TASK 2

a In groups, arrange interviews with or write letters to sole traders/partnerships in your local area, asking them why they decided to start their own business.

b Using your findings, produce a class report on what has motivated owners to run local, small businesses.

c Do your findings match the report by Coopers & Lybrand on page 27?

Private and Public Limited Companies

Unlike sole traders and partnerships, private and public limited companies enjoy the benefit of **limited liability**. This means that individuals contributing to the capital of a private or public limited company have their responsibility for the debts of that company limited to the amount of capital they invested. Most of this capital is made available through the sale of shares. The shareholders do not have to sell their private possessions to pay for the business debts, unless they need to do so to cover raising the finance of their original investment.

Various Acts between 1844 and 1862 made it possible to set up limited liability companies. Other Acts have been passed since and the provisions have been consolidated into the Companies Act 1985.

Limited liability companies have their own legal existence, unlike sole traders and partnerships where the business is the same as the business owner. A minimum of two shareholders and one director is required to form a limited liability company. The existence of limited liability means that some people setting up their own business will immediately set up as a private limited company, even if the business is small. However, a public limited company is certainly a form of business organisation suitable only for a large firm.

Any limited liability company must register with the Registrar of Companies. It must keep certain accounts and file an annual return with the Registrar of Companies which must include the names of the directors.

Private limited companies

A private limited company can sell shares privately; that is, usually to family, friends and employees. It may not publicly advertise the sale of its shares, and any shareholder has to be approved by the directors. Traditionally, it had a maximum of 50 shareholders but recent legislation has removed this upper limit. A private limited company must display Ltd after its name making it clear to anyone dealing with it that its liability is limited.

Public limited companies

A public limited company (plc) is a form of organisation only suitable for very large businesses. A public limited company has to have a minimum of £50,000 authorised share capital. It can invite the general public to purchase its **shares** and there is no limit to the number of **shareholders** a plc can have. Shares in plcs are quoted on the Stock Exchange. Its name must include the words 'public limited company', or the more commonly used abbreviation plc.

Franchise

Some small businesses might be tempted to set up on their own through the medium of a **franchise**. A franchise is the right to sell a good or a service produced by a large, possibly multinational, business on the payment of a fee plus a percentage of the profits. The small business has to agree to receive all raw materials and components from the **franchisor** and to follow the rules set out for the operation of the franchise. The small business buying the franchise is called the **franchisee** (see Unit 15).

Advantages of private limited companies

Members' liability is restricted to the amount of shares they own. They have limited liability.

Additional capital can easily be raised by selling more shares.

The company can continue to trade even if one of its members dies.

Shares can be bought and sold with directors' approval.

The private company has a separate legal existence from that of its owners. It can own property and sue and be sued.

This type of organisation has a much higher business status than a sole trader.

Disadvantages of private limited companies

Audited annual returns and accounts have to be made to the Registrar of Companies. All these documents are available for public inspection.

A private limited company is more expensive and time consuming to set up than a sole trader or partnership.

Professional help will be needed to set up a private limited company.

A company is limited to the type of business described in its professional documents.

There is a separation of ownership and control which means that the owners no longer make all the decisions.

There are limited opportunities for economies of scale.

Advantages of public limited companies

Members' liability is restricted to the amount of shares they own. They have limited liability.

Additional capital can easily be raised by selling more shares as there is no upper limit to the number of shareholders.

The company can continue to trade even if one of its members dies.

Shares can be bought and sold with directors' approval.

The plc has a separate legal existence from that of its owners. It can own property and sue and be sued.

A plc is able to exploit economies of scale due to its size.

This type of organisation has a much higher business status than a sole trader.

Disadvantages of public limited companies

Audited annual returns and accounts have to be made to the Registrar of Companies. All these documents are available for public inspection.

A company is limited to the type of business described in its professional documents.

There is a separation of ownership and control which means that the owners no longer make all the decisions.

Unwanted takeovers are possible as shares are openly bought and sold.

Plcs can be seen as remote from their customers.

If the plc becomes too large, it may suffer from diseconomies of scale, where unit costs begin to rise.

Advantages of franchises

Franchisors benefit as they are able to expand their business with limited finance.

Franchisees gain from the back-up support offered by the franchisor. This includes promotion, research and development, and administrative help.

Franchisors receive a proportion of income from the franchisee in the form of a licence.

Franchisees are able to keep any remaining profit and this can be a great motivator.

Franchisees are often starting a business that already has a well-known name and has been tried and tested in other areas. It is therefore less risky.

If franchisees set up as a limited company, they have the benefit of limited liability.

Disadvantages of franchises

Franchisees have to sign a contract with the franchisor and often this ties them to rules and regulations on stock, suppliers, layout of outlets and advertising, which leaves little room for individual flair and ideas.

Popular franchises can be very expensive.

Franchisees are often restricted to a specific site and for a specific time.

A royalty has to be paid to the franchisor, even when a loss has been made.

If franchisees set up as sole traders, or partnerships, they face unlimited liability.

Co-operatives

A co-operative is a group of people pursuing the same economic, social and cultural goals through a democratically controlled enterprise. Co-ops are the original people's businesses – set up by the people for the people.

The best known co-operative in the UK is the CWS (Co-operative Wholesale Society). CWS is a family of businesses made up of food shops, department stores, Co-operative Bank, CIS (Co-operative Insurance Society), Co-op Travelcare, CWS Funeral Services, Associated Co-operative Creameries, Co-op Eyecare, as well as engineering, farms, property and development and non-food manufacturing.

Co-ops are owned and controlled by their members, which makes them very different to other businesses. Instead of answering to shareholders or city bankers, co-ops are accountable to their members. Every co-op has a committee made up of members. They may form a workers', consumers' or producers' co-operative:

- In a workers' co-operative, the business is owned and controlled by the workers. Each member has one vote and puts in an equal amount of capital. Risk of failure and success can then be shared equally.
- A consumers' co-operative is usually formed where a group of consumers want to buy together in bulk to gain cheaper prices. In this way, they are able to share equally any gains that they make.
- A producers' co-operative occurs where producers join together either to create their own market or to take advantage of joint marketing or joint purchasing of expensive items of equipment.

In any co-operative there has to be a minimum of two owners and all members of the co-operative are considered equal.

Advantages of co-operatives	Disadvantages of co-operatives
Every member is a shareholder and therefore each is committed to the success of the business.	Democratic decision making can be slow and frustrating for members.
Members are able to set their own terms and conditions for the business including pay.	Members may disagree.
Members control all elements of the business, including recruitment, pricing and production.	Customers and members of the business and finance community may see co-operatives as low status.
The cooperative can benefit from the range of ideas and experience brought by its members.	Not everyone may have the same commitment to the co-operative.
	The committee that controls the co-operative may lack business experience.

Public sector

Although we live in an economy in which more and more goods and services are provided by the private sector there are still many which are provided by the public sector. The public sector includes central government through its departments and agencies, public corporations, nationalised industries and local government.

Nationalised industries were the most important type of public sector organisation from World War II up to the early 1980s. The majority of nationalised industries were created as a result of the compulsory purchase by the government of the assets of industries which had previously been in private hands. Many of these industries, e.g. gas and electricity, were natural monopolies. The government felt public sector ownership of the natural monopolies would prevent consumers from being exploited. Other industries, e.g. rail and coal, had the potential for **economies of scale** (see Unit 18) and the government felt that these advantages could best be realised through public sector ownership. Also, many of the industries nationalised required very large state investment after World War II. This investment was unlikely to be provided by the private sector at the time. Nationalised industries were set up through an Act of Parliament and are responsible, through a Board or Council, to a government minister.

When industries were nationalised the existing owners were paid compensation. Since 1980, the trend has been towards denationalisation or **privatisation**; that is, returning the nationalised industries to private hands by encouraging private individuals and firms to buy shares. Twenty years ago the electricity boards, the gas corporation and British Airways were nationalised industries. All three have since been privatised: the Gas Corporation in 1986, and British Airways in 1987.

The privatisation of British Rail was completed in the mid-1990s. The Bank of England and the BBC are still **public corporations**. Public corporations are owned by the government but run by a selected chairperson. Any profits that they make are returned to the government, but their aim is to serve the public interest.

Local government provides many goods and services. Some of these are funded through money provided by central government while others are funded from the council tax. Examples of public sector goods and services provided by local organisations are education, leisure facilities, roads, parks and other amenities, and refuse collection. Central government has, however, increasingly insisted that local government should not have a **monopoly** of these services but should tender to operate them, that is, put in a bid to run the service in the same way as private firms.

Given the part sale of previously state owned industries and the introduction of 'competitive tendering' it is becoming increasingly difficult to make a clear distinction between where the public sector ends and the private sector starts. Some services, such as defence and the police, are clearly part of the public sector. However, road maintenance, which is described as a public service, is mostly carried out by private contractors.

It is not always easy to reach a consensus view as to whether it is better to have goods and services provided by the private or public sector. There are economic, business and social factors to take into account, but ultimately the decision is a political one.

TASK 3

The Post Office is an example of an organisation in the public sector which has become more business orientated in its approach in recent years. Below is a brief history of the changes:

- Until 1969, the Post Office was a government department controlling the Royal Mail, parcels, post offices and telephones.

- In 1969, it became a nationalised industry with its own board.

- In 1981, the Post Office and British Telecom were separated and British Telecom was later privatised.

- In 1986, the Post Office was divided into three separate businesses: Royal Mail, Parcelforce and Post Office Counters Ltd. They each have their own markets and customer groups.

Royal Mail

Collecting, sorting and delivering letters within UK and overseas.

Parcelforce

Collecting, sorting and delivering parcels to businesses and private customers.

Post Office Counters Ltd

Operating 20,000 Crown, franchise and sub-post offices.

These three businesses come under the control of the Post Office Board. This is appointed by the Secretary of State for Trade and Industry, a member of the government. The government represents the interests of the UK public who ultimately own the Post Office.

During the early 1990s the government proposed the privatisation of the Post Office, but legislation was never carried through. There was particular opposition to the privatisation of the Royal Mail, because it was feared that a private company would no longer deliver to all parts of the UK at a single first or second class price.

In July 1999 the government gave the Post Office greater commercial freedom to do business. Under the new terms, the Post Office would receive an extra £600 million over the next three years and remain in the public sector whilst being allowed to make its own investments. An independent regulator would be appointed to protect consumer interests, regulate prices and ensure fair competition.

a Explain how the organisation of the Post Office differs from that of a plc.

b Why do you think that the Post Office was reorganised into three separate businesses in 1986?

c Consider each section of the Post Office. Identify any services they supply where they are a monopoly (the only) provider and where they are in competition.

d The future of the Post Office is still an area of great debate. Do you think that the Post Office should be in public ownership? Write down arguments in favour and against the Post Office remaining in the public sector. Make a final recommendation explaining your decision.

KEY TERMS

Co-operative – a group of people pursuing the same economic, social and cultural goals through a democratically controlled enterprise.

Economies of scale – the factors that allow unit costs to fall as the size of the firm grows. Internal economies of scale occur as a result of factors from within the firm. External economies of scale occur as a result of the firm being part of the market.

Franchise – a business format which allows a small business to trade in a well-known product or service in return for a share of the profits.

Franchisee – the holder of a licence who makes a payment to the franchisor.

Franchisor – the large organisation which offers others the right to sell its product or service in return for a share of the profits.

Limited liability – the responsibility for the debts of the company is limited to the amount of capital invested in the company.

Mixed economy – an economy that has both a private and a public sector.

Monopoly – where one supplier controls the market. By law, a monopoly is defined as any firm that has more than a 25 per cent share of the market.

Nationalised industry – industry owned and run by the government.

Partnership – between two and 20 people who form a business together. They all contribute capital, share the financial decisions and the profits.

Plc – public limited company

Private limited company – an organisation with limited liability which sells shares only to friends, employees and members of the family.

Private sector – the sector of the economy where all factors are owned by private individuals and firms.

Privatisation – denationalisation, or the process of returning a nationalised industry to private ownership.

Public corporation – an organisation owned and controlled by the government but run on its behalf by a board of governors.

Public limited company – an organisation with limited liability which sells shares to the general public through the Stock Exchange.

Public sector – the sector of the economy where all factors are owned by the state.

Share – a share in the decision making of an organisation in return for contributing capital.

Shareholder – a person who has bought shares in either a private or a public limited company.

Sole trader – a person who sets up a business.

Unlimited liability – total responsibility for the business's debts. Anyone in business with unlimited liability may have to sell his or her private possessions to meet the business's needs.

Youthful manifesto to unlock Enterprise Britain

by Alexander Garrett

Talking to Reuben Singh it's easy to forget just how young the guy is. One minute he's holding forth on the need for a more entrepreneurial culture in boardrooms, and reflecting on his meetings with Tony Blair and other grandees. The next, you remind yourself that six years ago, he was still taking his GCSEs.

But that is the point. For Singh, 22, who in February became one of the country's youngest-ever millionaires when he sold his Miss Attitude retail chain for a reputed £22 million, has made the quest to gain support and recognition for young entrepreneurs into something of a personal crusade.

'When I was 17 and studying at school and I wanted to start a business, I was told "you can't do it",' he explains. 'I went to see the banks and they wanted track record, management, security – and I had none of them. Even when I had eight to ten stores after the first year, it was still very hard because people thought this was a flash in the pan.'

But in the entrepreneurial stakes, youth has many advantages over experience, he says. The younger you are, the fewer responsibilities you have, the more prone you are to take risks, and the more commitment you can put into your business. 'When I started Miss Attitude, I would eat, sleep and drink it,' he says.

Singh's story is by now well known. He grew up in Manchester in a family that owned a fashion import business. In his early teens he was helping out and learning about business after school. He started Miss Attitude as a 17-year-old student during his A Levels, selling fashion accessories ranging from nail varnish to handbags, based on what was 'in' with the girls at school. Then, having grown it to a chain of around 40 stores, he sold out to Klesch Capital Partners.

Source: *Management Today*, September 1999

Q Questions

1 What factors motivated Reuben Singh to run his own business?
2 Reuben Singh could have left school and worked for someone before setting up his own company. What might have been the advantages and disadvantages of him doing this?
3 Reuben had the option of setting up his company as a sole trader, partnership or private limited company. Write a short report, explaining which option you think was most suitable, giving reasons why.
4 Why might Klesch Capital Partners have been keen to buy the Miss Attitude chain?

E Extension

1 Invest a notional £1,000 in up to three public limited companies to create a portfolio of shares. Keep a record of their share prices over the next two months.
2 What has made your share prices rise and fall?
3 How does your portfolio compare to others in the class? (Hint: You may wish to make your portfolio calculation easier by putting the information on a spreadsheet.)

Setting up in business

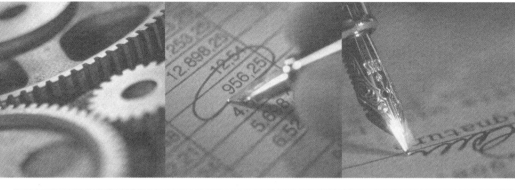

This unit is about how businesses are set up and the importance of business plans and legal structures in business.

At the end of the unit, students should be able to:

- understand the process of setting up a new business

- understand the strategies needed to start up a new business

- describe how business can protect its new ideas

- explain the need for a business plan

- explain and evaluate the range of possible legal structures that can be selected when setting up a business

- understand the factors that help business to succeed.

The process of setting up in business

The process of setting up a business involves four main phases.

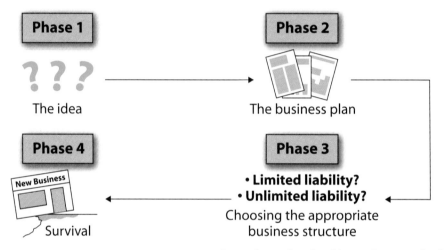

Four phases involved in setting up a business

Phase 1 The idea

To start a new business, the owner has to have an idea as to what he or she is going to do. This may involve research to find out what will sell, whether or not there is a market and how much the business will cost to set up. While some businesses succeed with little research, for most businesses this is a critical first step.

Phase 2 The business plan

For businesses seeking to raise capital through a bank, the need for a **business plan** is vital. However, even when the need to write a business plan is not a condition for a loan, the practice is still desirable. A survey by Cranfield Institute of Management in 1990 showed that 25 per cent of very new businesses had a business plan, with the figure rising to 95 per cent for businesses which had been in existence for five years or longer. Details about the benefits of having a business plan can be found later in this unit.

Phase 3 Selecting the appropriate business structure

The most important decision initially is whether to have limited or unlimited liability. This will be decided by the risk involved in the business. The riskier the investment, the greater the need for limited liability.

Phase 4 Survival

If by this stage, the business idea has not been abandoned, the first year will be the most difficult. The failure rate for new businesses is 50 per cent in the first 18 months, with only 33 per cent making it beyond the first five years. In certain industries, such as the restaurant trade, failure rates are much higher!

Starting up a business requires an **entrepreneur** – someone who can recognise an opportunity, raise money and take the risk involved. According to Brian O'Connor ('What can you learn from entrepreneurs?', *Works Management,* July 1999) most successful entrepreneurs display some of the following:

* They have a lot of energy and the ability to keep going to get results.
* They clearly visualise goals.
* They focus strongly on customers and their needs.
* They are modest about their achievements.
* They are willing to make mistakes.
* They react quickly to opportunities.
* They have a short attention span – are bored by repetitive work.
* They are impatient to grow the business.
* They are able to change direction.
* They underestimate how long it takes to achieve a goal.
* They believe in hands-on, practical experience rather than training.

Start-up strategies

Many small businesses are started by an entrepreneur who has an idea or an invention which will provide a good business opportunity. He or she should have carried out market research and as a result spotted a gap in the market or identified that consumers are likely to buy the good or service. Market research is a vital tool in business planning and can reduce the risk of starting up a business.

Another way of setting up in business is to buy an existing business. This is how many people get involved in retailing. They buy an existing outlet. In professional concerns such as solicitors, doctors and dentists it is usual to buy into an existing partnership. There are many advantages in buying an existing business, particularly if it is bought as a going concern. It will have accommodation, equipment, staff and customers, and the likely costs and possible profits can be estimated. This reduces the risk. The disadvantages include the fact that the cost of buying an existing business is likely to be substantial. Also the previous owner may have established business practices, including arrangements with customers and suppliers, which might not suit the new owner.

A third choice is to purchase a franchise. This means buying the right to make or sell a nationally recognised good or service. Franchises are covered in more detail in Unit 4. Again this reduces the risk but also reduces the potential profit as a proportion always has to be paid to the franchisor.

TASK 1

Choose an entrepreneur from the list below and write about what qualities he or she has that makes him or her so successful. You may wish to describe examples of the entrepreneur's success as well as your thoughts on the individual's personal characteristics. You may find evidence in textbooks, magazines, newspapers and on the Internet.

Bill Gates
Microsoft

Richard Branson
Virgin

Anita Roddick
The Body Shop

James Dyson
Dyson (vacuum cleaners)

Martha Lane Fox
lastminute.com

Stelios Haji-Ioannou
easyJet

Reuben Singh
Miss Attitude

Lawrence Ellison
Oracle

Tim Martin
J D Wetherspoons

Freddie Laker
Laker Airways

TASK 2

Lucy has worked for an insurance company for many years, but has just been made redundant. She has often thought of setting up her own business and the time seems right to do so. Having been to many weddings and seen how much it costs to buy a hat that is often worn only once, she thought that a hat hire shop might be a good idea. She has talked about this with one of her colleagues, Bryony, who also shared her enthusiasm.

a Write a list of 'things to do' for Lucy before she takes her idea to the bank manager.

b What might be the advantages of Lucy buying an existing business (which may be a hat shop rather than a hat hire shop) rather than setting up her own new business?

c Lucy is considering asking Bryony to come into partnership with her. If this happened, their combined redundancy money would mean that they would not need to take out a bank loan. Write a letter to Lucy, as a business adviser, offering her your views on whether to be a sole trader or partnership.

Protecting the idea

An entrepreneur may have created an idea that he or she wants to protect. There are four main ways in which he or she can do this;

- by **patent** – the right to be the sole user of an invention of a new product or process
- through design – a design can be registered if it has a unique appearance
- by **trademark** – a logo or symbol used to distinguish a firm's brand
- by **copyright** – this gives legal protection to an author, composer or artist and prevents others from copying the work.

The entrepreneur must also recognise that the idea may not be unique and therefore cannot be protected. Legal protection of ideas is also very difficult in the service sector as it is difficult to describe the item sold. This has been true for new technology and **e-commerce** industries where intellectual property rights are proving to be a matter of great debate. Intellectual property rights are the product and work of authors and inventors. It is difficult to protect their product as it may only be an idea of a phrase. If someone has the idea for a website that deals with bookings for last minute holidays, does this give them the right to copyright the idea?

There is more detail on this topic in Unit 16.

The business plan

A business plan sets out the objectives, policies and strategies for the business. It should help the business to look to the future and may be useful for planning and decision making. The benefits of business planning include:

- communicating to the bank's business adviser (or other potential investors) that the business has a well thought-out plan to help it succeed and grow
- reducing the number of mistakes which are likely to be made. The process of completing the plan requires the entrepreneur to have thought through his or her ideas carefully, identifying all probable costs.

Drawing up the business plan initially will make it easier to update and amend the business's strategy in future years.

The business plan should include details of the following:

- business objectives
- key personnel, including details of people's previous experience and current job role
- details of the product or service the business intends to offer and its possible place in the market
- premises, plant and machinery, including their costs, age, condition and policy on replacement
- any assets which are available as security, that is, as a back-up in case the business fails leaving loans outstanding
- financial requirements.

Extract from the NatWest Business Start Up Guide

Remember, to run your business efficiently, you need a plan to guide you.

Put yourself in the shoes of the person to whom you are making your proposal. Would you back the venture on the strength of your presentation?

Be as clear and brief as possible. Don't leave everything until the last minute. Give yourself plenty of time and send a copy of your plan in advance of a meeting.

Be realistic. Try to be objective. Look at things clearly and consider the need to include contingencies for the best and worst cases. Be ready to answer searching questions about the information you have assembled.

TASK 3

Visit the local branch of a high street bank to obtain a copy of its business start-up pack. (Only one pack is needed per group in the class.)

Lucy and Bryony have decided to go ahead as a partnership and set up a hat hire shop.

The business

(*Delete as appropriate)

a	Name	Top That
b	Address	6 Metcalfe St
		Bury
		BU3 7TN
c	Limited Company/Partnership/Sole Trader*	
d	Description/Activities	
		Hat hire
e	Date commenced trading	
	(Proposed date if new business)	7 September 2000
f	Date of termination	
	(If different from above)	
g	Objectives	
		To make a profit
h	Capital structure	

Partnership and Sole Trader Name	Amount of capital	% of Total
Lucy Riley	£12,000	60%
Bryony Page	£8,000	40%

Key personnel

Name, age & qualifications	Position held	Date joined	Salary
Lucy Riley, 34 BA Business studies	Partner Worker	7 Sept 2000	Not yet decided
Bryony Page, 38	Partner Worker	7 Sept 2000	Not yet decided

Sales and marketing

a Projected turnover for first year £ Don't know

b Sales breakeven figures

Total overheads x 100 £

Gross profit margin %

c Has your product or service been market tested? Yes/No*

We are offering a new shop to the area. We are aware of other hat hire shops but none locally

d Marketing and sales methods including the costs involved

We will be advertising in the local paper and doing a leaflet drop

e Buying

1 Who are your major suppliers? Department and millinery stores

2 Are there alternatives? Yes

3 What are the advantages of buying from the supplier shown in 1? They can offer a range of hats and give the customers a chance to compare the price of hiring and buying.

Business premises

Freehold/leasehold*

a Valuation (give basis and date) £17,500

Mortgage outstanding plus name of mortgage

£

Rates	per annum	£
	dates payable	

b Size (in sq ft) 300

Comprising	1 Production space	200
	2 Office space	100

If leasehold, terms of lease	Not known
Period outstanding	875 years
Options to renew	Yes/No*
Present rent per annum	£1,800
Frequency of payment	Monthly
Next rent review	1 April 2001
Frequency of review	Not known

Who is responsible for repairs?

internally

externally

a Using the business start-up pack, create a presentation to Lucy and Bryony, advising them on the five key areas on which they need to concentrate when producing their business plan. (You could use video, flipchart or a software application package such as Powerpoint to make your presentation.)

Look at the extract from the business plan which Lucy and Bryony have prepared.

b Do you think that this is a well-prepared business plan? What criticisms would you make of it?

c Prepare some questions that you think the bank's business adviser might ask Lucy and Bryony. The questions should be based on the evidence provided. (You may extend this into providing suitable answers or role playing the interview.)

The legal structure

Once the decision to set up the business has been made, the owner(s) will need to decide on the appropriate form of ownership. Initially, the owners must decide whether they want **limited** or **unlimited liability**. Having decided this, they must then opt for the particular format that suits their needs. The options for a new business usually are:

- sole trader
- partnership
- private limited company
- franchise.

If the owners have bought an existing business as a private limited company, they may also wish to look into a further option of **going public** and setting up a public limited company.

Unit 4 has already looked at the advantages and disadvantages of such options. In this unit, we will look in more detail at the legal requirements of setting up these organisations.

Sole trader

For a sole trader, there is no distinction between the private person and the business. The business is an extension of his or her private concerns. There are, therefore, no legal considerations to take into account when setting up as a sole trader, particularly as initially the business is likely to be too small to have to register for VAT. No public accounts have to be kept although the business must keep accurate financial accounts.

Partnership

As a partnership involves more than one person, there are legal regulations to follow. These are set out in the Partnership Act of 1890 which provides a framework for an agreement. The Partnership Act applies when no other partnership agreement has been drawn up. The partners can go to a solicitor to draw up a **Deed of Partnership** which can vary the requirements of the Partnership Act to suit specific partnerships. A Deed of Partnership can cover the following aspects of the business:

- How profits and losses are to be shared. For example, if there are three partners putting in £10,000, £20,000 and £50,000 respectively, then profits will be shared among them in the same proportions as the capital invested, that is, 12.5 per cent, 25 per cent and 62.5 per cent.

- How much money can be withdrawn. It is important to have rules about this so that the business can continue to grow as a result of profits being reinvested.

- Arrangements about holidays, time off and illness.

- How long the partnership is expected to last.

- Getting rid of a partner or taking on another partner. The consent of every partner is required to bring another partner into the business. A court order is required before a partner can be got rid of.

- Dissolving a partnership. A partnership usually automatically dissolves on the death or bankruptcy of a partner.

- Getting capital out of the business. When a partnership is dissolved the remaining partners are allowed to sell the assets and share the proceeds in the proportions in which they contributed any capital. If the partnership has debts at its dissolution, then the partners must share the debts in the same way.

Sometimes partners are prepared to contribute capital to a partnership but do not want any part in the running of the business. Such a partner is known as a sleeping partner and can register a limited partnership with the Registrar of Companies. This means that he or she is not personally responsible for any debts the partnership might incur and will not therefore have to sell any personal belongings.

TASK 4

Using the information from the business plan, draw up a Deed of Partnership for Lucy and Bryony. Try to make it look like a legal document and add any clauses, in addition to the key areas covered in the book, to stop any problems emerging between the partners.

Private Limited Company

A private limited company can be formed from scratch or more usually from a sole trader or partnership. Its legal status is established by registering the company with the Registrar of Companies.

The following documents are required:

- **Memorandum of Association** – this is the company's charter which sets out its relationships with the rest of the business world. It contains a note of the company's name, the place of its registered office, the purpose of the business and the amount of its share capital.

- **Articles of Association** – these are the internal rules of the company. They establish the relationship between the company and its shareholders by setting down such things as voting rights at meetings, the power of directors and the amount the company may borrow without seeking the permission of the shareholders.

- A statement of the amount of the share capital.

- Details of the company director and the company secretary.

- The address of the company's registered office.

These rules and regulations exist to protect those who invest money in the company by, for example, restricting the company to the type of business stated in the Memorandum of Association.

Franchise

The British Franchise Association claims that franchising now accounts for 20 per cent of all retail trade in Britain, employing around 275,000 people (*Management Today*, December 1998).

Franchises are advertised in the press, on the Internet and through specialist publications such as *UK Franchise Directory*. To become a franchisee, potential owners must apply for the franchise and undergo rigorous interviews, tests and training. If they pass these, and can provide the necessary fee for the purchase of the franchise licence, they can become a franchisee. The franchisor will still earn a royalty from the franchisee, based upon the turnover of the franchise. Franchise licences vary according to the type of business involved. In 2000, a Rosemary Conley Diet and Fitness club franchise might cost £15,000, whereas a McDonald's franchise would cost several hundred thousand pounds. Each business outlet is owned and operated by the franchisee. However, the franchisor retains control over the way in which products and services are marketed and sold, and controls the quality and standards of the business.

Public Limited Company

A public limited company is most usually formed from a private company. This process is known as going public. The general public are invited to buy shares, thus providing the company with capital. The invitation is contained in a prospectus which provides considerable detail about the company's business. Those who want to buy shares complete an application form, and provided the offer is not oversubscribed, will receive the quantity requested. Provided enough capital is raised, the company can begin trading and shares can be bought and sold on the Stock Exchange (see Unit 22). The Registrar of Companies will issue a Certificate of Trading.

A less risky way of launching a public limited company is for a merchant bank to buy all the shares instead of inviting the public to do so through the prospectus. The bank then advertises an Offer for Sale which contains the same information as would be found in a prospectus and the public buy the shares from the bank. This method allows some of the shares to remain unsold but in the hands of the merchant bank.

Most large retail chains are public limited companies

Success in business

No one can guarantee a successful business, even if he or she follows all the correct procedures. However, there are some tips that can be followed which might make failure less likely:

- Ensure that you have carried out adequate research before opening the business. How big is the market? What are the market trends? What is the competition? These are questions that should be answered, even if the research is costly in terms of time and money.

- A business is more likely to survive if the market is well defined and customers are easily contacted.

- Businesses benefit from having a unique selling proposition (USP). To attract customers it helps to be selling something that is different from your competitors. This does not mean that your idea has to be new, but you should aim to have something that makes it different from the rest, e.g. food products that contain no genetically modified ingredients.

- The business should be established in a market that is expanding rather than contracting.

- Start-up costs should be reasonable.

- There should be a well thought-out business plan.

- Most entrepreneurs will tell you that luck is the final factor.

KEY TERMS

Articles of Association – the internal rules of a company.

Business plan – a document which sets out all the factors which someone starting their own business will have considered. For example, objectives, finance, premises, employees, product, market, and suppliers.

Copyright – the exclusive right to use or authorise others to use literary, dramatic, musical and artistic works, sound recordings, films or radio and television broadcasts.

Deed of Partnership – a legal document which states the rights of the partners in the event of a dispute.

E-commerce – retailing that takes place over the Internet.

Entrepreneur – a person who takes the risk of setting up in his/her own business.

Going public – the act of becoming a public limited company with shares quoted on the stock exchange.

Limited liability – the responsibility for the debts of the company is limited to the amount of capital invested in the company.

Memorandum of Association – a statement which sets out the company's name, place of trading, business purpose and amount of share capital.

Patent – an authority from a government giving the person to whom it is addressed the sole right of making, using and selling an invention for a certain period.

Trademark – A legal protection to stop others using a logo or symbol; obtained by registering the trademark at the Patent Office.

Unique selling proposition (USP) – the aspect of a business's activity that makes it distinctive and sets it apart from the competition.

Unlimited liability – total responsibility for the business's debts. Anyone in business with unlimited liability may have to sell his or her private possessions to meet the business's debts.

Liverpool's most valuable home draw

Littlewoods began as a football pools business in 1923 when Sir John Moores and two work colleagues each put £59 towards the cost of printing the company's first pools coupons. After their first season the business failed to make a profit and Sir John bought out his friends. The next year saw the first profits being made. In 1932 Littlewoods home shopping business was founded and in 1937 the first Littlewoods store was opened in Blackpool. The first Index store opened in 1985.

The Littlewoods Organisation remains based in Liverpool. Today, Littlewoods employs some 27,000 people, with over half employed in the north west region.

The Moores family business currently has annual sales of £2.8 billion and after-tax profits of £77 million. There are only 32 shareholders, all members of the Moores family.

The Littlewoods group is managed principally through two main bodies: the Group Board and the Executive Management Team.

The Group Board, headed by non-executive Chairman James Ross, has overall responsibility for the group's strategic direction, approval of annual budgets and plans, and performance appraisal.

The Executive Management Team, headed by the Group Chief Executive, is the team responsible for the day-to-day management of Littlewoods and the delivery of performance targets.

In 1989 discussions within the family seemed to indicate that they were in favour of a stock market flotation as a way of realising their money. In December 1995 an outsider offered £1.2 billion for the business. Some of the family members were in favour of a sale, others were not.

However, pre-tax profits for 1996 fell as the mail order business was hit by bad debts among its low income customers and the lottery had a significant effect on pool revenues. By 2000 things had improved. Littlewoods Retail was one of the UK's leading retail companies:

- It had retail sales of some £2.5 billion.
- It was the second largest home shopping business.
- It was the third largest clothing retailer.
- It was the fifth largest non-food retailer.
- It had some 5 million sq. ft of retail selling space.

While there were still concerns over clothing sales, the company was continuing to expand and look to refurbish existing stores.

Questions

1 What form of legal organisation does Littlewoods have?
2 What advantages are there in this form of ownership for Littlewoods?
3 Write a report to the shareholders of Littlewoods, offering your advice on the advantages and disadvantages of going public.
4 If Littlewoods did go public, how might it use the extra finance raised by the flotation?

E Extension

In the early months of 2000, some companies including Arjo Wiggins, MEPC, Hogg Robinson and Allied Textiles have returned to being private limited companies. Why has this happened?

Business and the market

The nature of different markets

In Unit 1 we discovered that we all have needs and wants that are met by business. When a good or service is bought or sold, we can act as a consumer, that is, the person who buys the item, or as a seller. When sellers and buyers meet, a **market** is created. The items that we need and want are varied. We may want a good or a service, it may be produced locally or abroad, it may require spending thousands of pounds or just a few pence.

Because we have such a wide range of needs and wants, different markets have evolved. Each market has a special function to meet these needs and wants and hence our economy is made up of many different markets. It is important to remember that business has its own needs as well as trying to satisfy the needs of consumers.

Some markets are provided by the government rather than privately owned businesses. This is because we are in a **mixed economy**. Some goods and services are provided by the **private sector** and some are provided by the **public sector**. You can review this in Unit 1.

Satisfying the needs of consumers and producers

Needs and wants are met through consumers and producers meeting in a market place. The type of need or want will determine what and where the market place is, e.g. if you wanted fruit and vegetables you may be able to buy them from your local market but if you wanted to buy an exotic fruit or an unusual vegetable you may have to go to a large supermarket.

Businesses, too, may have to 'shop around' to meet their needs. If they want to hire two clerical staff they may advertise in the local paper or job centre, but if they want a new marketing manager they may advertise in a national paper or specialist magazine such as *Marketing Weekly*.

As consumers we face a similar dilemma to that of the business. We may have needs and wants that are not satisfied in the local area and this may cause us to look at markets that are in other parts of the country or abroad. For example, a collector of stamps may have to go to a town many miles away from his or her home in order to find a specialist stamp dealer. A wine merchant may need to travel abroad to select the right wine stock for a restaurant.

The table shows some examples of such items and possible reasons why they are not available from a local producer.

Item	Reason
Bottle of champagne	Has to come from the Champagne region of France to be called champagne Years of tradition and skill are involved in making the wine
Motorbike	No significant British motorbike manufacturer
Banana	Climate

Business and the market

E-commerce now means that consumers are able to look to have their needs and wants satisfied through a global market. By using the Internet, consumers have greater access to goods and services all over the world and are also able to compare prices more easily. The last few years have seen an enormous growth in the number of dotcom companies that have been set up to meet customers' needs and wants. This also extends to businesses, who are able to contact and compare suppliers on the Internet.

In summary, all businesses try to meet the needs and wants of their customers but the market to meet these needs and wants may not be local and for some items may not even be national. Since we have a choice of markets in which we can buy the good or service we want, consumers may even choose a non-local item in preference, due to factors such as quality, reliability of supply etc.

Demand and the price system

So far, we have looked at the needs and wants of the consumer without looking at factors that may alter them. One of these factors is price. If, for example, the price of CDs falls and the price of cassettes does not, it is likely that the number of people demanding (wanting) CDs will rise. The way in which we as consumers react to price changes will create the **demand** for the good.

This simple idea of demand for a good rising as price as falls and vice versa can be shown on a diagram. It should be remembered that some goods do not keep to this simple rule but these are exceptional cases.

The diagram shows that if the price of CDs was reduced from £15 to £10, the consumer (possibly you or I) would buy an extra 4 CDs per year.

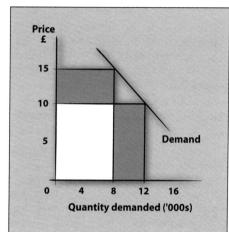

Demand curve for CDs

Business needs to be very aware of how consumers react to changes in the price of a good or service. Some items may have a price increase but consumers will still buy the product. With other items, however, even a small increase in price leads to a huge drop in demand.

Supply and the price system

Just as consumers react to changes in the price of a good, as do producers. As the price of a good or service rises, more will be supplied (available) on the market. This is because producers will be keen to sell their goods and services at a higher price with greater potential for profit.

The reaction of **supply** to **price** changes can also be shown on a graph.

The diagram shows that as the price of CDs rises from £10 to £15, the producer of CDs makes available an extra 6,000 CDs on the market.

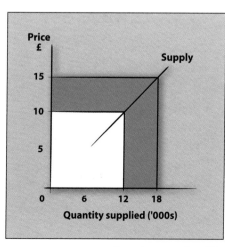

Supply curve for CDs

TASK 1

You are the manager of a shoe shop in the high street of your local town. You have carefully thought out your needs and wants over the next month and the list includes the following items:

- a loan
- a new part-time employee
- an accountant to help you with the paperwork
- shoes!!
- carrier bags
- electricity
- light refreshments for the workers on their breaks
- legal advice as the shop is being sued by an irate customer
- you are worried about the health and safety standards of the workplace so you need to put the shop in order in case you are visited.

Using the list of needs and wants, find out the following:

a the names and addresses of suppliers within your local town

b suppliers located more than 20 miles away

c three reasons why it might be better to get the items locally and three reasons why it might be better to get the items from further afield.

A market economy

A **market economy** is one where the consumer indicates to the producer what is needed on the market. As a result, producers will make the goods and services that are needed, provided that a profit can be made.

The characteristics of a market economy are as follows:

- Most or all factors of production are privately owned.
- The consumer dictates to the producer what will be produced through their demand. This means that if the consumer has a need or want, the producer will aim to satisfy it. Any changes in the demand for a good or service will have to be met by a change in the producer's supply.
- Profit is the motivating factor for producers.
- Goods and services are allocated through the price system.

There are many examples of market economies throughout the world and the USA comes perhaps the closest to a pure market economy. Many eastern European economies and China which were previously **planned economies** have recently begun to run parts of their economy through a market system.

They have done so because they believe that the price system is an efficient way to run an economy. How does such a system work?

Imagine the effect of having too high or too low a price in the market. If the price was too high (e.g. £16 for a CD), then more CDs are supplied on the market than people will want to buy. In order to get rid of the unsold stock, producers are forced to lower their price. This discourages future supplies and encourages demand. On the other hand, if the price is too low (e.g. £9 for a CD), more people will want to buy the CDs but fewer will be available on the market. Because the CDs are in short supply, their price will rise. The rise in price due to scarcity will encourage more suppliers to make CDs in the future and discourage people from buying as many.

The price system therefore keeps demand and supply in balance. When quantity demanded and supplied are equal, equilibrium prevails, that is, there is no tendency for change. At any price above or below the **equilibrium price**, a movement in either demand or supply will occur in order that equilibrium can be restored.

In the diagram, the equilibrium price is P with Q units being supplied and demanded. If the price rose above P, too much would be supplied and hence the market price would fall again. If the price sank below P, there would be shortages as demand would outstrip supply and hence the price would rise again.

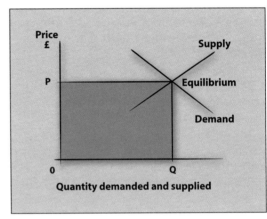

Equilibrium in the market

TASK 2

Assume that there are 850 buyers of CDs in your school. Of these consumers, 800 will buy (demand) at the lower price of £10 and 375 will buy at the higher price of £15. The producers, however, will make 925 available at £15 and only 425 at £10.

a Draw both the demand and supply curves for CDs on the same graph.

b Work out roughly what the equilibrium price will be (where the supply and demand curves cross).

c What would happen to both supply and demand if the producers set the price at £14?

d What would happen to both supply and demand if the producers set the price at £6?

Changes in price

Earlier in this unit, you saw how the market creates a price. When demand and supply are equal, the price that the market settles at is known as the equilibrium price because there is no tendency for change. There are however likely to be changes in the market that will affect the equilibrium price. Such factors can be classified into four areas.

An increase in demand

This is defined as more being demanded at the same price and is shown by the demand curve shifting to the right. It can be caused by a variety of factors such as increased living standards, advertising campaigns making an item more popular, changes in fashion and so on.

The top diagram shows that an increase in demand will raise the equilibrium price to P1 and the quantity demanded and supplied to Q1.

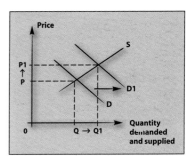

A decrease in demand

Factors such as unemployment, items becoming unfashionable and health scares can cause the demand for a good to fall, that is, less is bought at the same price. This shifts the demand curve to the left, hence equilibrium price falls to P1 and demand and supply to Q1.

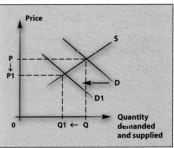

An increase in supply

When more is supplied at the same price there has been an increase in supply. This can be caused by better production methods, new technology, government subsidies and, in the case of agricultural items, favourable weather conditions. An increase in supply is shown by the supply curve moving away from the origin.

The effect of an increase in supply is to lower equilibrium price to P1 but to increase the quantity demanded and supplied to Q1.

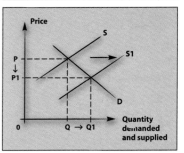

A decrease in supply

A tax on production, a strike or a bad harvest due to disease may cause supply to decrease. The effect of this will be to shift the supply curve from S to S1 and hence increase equilibrium price to P1 and decrease the quantity demanded and supplied to Q1.

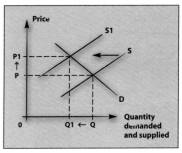

TASK 3

Look at the statements below.
Use demand and supply diagrams plus a written commentary to explain what has happened.

a Local greengrocers are forced to alter the price of apples as a medical journal provides evidence to suggest that an apple a day really does keep the doctor away.

b Share prices in Marks & Spencer rise after record profits are announced.

c Apple trees are hit by a new disease that has killed off half the trees.

d Agricultural research has produced a wheat strain that can produce 50 per cent more wheat per hectare.

e Government ministers decide to tax firms that pollute the local environment.

Hint: For each statement, decide if the situation affects supply or demand (it will only affect one). When you have decided this, you then have to decide if the situation will cause an increase or a decrease.

Failures in the market

You have already seen that the problems of planned economies led many countries, including the former Soviet Union, to change to a market system. This is because the market is believed to be the most efficient way of producing and distributing goods and services. The system is not perfect however and some problems do emerge.

It is important to recognise that all economic systems have advantages and disadvantages. The market system aims to allocate resources through the market or price system whereas the planned system aims to allow the state to control the allocation of resources and the setting of prices. Many economies are still trying to get the right balance between private provision and state provision. Having looked at both sides of the argument it is for you to decide what you think is the best system or whether there is another economic system you would prefer.

Food shortages were common in the planned economy of the Soviet Union.

But an unregulated market economy can mean low pay and very unpleasant conditions for workers.

TASK 4

The Small Island economy is run as a market economy. All the factors of production are privately owned and there are nine large business owners on the island. All the workers are employed from the island but because the businesses meet the changing need of the islanders, their production is never stable. One of the large businesses, the TV station Isle TV, has no rival and has recently put up its fee for viewing by 30 per cent.

The island has an education and health care system that is run privately. The sick, young and elderly who are not in employment become a burden on their family or charity and as a result rarely receive the treatment that they need.

A newspaper reporter recently investigated pollution on the island. Many factory workers from one particular company were receiving medical care for lung complaints. The reporter found that they had been working in unhealthy conditions for many years. The company director commented that the business had to make a profit to stay in business and that workers would find themselves without work if the company had to change its production line as this would lead to a huge increase in costs.

The employed of the island have few complaints about the goods and services available to them on the island and many are pleased that they are able to get the items that they see advertised on Isle TV.

a Using the information above, list the disadvantages of the market economy.

b How might planned economies, where all factors are owned by the state, overcome some of these problems?

c Some of the disadvantages you listed in your answer to **a** exist in the UK. What is done to solve these problems ?

Privatisation

One way in which a mixed economy can open up the market system more effectively is to privatise what were nationalised industries. The process of privatisation returns state owned, public sector industries to the private sector.

These industries are relaunched as public limited companies. Both private individuals and financial institutions are invited to buy shares in them, often through a large-scale advertising campaign. Ownership of these companies is transferred to the private sector and a board of directors is put in charge as with any plc.

Since the 1980s, there have been many examples of privatisation. Some of the best known are shown below:

Date	Corporation
November 1984	British Telecom
December 1986	British Gas
February 1987	British Airways
December 1988	British Steel
December 1989	Regional Water Authorities
December 1990	The National Grid and Regional Electricity Companies
December 1994	British Coal
Commenced 1996	British Rail

Once privatised some of these firms have had to compete with other firms. For example, the government has encouraged the deregulation of the telecommunications market so that BT now has to compete with many other telecoms businesses.

There is competition in the gas supply market. There are also several operators now providing services on the railways.

However, in some industries, notably gas, water and electricity supply, the privatised companies have not faced substantial competition and have been able to make large profits for their shareholders. The directors of

British Rail has been privatised and split up into several new companies, including Virgin.

these businesses have come under considerable criticism for paying themselves excessive salaries and bonuses. There is still debate as to whether privatisation of these industries has benefited the public.

KEY TERMS

Demand – the amount of a good or service that consumers are prepared to buy over a given period of time.

Equilibrium price – where the price has no tendency to change. At equilibrium price the quantity demanded equals the quantity supplied.

Market – where buyers and sellers come together to exchange goods and services.

Market economy – an economy where prices are set by the forces of demand and supply and not by state intervention.

Mixed economy – an economy that has both a private and a public sector.

Planned economy – an economy where decisions about what, how and for whom goods and services are to be made are taken by the state.

Price – the amount of money that a consumer has to pay for a good or service.

Private sector – the sector of the economy where all factors are owned by private individuals and firms.

Public sector – the sector of the economy where all factors are owned by the state.

Supply – the quantity of a good or service that a producer makes available to the market over a given period of time.

Houses too pricey for 'backbone of Britain'

Teachers, nurses and bus drivers are having more difficulty than before buying homes close to where they work, says a report from the Labour Research Department.

Its inquiries show that people in vital services who are on average earnings cannot afford to buy a house in many areas, with those in London and the South East the worst hit.

The Government has proposed a Starter Home initiative designed to help 'key workers' and others on low incomes buy their own homes in areas of high house prices. Last week it announced that £500 million was to be made available to provide affordable housing for those working in essential services.

John Edmonds, general secretary of the GMB union, which commissioned the research, said that although the additional money was 'a move in the right direction' it was not necessarily

enough. He said: 'It is a scandal that such huge gaps in affordable housing exist. These workers are the backbone of this nation, they serve their communities day and night and deserve the chance to buy a home close to where they work.'

In much of London, two people on average earnings would be almost £31,000 short of the amount needed to buy a house. Only nine of London's 32 boroughs had house prices that could be afforded by people on average earnings.

Hospital porters could not afford to buy a house anywhere in the South East. In the West Midlands bus drivers and hospital porters would find only Stoke-on-Trent affordable, and in the South West, hospital porters are priced out of the housing market, while bus drivers can afford to buy only in Plymouth.

Source: *The Independent*, 3 August 2000.

Region	Average price	Quarterly change	Annual change
East Anglia	£83,751	2.8%	18.9%
East Midlands	£68,407	0.3%	10.0%
Greater London	£145,104	-2.4%	19.5%
North	£56,228	-0.7%	1.4%
North West	£62,040	0.5%	6.9%
Northern Ireland	£67,021	1.3%	10.4%
Scotland	£60,689	-5.9%	-2.3%
South East	£129,453	4.5%	22.7%
South West	£95,677	2.4%	19.4%
Wales	£64,034	1.6%	8.4%
West Midlands	£78,561	-0.1%	10.1%
Yorkshire & Humberside	£55,494	-3.2%	1.8%

House prices by region, April to June, 2000. Source: Halifax

Month	Average price	Monthly change	Annual change
September '96	£64,457	-0.1%	5.2%
September '99	£79,162	0.0%	8.8%
June 2000	£83,903	-0.4%	9.2%

House prices, 1996–2000. Source: Halifax

UK house prices levelling

The sharp recent rises in house prices are starting to level off, but homes are still cheaper in real terms than in the last boom in 1988, according to Berkeley Group.

Tony Pidgley, managing director, said the renewed popularity of city-centre living meant there was strong demand for apartments in 'life-style' developments which featured restaurants, shops and leisure facilities.

Berkeley, the largest UK housebuilder in terms of market capitalisation, focuses on London and the South East, and has plans to expand its operations in the Midands, the north of England and the West Country .

Berkeley, a pioneer in the area of brownfield developments, which accounts for 90 per cent of its business, sees the potential for new town-centre developments that would appeal to young professionals in smaller towns.

The company has begun developing a scheme in Swindon. 'There are lots of hi-tech industries around Swindon, but there are no 'life-style' units in the town,' said Tony Carey, managing director of the St George subsidiary. 'There is no town centre.'

But Mr Pidgley warned councils against imposing unduly restrictive conditions on private developers. Requiring too much social housing on a scheme could render it unviable, he said.

Berkeley completed 2,915 homes last year, a three per cent increase, at an average selling price of £251,000, 8 per cent up on the year before. It sold one home for £3.4 million and 20 for more than £1 million each.

It has a land bank of 18,200 plots, up from 14,300, and bought several large brownfield sites last year including the Woolwich Arsenal, with room for 711 homes. It has 2.5 million sq ft of commercial schemes under development.

Source: *Financial Times*, FT.com, 27 June 2000

Q Questions

1 What factors affect the demand for housing in the UK?

2 What does the data show about house prices across the UK?

3 Explain the differences in regional house prices by using demand and supply.

4 While the government is keen to help people on low incomes buy their own homes, it is not seeking to build more public sector housing, that is, council homes for purchase. What problems might be caused by providing more low rent council housing?

E Extension

A lot of companies, including Ikea and McDonald's, are opening stores in the former Eastern bloc countries . What gains are there for companies either selling goods or producing in these previously planned economies?

Government influence on business

This unit is about the effects that government policy and European Union policy may have on business.

At the end of the unit, students should be able to:

- understand the main government economic objectives

- explain how the pursuit of government objectives can affect business

- outline briefly fiscal, monetary, regional and monopoly policy

- explain how business affects and is affected by international trade and exchange rates

- understand the role of the European Union

- evaluate the case for UK adoption of the euro.

How does the government affect business?

Like business, government has objectives. This unit looks at the economic objectives of government and how they may affect business. Unit 8 looks at the social objectives of government.

Economic objectives include:

- aiming towards full employment, that is, aiming to have as many people with jobs as possible

- a low level of inflation, that is, a low rate of increase in the general level of prices

- a stable balance of payments, that is, trying to balance the value of imports against the value of exports

- improving the standard of living, that is, trying to make everyone better off

- closing the gap between the rich the poor, that is, trying to give everyone a more equal income.

It is very difficult for the government to achieve all these objectives at once. This can be shown by the simple example in the diagram.

Governments usually try to meet the five objectives but because they cannot achieve them all at once, they may have to make choices.

Problem
UK needs to increase long-term growth

Solution
Reduce the rate of interest to encourage investment

Effect 1
Firms borrow money as the rate of repayment falls and invest in new technology

Effect 2
Lower mortgage repayments encourage people to buy new homes or move up the property ladder

Outcome
The economy enjoys short-term growth but interest rates rise again quickly to remove it. House price inflation

TASK 1

Sam's Footwear is a shoe manufacturing business. It employs 20 people and has made a reasonable profit in the last ten years. The business is expanding and has bought new equipment which it has financed with a loan.

a How might increasing consumer expenditure affect the business? You could consider what may happen to the demand for shoes and what this might mean for the business in terms of production, employment and profit.

b How might a change in income tax from 25 per cent to 20 per cent affect the business?

c What might happen if the government extended VAT to children's shoes?

d What might happen to the business if the rate of interest rose from 6 per cent to 12 per cent?

Task 1 shows how government can affect business through changing taxes and interest rates. Changes that the government makes can have both harmful and helpful effects for business. The government is constantly trying to make the best decisions both for the economy, consumers and business. It is not an easy balance to get right.

In order to achieve any of the objectives, the government needs to influence the economy. Economic policies fall into three main categories:

- fiscal policy
- monetary policy
- direct controls.

Fiscal policy

Fiscal policy involves the government adjusting the level of demand in the economy by altering government spending and taxation. Government can influence the level of activity. If it can help to raise demand, firms will produce more and employ more people. This can be achieved by lowering taxes so that people will have more money to spend and this will increase demand. Or, the government can spend more on building roads and so forth and create more demand. In these examples, fiscal policy has been used to create demand and thereby reduce unemployment.

The government sets out its expenditure and taxation plans each year in the Budget. The Chancellor of the Exchequer will prioritise objectives and try to make changes in the economy that might create more jobs, keep prices stable, reduce imports and make everyone better off. The Budget aims to raise revenue through taxation in order to finance government expenditure.

Monetary policy

Monetary policy involves the control of the economy through interest rates and the money supply. The aim is to control inflation as monetarist economists believe that inflation causes many problems for the successful management of the economy. The government sets a target rate for inflation and it is the job of the Monetary Policy Committee (MPC) to set the level of the interest rate and supply of money to meet this target. The MPC may raise the rate of interest if it wants to control inflation. This will reduce the amount of money the banks lend out and will reduce demand in the economy and discourage people from borrowing. Furthermore, firms will have to reduce costs when demand falls in order to attract buyers with lower prices. As a result of all of this, prices may fall.

TASK 2

Look at the two graphs showing inflation and the rate of interest over the last 10 years.

a What do the two graphs tell you about the possible link between inflation and the rate of interest? (*Hint*: There may be a time delay between altering the rate of interest and the final effect on inflation.)

b How might the change in interest rates between 1991 and 2001 affect:

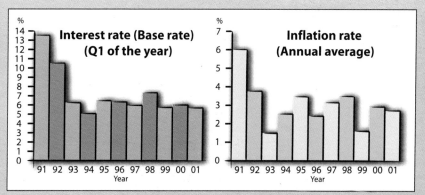

i a large business making household appliances

ii a retail outlet that sells the appliances?

c How might a lower rate of interest affect your parents or carers?

TASK 3

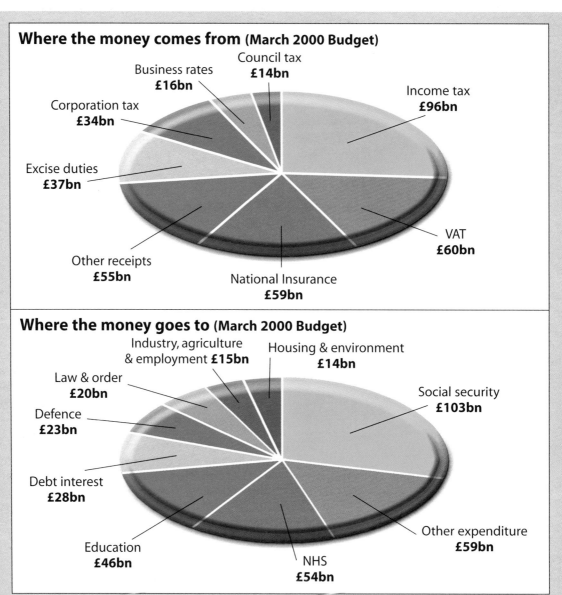

Where the money comes from (March 2000 Budget)

- Council tax **£14bn**
- Business rates **£16bn**
- Corporation tax **£34bn**
- Excise duties **£37bn**
- Other receipts **£55bn**
- National Insurance **£59bn**
- VAT **£60bn**
- Income tax **£96bn**

Where the money goes to (March 2000 Budget)

- Industry, agriculture & employment **£15bn**
- Housing & environment **£14bn**
- Law & order **£20bn**
- Defence **£23bn**
- Debt interest **£28bn**
- Education **£46bn**
- NHS **£54bn**
- Other expenditure **£59bn**
- Social security **£103bn**

Source: *The Independent,* 22 March 2000.

a Look at the pie chart 'Where the money comes from'. This gives a breakdown of the various sources of revenue for a government and the importance of each source in terms of overall monetary contribution to the Budget. Find out what each of the following taxes is, the present rate and how each affects business:

- income tax
- corporation tax
- value added tax (VAT)
- excise duties
- business rates.

b Look at the pie chart 'Where the money goes to'. List the four largest expenditure items in order. Will the order change over the next few years? Can you think of any reasons why?

c In the March 2000 Budget, the Chancellor raised spending on health and education. In groups, or individually, list four different ways of funding this increase in expenditure and the advantages and disadvantages of each method. Report to the class on your proposals. Write an individual report on three of the options having listened to all the other proposals.

d Overall was the government planning to spend more or less than it received in taxation in 2000? Show your calculations.

Direct controls

Fiscal and monetary policy are both directed by government but their effects may be unpredictable and they do not control all aspects of the economy. In order to influence the economy in areas other than demand the government may wish to use direct controls. There is a wide range of controls that government can use in order to influence the economy. These include regional policy and monopoly policy.

Regional policy

Over the years the staple industries of the UK economy such as iron and steel, coal and shipbuilding have declined. Due to their need to locate near to raw materials many of these industries based themselves in the North. As they began to decline, new, footloose industries began to develop. These are industries that are free to locate wherever they choose. They chose to locate in the South, nearer to export markets in Europe and the large domestic market of the capital city. This led to certain areas of our economy such as the North East, South Wales and Scotland developing high rates of unemployment. Governments have directed financial policies towards these areas. Two schemes that have been created to help these regional areas are Regional Selective Assistance and Enterprise Zones.

Regional Selective Assistance offers grants (e.g. £3,000 per new job created) in order to encourage firms to locate in a development area. Development areas include Merseyside, the Highlands of Scotland, South Wales and Tyneside.

Enterprise Zones were created in the 1980s offering rate-free accommodation and tax advantages to firms that moved into the zone. Enterprise Zones that have been created include Swansea, Corby, Salford and Trafford, and Clydebank and Glasgow.

The effect of regional assistance has meant that employment patterns are changing. Traditional areas of high unemployment such as Scotland have seen a great development in high-tech engineering. 50,000 people in Scotland are now employed by 400 electronics companies.

Grants from the European Union (EU) are also available to regions that qualify for UK grants. The European Regional Development Fund (ERDF) funds disadvantaged regions which are categorised by their objective status.

- Objective 1 is the development and structural adjustment of regions whose development is lagging behind.
- Objective 2 is the economic and social conversion of areas facing structural difficulties.
- Objective 3 is the adaptation and modernisation of national policies and systems of education, training and employment.

The ultimate aim of the ERDF is to create jobs by fostering competitive and sustainable development.

TASK 4

The London Lee Valley regeneration programme

The Lee Valley corridor, which extends from the M25 in the north, to the Thames at Leamouth, in the south, has EU Objective 2 status, with European funds to assist the regeneration of its industrial base and employment potential.

The Lee Valley potential

- It has an established and diverse industrial economy.
- It is in a strategic location linking the M25 and the Stansted–Cambridge corridor to the developing areas of the Docklands and East Thames.
- It has extensive transport improvements – road, rail and air links are in place and provide excellent access to local, national and international sites.
- The River Lee and the Lee Valley Regional Park offer environmental quality.

The regeneration strategy

The regeneration of the Lee Valley seeks to promote the opportunities which are present and exploit these through a strategic and integrated approach. The regeneration programme provides an opportunity to:
- establish the Lee Valley as an attractive location for new investment and development
- exploit the linkages between the proposed transport network and development opportunities
- restructure its industrial areas to meet modern business expectations through improved service roads, parking and business accommodation
- support businesses in the areas of innovation, new technology, design and telecommunications
- preserve and enhance the environmental qualities of the area by improving parkland, waterways and to expand leisure facilities in the area.

Source: www.leevalley.co.uk

a What might the Lee Valley Regeneration Programme do with a grant from the EU?

b How would the grant benefit the local business community?

c Create an advertisement designed to attract business to locate in the Lee Valley. (If available, use a DTP package to do this.)

Monopoly policy

The government is able to influence not only where a firm locates but also the way in which it competes both domestically and internationally. This may not always be necessary as competition may benefit the consumer, e.g. lower prices, better service, better quality. However, if a firm does not have to compete it may not provide a good service to the customer. A firm that controls the supply of a good or service is known as a **monopoly**. This control over the market may mean that, without intervention by government, the firm can limit supply, raise prices and offer a poor quality product. The consumer is left with only two choices: either buy the good or service in the condition offered or go without!

Many industries in this position used to be owned by the government in order that they could watch over the industry to ensure that the consumer would not be exploited. During the 1980s many of these industries were privatised (the majority share ownership was transferred into the private sector), leaving the consumer open to possible abuse. In order to avoid any problems, all privatised companies are monitored by their own regulator body, e.g. OFGAS which was set up to investigate complaints by the customers of Centrica (formerly British Gas plc) which has been privatised but still has few competitors.

As a further precaution all industries may be subject to investigation by the Office of Fair Trading and the Competition Commission.

The Office of Fair Trading was established in 1973 to ensure that all businesses compete fairly. It will investigate accusations of price fixing (where firms agree to sell a product at a fixed price that only they will benefit from) and cartels (where a group of firms get together to restrict output and hence keep the price high) and if such practices are found to exist and are harming the customer, the practice will be made illegal.

The Competition Commission will investigate any proposed merger (where two companies agree to join their organisations together) or existing monopoly that is believed to be against the public interest. The Commission can recommend action to the Secretary of State who may ban an unfair practice or stop a merger that is found to be against the public interest.

This will be covered in more detail in Unit 8 (page 62) and Unit 18 (page 135).

International trade

Governments are also able to influence the behaviour of firms in the international market. The ability of firms to trade and exchange currency is influenced by government policy in the same way that domestic trade is. To be able to understand how and why governments intervene it is important to know the mechanisms of trade and exchange.

We are unable to buy all the goods and services that we need to maintain our standard of living from domestic producers. Manufacturers also want to buy raw materials, semi-manufactured goods and certain services from abroad. Similarly consumers and producers from other countries buy UK goods. The measurement of the value of these flows of trade forms the **balance of payments**.

The balance of payments is the difference between the value of all our *exports* (UK goods and services bought on the international market) and *imports* (internationally produced goods and services that are purchased by the UK).

Trade in raw materials and manufactured goods is known as **visible trade**, while trade in services such as tourism, banking and insurance is known as **invisible trade**.

Tourism – an invisible trade

The UK tends to have a trade surplus in invisibles (it sells more exports than it buys imports) and a trade deficit in visibles (it buys more imports than it sells exports).

If the UK imports more in total than it exports we have a balance of payments deficit. When this occurs, the government may intervene because:

- UK industry will suffer as more imports are bought, hence employment levels will fall

- the UK may be losing strategically important industries such as shipbuilding and defence

- new UK industries such as electronic or light engineering firms will not be able to establish themselves.

In order to help UK industries the government may introduce controls on imports. These include the following:

- *Tariffs* – a tax on the imported goods. The tax makes the import more expensive so that UK residents will be discouraged from buying it.

- *Quotas* – this sets a limit on the number of imports that can be allowed into the UK.

- *Trade embargos* – this is where there is a complete ban on trade with a particular country or a particular good or service. It can be due to either political or social reasons.

It should be remembered that many controls are now impossible to introduce in the European Union due to membership of the EU and through world free trade agreements such as the World Trade Organisation (WTO). In any case, the UK may not benefit from the use of import controls if other countries decide to retaliate.

Exchange rates

When goods and services are exchanged on an international level, payments have to be made in currencies. When currencies are exchanged in this way a rate of exchange has to be determined. This is done through the foreign exchange market and the 'price' of each currency will depend on the demand and supply of the currency relative to others.

This rate of exchange between currencies determines the price of exports and imports in their different markets. For example, if the exchange rate is £1 = $1 and it then moves to £1 = $2, UK exports to the USA will become twice as expensive and USA imports into the UK twice as cheap. A rising exchange rate is therefore bad for UK companies exporting and good for international companies exporting to the UK.

The UK government is able to influence these movements in the exchange rate of sterling in order to make the exchange more stable. This enables business to know the price of an export more accurately and this helps it to plan for the future. The government can alter the exchange rate in three main ways:

- It can buy and sell currency on the world market. Selling sterling would help to keep its level low.

- Altering the rate of interest will alter the demand for a currency. If the interest rate is lowered, then international financiers will move their money out of the UK and into an economy with a higher rate of interest. This will lower the demand for sterling, increase supply and hence lower the price of the pound on the foreign exchange.

- The government can also help industry by entering a more stable exchange rate system. In fixed exchange rate schemes the price of a currency is fixed against other currencies, hence there is no uncertainty in exchange.

The European Union

Britain joined the European Union (formerly called the European Community) in 1973 in order to gain from free trade between the member countries. There is a wide range of rules and regulations that are imposed on all firms trading in the EU and in particular the free trade agreement means that there are no customs duties on goods and services traded in the area. A common external tariff is placed on all imports coming into EU countries.

Since becoming a member of the EU, many regulations that affect business are monitored by the European Parliament rather than the British government. These include:

- legislation to support free competition between firms and hence ban practices such as price fixing and other anti-competitive practices

- a guaranteed (fixed) price to farmers for most agricultural products

- additives in food, packaging and other legal/technical aspects

- location of business through the use of loans and grants available from the European Regional Development Fund.

The EU currently has 15 member countries, but another 12 countries (mostly from Eastern Europe) have applied to join. The introduction of new members is complex, but if and when they join, the free trading market will become vast.

The Euro

On 1 January 1999 the euro (€) became the official currency of 11 member states of the EU, with a fixed conversion rate into their national currencies. Greece became the 12th euro member in January 2001. Euro notes and coins were not due to appear until 1 January 2002, but the new currency could be used before then by consumers, retailers, companies and public authorities in non-cash form. This meant that goods in the shops were priced in euros as well as the national currency. Member countries also agreed to share a single interest rate, set by the European Central Bank (ECB), and a single foreign exchange rate policy. The euro was set to have a major impact on the business environment both within these countries and throughout Europe.

Even though the UK did not join the single currency on 1 January 1999, the introduction of the euro directly affected many UK businesses, especially those which buy and sell products throughout Europe. The euro will probably be used in some business transactions within the UK itself, particularly in supply chains dealing with multinational companies.

KEY TERMS

Balance of payments – the value of exports from the UK minus the value of imports into the UK.

Euro – the single currency to be used for all exchanges in 12 member states of the European Union.

Exchange rate – the price at which one currency is exchanged for another.

Fiscal policy – the use of taxation and government spending to change the level of demand in the economy.

Invisible trade – the trade in services.

Monetary policy – the use of policies to change the level and value of money and hence influence the economy through lowering inflation.

Monopoly – where one supplier controls the market. By law, a monopoly is defined as any firm that has more than a 25 per cent share of the market.

Regional policy – the use of grants and loans to influence the location of industry.

Visible trade – the trade in goods.

Japanese have no yen for euro-less Britain

Foreign firms are fighting shy of investing in British industry because ministers have failed to steer the country firmly towards membership of the single European currency, according to a secret telegram published today.

The leaked message from Sir Stephen Gomersall, Britain's ambassador to Japan, to senior government officials, says many Japanese investments in the UK have been 'affected' by the high value of the pound to the euro.

They feel that further investment in the UK carries 'unnecessary risks'.

Sir Stephen said any backtracking on the government's timetable for euro membership could 'trigger a much stronger move towards disinvestment' by Japanese firms.

In the telegram Sir Stephen says 'losses on the bottom line of manufacturers have brought about some closures, plans to increase sourcing from outside the UK and consideration of re-weighting of operations and headquarters towards Eastern Europe and the euro-zone.

'Some significant projects are at risk.'

There are 'brighter spots' in research and development where the UK has particular skills to offer, Sir Stephen says.

'But uncertainty about UK policy on the Euro has fed a generalised perception that until the UK is clearly on a track to join the single currency, further investment in the UK carries unnecessary risks.'

Source: Adapted from *Manchester Evening News*, 4 July 2000

UK economy risks 'lagging Europe'

Failure to join the single currency and over-generous government spending plans could turn the UK economy into the 'sick man of Europe' once again, a report warns.

The quarterly Item Club report was prepared by accountants Ernst & Young and is based on the Treasury's own economic model.

The report's authors argue that Chancellor Gordon Brown's recently announced spending spree – with £43 billion going to education, health and transport – will make future tax rises 'inevitable'.

Those taxes would sap private demand and cause an economic downturn.

This in turn could herald the return of old-style tax-and-spend economics, just at a time when the single currency is forcing governments on the Continent to reform and cut their taxes.

'With all of Britain's advantages as a low tax economy seeping away, Germany's increasingly dynamic market economy – given added zest, of course, because it functions in the single market – will eclipse that of Britain, which will look increasingly backward,' the report says.

The report concludes that the UK could be 'left behind', while eurozone economies regain their strength.

EU Commissioner Chris Patten, meanwhile, told the *Financial Times* that the UK would sacrifice economic success and international influence if it did not join the euro. The former chairman of the Conservative Party said the government should speak out more in favour of the euro: 'It's a very curious description of sovereignty to say that in return for Bank of England governor Sir Eddie George still being able to set interest rates in Britain ... it is worth us paying a price in which the euro group of countries set macro-economic policy without consulting us.'

Source: *BBC News*, 31 July 2000, http://news.bbc.co.uk

75% of British voters say euro is a failure

British hostility to the euro has hardened since its launch last year, according to a Gallup poll for the *Daily Telegraph* today.

Three-quarters of the electorate believe the single currency is a failure and the pro-euro lobby would be outvoted 2–1 in a referendum on scrapping the pound. The proportion of the electorate opposed to British membership of the euro has risen to 69 per cent, amid a growing mood of scepticism about the way the European Union has conducted itself.

A large proportion of voters fear their standard of living would fall if Britain left the EU entirely, and fewer than 20 per cent favour pulling out altogether. Nevertheless a significant proportion, 31 per cent, said their opinion of the EU had gone down over the past few months.

Many cited excessive EU interference in Britain's internal affairs and mounting evidence of mismanagement and corruption in Brussels.

Britons and the Euro		
From what you know, has the single European currency been a success?		
	June 1999%	Now %
Yes it has	21	16
No it has not	59	75
Don't know	20	8
In a referendum on the euro, how would you vote?		
In favour of Britain joining and abolishing the pound	29	27
Against	66	69
Don't know	5	3

Source: *Daily Telegraph*, 13 March 2000.

End of unit ASSESSMENT

UK Inflation and Growth, 1996–2002

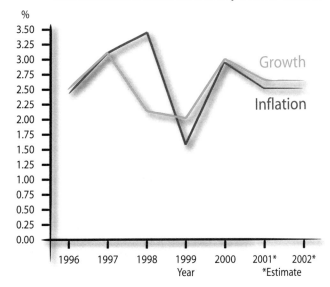

%
3.50
3.25
3.00 — Growth
2.75
2.50
2.25
2.00 — Inflation
1.75
1.50
1.25
1.00
0.75
0.50
0.25
0.00

1996 1997 1998 1999 2000 2001* 2002*
Year
*Estimate

UK Balance of Payments, 1997-2002

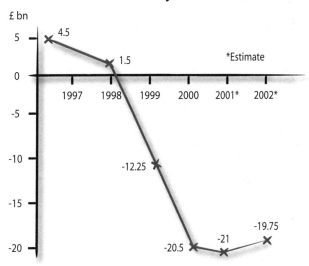

£ bn

5 — 4.5
        1.5   *Estimate
0
   1997 1998 1999 2000 2001* 2002*
-5

-10
              -12.25

-15
                                        -19.75
-20   -21
              -20.5

UK Unemployment, 1996–2002

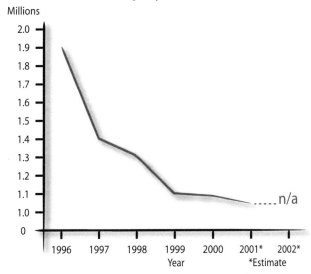

Millions
2.0
1.9
1.8
1.7
1.6
1.5
1.4
1.3
1.2
1.1 ......n/a
1.0
0

1996 1997 1998 1999 2000 2001* 2002*
Year
*Estimate

Source: HM Treasury.

Q Questions

1 Produce a leaflet, outlining the basic facts about the European single currency and the pros and cons for British business of the UK joining the euro. (*Hint:* You will find a lot of useful information in textbooks and on the Internet as well as the data provided.)

2 What other factors might persuade investors to locate their business in the UK, despite our current non-membership of the euro?

3 Explain why manufacturing businesses are worried about 'the strength of sterling'.

4 Using the statistics provided, discuss how each of the four economic variables affects and is affected by UK companies. Do you think the economic conditions shown have been good for UK companies?

E Extension

Research the most recent Budget. What has the Chancellor done to help business? What was the reaction of the City to the Budget? Do you think it was a good Budget for business?

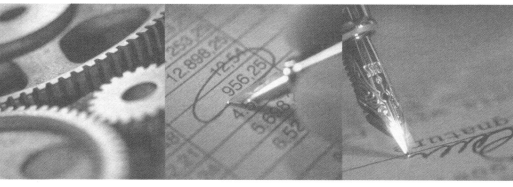

Business and the community

This unit is about the relationship between business and the community.

At the end of the unit, students should be able to:

- describe, with relevant examples, the social costs and benefits of business activity

- compare social costs and benefits with private costs and benefits

- understand the need for consumer legislation and explain how such legislation affects business

- explain the role of pressure groups in relation to business activity

- understand the need for competition policy and explain how such legislation affects business

- understand the need for environmental policy and explain how such legislation affects business.

Social costs and benefits of business activity

Whenever a business undertakes a major course of action, such as opening a new outlet or extending a factory, there are costs and benefits both to the business and to society. The costs and benefits to the business itself are called **private costs** and **private benefits** and can usually be worked out in financial terms. The costs and benefits to society are called **social costs** and **social benefits** and are difficult to work out in financial terms. The process of looking at the costs and benefits of a particular course of action is called cost-benefit analysis.

If a large organisation wishes to undertake a new project which is likely to stir strong feelings in the local community, e.g. extending a factory site, it would be helpful for the organisation to have carried out cost-benefit analysis. This will enable the organisation to have considered the social costs and social benefits as well as the benefits to itself. It will then be able to present arguments in favour, the social benefits, to any local objectors. It will also have identified the social costs which may form the basis of local objections. The organisation may be able to find ways in which it can compensate the local community.

AGAINST   FOR

The social costs of extending a factory site might be:

- the inconvenience and possible danger to local residents while construction was taking place
- the noise and dirt from the construction
- the loss of open, green space
- the unpleasant sight of a factory building once completed
- the noise and pollution from the factory once in use
- the increased traffic to and from the factory once in use.

The social benefits of extending a factory site might include:

- an increase in the number of jobs for local people both during construction and once the factory is open
- increased spending in local shops by construction workers and by the workers employed in the new factory
- use by the local community of the accompanying new sports and social facilities
- pleasant landscaped factory grounds.

TASK 1

Identify the social costs and benefits of the opening of an out-of-town superstore. You will be able to use much of the information in this article but may also wish to use local information if there is a superstore development near you.

Superstores in search of new frontiers

In October 1995 two huge new superstore developments in south Manchester were opened on the same day. The schemes, both opposed at first, provide 445,000 square feet of shopping space spread over almost 70 acres of land. They have had the biggest impact on local employment in years, creating about 1,900 new jobs.

There is a free bus service to one of the sites. 144 regular buses per day have had their routes diverted to include both sites.

A new bypass which had been planned for years has been built because the supermarket chains have made substantial contributions to the cost of building the road. This contribution enabled planning permission to be granted.

On one of the sites the John Lewis Partnership has built the largest new department store in Britain in the last five years. It will be the third biggest private sector employer in Stockport and the biggest single job creator in two decades.

But many villages and small town shopping centres, already hit by competition from existing supermarkets and the advent of Sunday trading, feel it could just be the final nail in their coffin. A delicatessen in nearby Cheadle Hulme has been on the market for the last three years. The owner is not surprised that it hasn't sold. 'Who wants to buy a business like this when these superstores are around the corner?' she says. 'We can't compete with them for price and most people will shop where the price is lowest.'

The Chief Executive of Manchester Chamber of Commerce agrees that the effect on small businesses is a matter of concern. 'Superstores like these take away individual choice when small businesses close. It is not always possible to bring these small shops back. Another concern is that it is the elderly, the less mobile and the less well off who don't have the freedom to travel who are hit once again.'

Source: Adapted from *Manchester Evening News*, 20 October 1996

Consumer legislation and its effects on business

Business generally has always been more powerful than a single consumer and this power is increasing. In the last two decades multinational businesses, often with turnover equal to the value of the total goods and services produced by a country such as Sweden, have increased in number. In order to protect consumers in their dealings with business and to try to ensure that consumers are not exploited, various Acts have been passed. The most important Acts – important both in terms of the protection offered to consumers and because of their effect on the operation of business – are as follows.

The *Sale of Goods Act 1974* requires businesses to sell goods which are of **merchantable quality**, that is, they must not be defective or damaged. Goods must also be **fit for the purpose**, that is, they must be suitable for the purpose for which they are sold. For example, a pair of sports shoes must not begin to disintegrate after a few games of squash. Consumers are entitled to their money back or to replacement goods if their rights are breached. It is therefore in the interests of business that goods are in perfect condition and are correctly designed.

The *Trade Descriptions Act 1968* protects the consumer against a business falsely describing its goods or services. For example, a consumer may claim against a holiday company which describes a hotel as having an extensive pool and leisure complex when these are still under construction.

The *Weights and Measures Act 1951* protects consumers against purchasing goods which fall short of the weight or measure required. Businesses are not only compelled to give full weight or measure but also to indicate the weight or measure on pre-packaged goods.

The *Food and Drugs Act 1955* deals with the content of foodstuffs and their accurate labelling.

The *Consumer Credit Act 1974* protects consumers in the way they make their purchases. Many people buy large items on credit, that is, they pay for the item over a period of time. The Consumer Credit Act ensures that the consumer is aware of the annual rate of interest charged on the money that they have borrowed. This rate is known as the **APR – annual percentage rate**. The Act is important because otherwise businesses would be able to quote interest rates in ways which make the opportunity to borrow seem much more attractive, e.g. by using the monthly rate.

The *Consumer Protection Act 1987* deals mainly with the safety of goods. If, for example, a personal computer blows up and injures someone, or burns a carpet in the home, the consumer is entitled to claim for costs and damages against the manufacturer of that computer. Mail order customers have also been protected under schemes run by the Mail Order Protection Association. Its code of practice states that as customers do not benefit from seeing the goods before they buy them they can get their money back within 14 days.

TASK 2

Take care with food claims

Like advertising, food labels should be honest and not misleading. But that is where the law stops. There are few detailed rules outlining what manufacturers can and can't say about their products. This means that a 'low fat' burger can have twice as much fat as a 'low fat' fish fillet and the door is left wide open for manufacturers to make a host of dubious health claims about their foods.

Food claims can also be confusing because they are allowed to be selective about the information they give. Foods which claim to be 'low fat', for example, may not point out that they are also high in sugar or salt. And a 'low fat' or 'low sugar' food won't necessarily be any lower in calories – it might even have more.

Since October 1993 all foods making claims must also provide nutrition information on the pack. However, this doesn't help consumers understand more general health claims like 'good for you' or 'healthy'. These are often nothing but marketing ploys.

'Reduced Sugar'
Sainsbury's reduced sugar digestives do contain less sugar – what the label doesn't tell you is that they also contain more calories

'A Low Fat Food'
Cornflakes have always been low in fat – they contain less than 12g fat per 100g. Apples, too, are 'a low fat food'.

'Lower Fat'
These crisps contain 30 per cent less fat than Tesco's standard crisps – but they still have 26g of fat per 100g

'Low fat'
These chips have been made so that they contain little fat – less than 5g per 100g

Source: Adapted from *Which?*, May 1993.

 Ministry of Agriculture Fisheries and Food

Better food labelling

What do you think should be included on food labels?

We would like to hear your views.

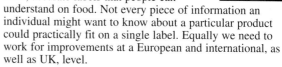

Food is an important issue for us all – and in making choices about what we eat we need clear information.

This Government is committed to giving consumers informed choice – and that means clear, accurate labels that people can understand on food. Not every piece of information an individual might want to know about a particular product could practically fit on a single label. Equally we need to work for improvements at a European and international, as well as UK, level.

We want to know more about your priorities on labelling, the improvements you would like to see, so that our overall strategy and policy on specific issues can reflect these views. I will be making sure the Food Standards Agency, the new independent body we have set up which will have responsibilities in this area from April, receives a full report on the results of this 'listening exercise' – so please do let us know what you think.

Helene Hayman

Helene Hayman, Minister for Food Safety

Turn over for more information and where to send your comments.

Source: Ministry of Agriculture, Fisheries and Food

Despite the range of legislation designed to protect the consumer, manufacturers are still able to entice consumers to buy by making claims for their products which may be misleading. Another way of increasing sales is to make a truthful claim about 'lower fat' or 'low sugar' products without explaining the extent of the other ingredients.

a What information on the label is important to the consumer and why?

b What does the *Which?* article mean by 'marketing ploys'? Use an example to help illustrate your answer.

c If the label makes a claim about food (e.g. it says that it is low fat), should this be controlled?

d Research an example of where a product description has been misleading. (*Hint*: TV programmes such as *Watchdog*, consumer magazines such as *Which?* and the Consumers Association may be of help.)

The role of pressure groups

A **pressure group** is an organisation which tries to influence or change the course of events. Pressure groups can be local, national or international. A local group of protesters in Didsbury, Manchester, prevented the pub chain J D Wetherspoons from converting a former hardware store into a pub with beer garden. The local protesters fought the company in the courts and won their protest (see Task 3).

Many national pressure groups are charities such as the National Society for the Prevention of Cruelty to Children (NSPCC). Most of the time the charity engages in practical action and fund raising, but it may try to bring pressure to bear on the government when specific cases of child neglect are publicised. For example, well-publicised cases of children being left alone while parents go to work highlighted the need for the NSPCC to campaign for parents to be able to claim child care fees as a tax deductible expense.

Friends of the Earth is an example of an international pressure group. It tries to pressurise national and international business to behave differently. Recent campaigns have drawn attention to how we produce our food including genetically modified foods, the use of pesticides and organic farming. The Real Food campaign aims to make a difference to the food we eat and Friends of the Earth provides information on supermarket policies towards GM-free, pesticide-free products, where GM crops are grown and how to influence supermarkets through an e-mail petition.

A business can suffer adverse publicity and incur costs because of the actions of pressure groups. A local group of protesters in Bolton tried to prevent the housebuilders, Barratt, from building an estate of houses in a beauty spot. Barratt had to fight the pressure group in the courts, incurring legal fees.

Trade unions are the pressure group which businesses are most likely to come into contact with. Trade unions exist to protect the rights of workers in the workplace and will fight business where it is felt that workers have not been fairly treated. Trade unions are dealt with in more detail in Unit 32.

Not all pressure groups are directed at business by consumers. Businesses have their own pressure groups or watchdogs to ensure that the majority of businesses adhere to a voluntary code of practice. The *Advertising Standards Authority* is a pressure group funded by the advertising industry to ensure that all press adverts are legal, honest, decent and truthful. It responds to requests from the general public and can ask its members to withdraw adverts which are found to infringe the code.

TASK 3

Pub battle set for showdown

A developer is set to go head to head with the City Council in a controversial proposal to build a large pub in Didsbury.

The battle is being viewed as a stand-off between those who believe there are already too many licensed premises in Didsbury village and the big chains keen to take advantage of its growing reputation as a centre for food and drink.

A public inquiry is due to hear an appeal against the Manchester City Council's refusal to grant Wetherspoons approval to build a pub on Didsbury's largest retail site – the former Griffiths DIY store.

And Wetherspoons have caused further anger by submitting a last minute adjustment to their proposal with a beer garden added to the back of the premises adjacent to neighbouring funeral directors Peacocks.

Councillor David Sandiford said he was outraged by the idea. He added: 'Wetherspoons have submitted new plans to the town hall in the past week, only three weeks from the public inquiry and have announced that they will be asking the Inspector at the inquiry to rule on these new plans.

'I am totally opposed to this – Didsbury residents are not properly informed about the new plans and have not been given a sensible opportunity to consider them.

'The idea of a beer garden shown in the plans, next to the neighbouring undertakers' Chapel of Rest is abhorrent. The last minute manoeuvre by Wetherspoons is a desperate attempt to short cut the normal democratic procedures that must include full consultation.'

A spokesman for Peacocks Funeral Directors said they were extremely concerned by the application because of the effect that beer swilling Wetherspoons clients may have on their business.

He added: 'Our priority is to protect our clients who wish to pay their respects to a loved one in a dignified manner at what is a very distressing time.'

Planners originally suggested the proposal be refused because there were no acceptable provisions for a loading area for vehicles bringing beer to the pub.

Campaigners are hoping the Planning Inspectorate will rule against any new proposals to bring wagons down a narrow passageway between the premises and a funeral directors next door.

Source: Adapted from *Manchester Evening News*, 20 October 1996

a What arguments might the pressure group use to persuade people about its cause?
b What actions might the local pressure group take?
c What arguments might Wetherspoons use to oppose the pressure group in court?

Other legal controls on business activity

Some legal controls have a direct impact on business activity rather than working to protect groups with which business comes into contact. Some of the legal controls are aimed at large businesses but others affect all businesses whatever their size. Two government bodies exist to prevent businesses acting against the interests of consumers by restricting the amount of competition. The two bodies are the Office of Fair Trading and the Competition Commission.

The *Office of Fair Trading* can take action against a business or group of businesses which are engaging in unfair practices likely to restrict competition. The Competition Commission is an independent public body established by the Competition Act 1998. The Commission replaced the Monopolies and Mergers Commission (MMC) on 1 April 1999.

The Commission has two distinct functions:

- It has taken on the former MMC role of carrying out inquiries into matters referred to it by the other UK competition authorities concerning monopolies, mergers and the economic regulation of utility companies.

- The newly established Appeal Tribunal hears appeals against decisions of the Director General of Fair Trading and the Regulators of utilities in respect of infringements concerning anti-competitive agreements and abuse of a dominant position.

There are two Acts which prevent businesses engaging in anti-competitive behaviour: the *Restrictive Trade Practices Act* and the *Resale Prices Act*. Complaints falling under the two acts are dealt with in the courts. The Restrictive Practices Act deals with any activity between businesses which could prevent them from operating independently. The Resale Prices Act prevents business from setting minimum prices at which goods can be sold.

There are also legal controls on manufacturing firms and their impact on the environment. The *Environment Protection Act 1990* created two new systems for regulating industrial pollution. More than 5,000 existing industrial processes which are likely to cause the greatest industrial pollution are regulated through the Integrated Pollution Control, so named because it monitors pollution to air, water and land. An Inspector of Pollution is responsible for enforcing this aspect of the legislation. In addition, local authorities have the right to ensure that action is taken in relation to a large number of complicated processes which result in air pollution.

TASK 4

50 ways to give the customer better deal

Don Cruickshank's plan to shake up Britain's banks contains more than 50 recommendations, aimed at securing a better, cheaper service for customers by ensuring more competition in the industry.

Mr Cruickshank was asked to examine the way banks work, amid claims that their record profits were excessive. The banks said their profitability was merely an indication of a healthy economy.

Yesterday's report is evidence that they have failed to persuade Mr Cruickshank that they do not conspire to operate a monopoly in several key areas.

Key points of the 344-page report are:

- Individual customers and small businesses get a poor deal, with most households paying up to £400 a year more than they should.
  The massive profits are all returned to shareholders, leaving customers with low rates of interest for savings and higher rates for borrowing.
- No government intervention is needed because new players – such as Standard Life, Egg and Internet banks – are offering better deals.
- Banking services for small and medium enterprises should be referred to the Competition Commission. This could lead to the break-up of the dominance of the big four high-street banks in that market.
- There should be a new watchdog, Paycom, to oversee charges from cash machines, standing orders, direct debits and cheque clearing.
  Some banks, led by Barclays, have been attempting to impose a £1 fee for each time a non-customer uses its cash machines. Mr Cruickshank said such charges should not exceed 30p.
- Mergers should be more closely scrutinised to check they are in the consumer interest.

	Small business charges	Personal charges for an unauthorised overdraft	Charge for return of each unpaid cheque or standing order made while overdrawn
Abbey National	Free banking (but no overdraft facility)	£15 fee and 29.9% equivalent annual interest	£30
Barclays	£2.50 monthly maintenance fee. Automated transactions 45p each, non-automated 64p each	Over £20 or three days, £20 fee and 29.8% equivalent annual interest rate	£25
First Direct		£37.50 charge for first day of unauthorised overdraft, plus £9 for each subsequent day; 29.5% equivalent annual interest	£37.50
HSBC	£2.50 monthly fee. 60p for each cash transaction and 35p for each automated item.	£27.50 per month; 29.5% equivalent annual interest	£28 flat fee, plus £28 per item
Lloyds TSB	£2.50 monthly fee. 59p for each cash transaction and 42p for each automated item.	£10 charge when overdrawn by £10 or more, plus 60p for each transaction	£27.50
NatWest	£5.75 monthly fee; 67p for each cash transaction; 40p for automated paying out transaction and 22p for paying in	£5 per month when more than £50 overdrawn, plus £3.50 for each day; 33.8% equivalent annual interest	£27.50
Royal Bank of Scotland	No monthly fee. Automated credits 25p, non-automatic credits 64p, automatic debits 40p, non-automatic debits 55p	£15 fee and 33.7% equivalent annual interest	£30

Source: *Daily Telegraph*, 21 March 2000.

a In what ways does the article suggest that banks are behaving in an anti-competitive way that is harming the customer?

b What might customers have done to oppose the behaviour of the banks?

c Describe three measures that you think the Competition Commission could take to break up the dominance of the four main banks in the small and medium businesses' market.

d What arguments might banks put forward to oppose the loss of their dominant position?

KEY TERMS

APR – the annual percentage rate of interest charged on money borrowed.

Fit for the purpose – a requirement of the Sale of Goods Act is that goods are suitable for the purpose for which they are sold.

Merchantable quality – a requirement of the Sale of Goods Act is that goods are not defective when offered for sale.

Monopoly – where one supplier controls the market. By law, a monopoly is defined as a company that has more than a 25% share of the market.

Pressure group – an organisation which tries to affect the way another group, usually business or government, operates.

Private benefits – the benefits to the investor, usually easy to measure in terms of money.

Private costs – the costs to the investor, usually measured in financial terms.

Restrictive practices – business activity which is designed to restrict competition.

Social benefits – benefits to society in general; difficult to calculate in financial terms.

Social costs – costs to society in general; difficult to calculate in financial terms.

The story of Manchester airport

Today, Manchester Airport is one of Britain's, and the world's, principal airports, handling millions of passengers each year, connecting the North of England with global destinations. Still growing, Manchester Airport has an exciting and promising future, but it has an equally illustrious past, which began in 1928.

1986 The World Freight Terminal opens.

1993 Terminal 2 is opened by HRH the Duke of Edinburgh, doubling Manchester Airport's terminal capacity to around 20 million passengers a year.

1997 Approval for the building of the second runway is granted and work on building the second runway commences.

2000 Work starts on the £60 million Integrated Public Transport Interchange and the government gives the go ahead for a £289 million Metrolink extension to the airport.

Source: Manchester Airports plc, 2000

Introduction to Runway 2

Manchester Airport is enjoying unprecedented growth, but in many ways it is just the beginning. A £172 million investment in a new second runway will offer vital extra capacity to the airlines, tour operators and freight companies, allowing them to respond to an anticipated increase in passengers to 30 million over the next ten years.

The single runway has been operating at capacity in the peak period for a number of years and can handle up to a maximum of 48 aircraft movements per hour. If the airport is to continue to grow and serve the travel needs of the North of England, additional runway capacity is needed. This will provide capacity to enable airlines, particularly those operating scheduled services, to grow and develop new services at Manchester Airport. This development will not only serve the needs of the region's travellers, but will help to stimulate economic growth through the creation of thousands of new jobs.

Source: Manchester Airport plc, 2000

The argument against Runway 2

The principal argument put forward to convince the public that the second runway is a good idea is that employment would be created. However, with the same amount of investment in other areas many more jobs could be made, to improve quality of life rather than damage it through pollution and destruction.

Some air travel is beneficial, but much is extremely unnecessary. Seven-eighths of business passengers' flights from Manchester Airport are internal flights – why can't they use the train? (Source: MAJAG)

Food is flown in when it can be grown here! Many foreign holiday journeys could also be made by train, or be taken in one of the many beautiful parts of the UK, if only we'd preserve them! These alternatives would benefit local economies, rather than flying money out of our already impoverished city.

Air pollution causes health problems. The growth in air transport will lead to increased problems of air pollution. A second runway with the projected extra passengers is estimated to increase road traffic by more than 100%. (Source: GMTAG) That means MORE road building, MORE pollution and MORE accidents.

'Today 1 in 7 children has asthma. In some inner-city areas 1 child in 3 suffers'. (Friends of the Earth, 1995)

Source: Coalition Against Runway Two, Manchester Friends of the Earth, 2000.

Manchester Airport

Manchester Airport's plans for the environment

As part of the Green Charter for the second runway, a detailed environmental mitigation package was developed. It includes planting six new trees for every one removed, providing or improving two ponds for every one lost, planting or restoring over 36 km of hedgerow, and creating new areas of wild flower grassland and woodland. Additional special measures have been undertaken to deal with the protected species identified within the site.

A 15-year management plan (with 1- and 5-year action plans) has been developed to protect and improve over 850 acres of countryside around the Airport. Progress is monitored and reviewed by the Nature Conservation and Landscape Steering Group, which meets regularly and brings together the Airport Company, local authorities, specialist bodies (e.g. English Nature) and representatives of the local community.

Source: Manchester Airport plc, 2000.

Runway two: an untold environmental disaster

Manchester Friends of the Earth today condemned the (likely) decision to allow Manchester Airport plc to destroy thousands of acres of Manchester's greenbelt. The expensive public relations exercise conducted by Manchester Airport plc and Manchester City Council has failed to mention these:
- Increased road traffic.
- More road-building.
- Emissions of global warming gases.
- Loss of green space and recreation area.
- Destruction of wildlife habitats.
- Increases in air pollution, from air traffic and road traffic.
- Increase in noise pollution.
- Associated out-of-town developments.
- Promotion of an unsustainable form of transport.
- The creation of little local employment for gross environmental destruction.

Source: Campaign Against Runway Two, Manchester Friends of the Earth, 15 January 1997.

Noisy defeat, silent victory!

With physical eviction from the site of Manchester Airport's second runway expected at any moment, environmental activists today confirmed their continued opposition to the most environmentally damaging construction project the north-west has ever seen.

Tree-house-based campaigner Phil, based at Flywood Camp, said: 'Our campaign to highlight the local and global environmental costs of continual air transport growth is succeeding. The issues of noise pollution, air pollution irretrievable and irreversible damage to the countryside, coupled with the huge and growing global warming effect of air transport are really beginning to be understood by everybody. Our noisy defeat will lead to a silent victory as people use planes less.'

Phil continued: 'We hope the impact and legacy of our campaign will be to change forever people's attitude towards the seductive allure of foreign holidays and business travel.'

Source: Campaign Against Runway Two, Manchester Friends of the Earth, 9th May, 1997.

Q Questions

1 Write a report, outlining the social costs and benefits of building a second runway.
2 Why do you think that the second runway proposal was accepted?
3 Explain, using examples, what legislation might affect:
   a Manchester Airport plc and its relationship with the local community
   b a customer flying with an airline such as BA or Ryanair
   c an outlet selling drinks to passengers waiting to fly.

E Extension

The media often cover stories on big business being investigated for anti-competitive practices, a recent case being that of computer software giant Microsoft.

1 Investigate a case that has been referred to the Competition Commission and find out:
   a the claims made by the two sides in the case.
   b the final verdict by the Competition Commission.
2 Did you agree with the verdict? If not, explain why.

Globalisation of business

This unit is about the development of globalised businesses, global brands and whether there is a future for the small, localised company.

At the end of the unit, students should be able to:

- understand what is meant by globalisation in a business context
- give examples of globalisation
- explain why globalisation has developed over the past 20 years
- identify the advantages and disadvantages of globalisation from a range of perspectives
- explain the need for local and transnational companies.

What is globalisation?

Over the past 20 years, much has happened to the world economy to open up opportunities for trade. The reforms in eastern Europe and the continuing growth of the east Asian economies have played a large part in the expansion of world trade. Between 1980 and 1993, world trade grew from US $4 trillion to $7.5 trillion, a rate of 87.5 per cent! Of this, approximately 70 per cent involves trade by transnational companies.

During this time, companies have also seen tremendous changes in the way in which they operate. Developments in new technology, transportation of goods, quicker and more efficient communications systems and the reduction of world **trade barriers** have made it easier for companies to buy and sell in the world market. As a result, the number of transnational companies rose from 7,000 in 1970 to 40,000 in 1995. A **transnational corporation (TNC)** is defined as a company which operates in several countries. The best known TNCs include Coca Cola, IBM, McDonald's and Sony.

McDonald's fast-food restaurants can be found in towns all over the world

TASK 1

a Identify what each company shown in the table sells on the world market. (*Hint:* You may need to look up some of these companies on the Internet.)

b Describe, using examples of goods and services sold by the companies listed in the table, how the marketing department may find selling on a world market to be a great advantage. (*Hint:* Try to cover price, advertising, branding, the product/service, and meeting customer needs.)

c Describe, using examples of goods and services sold by the companies listed in the table, how the marketing department may find it difficult to sell on a world market.

Brand	Value (US$bn)
Coca Cola	47.99
Marlboro	47.64
IBM	23.70
McDonald's	19.94
Disney	17.07
Sony	14.46
Kodak	14.44
Intel	13.27
Gillette	11.99

The most valuable global brands, 1998. Source: *The Economist*, 12 June 1999.

Why has globalisation developed?

Globalisation has developed over recent years as a result of the following:

- Globalisation offers the benefits of **economies of scale**. As firms are able to produce goods and services for a world market, they are able to enjoy the benefits of reduced production costs through bulk buying and international **marketing**. In addition, costs are often reduced by choosing low cost locations offering advantages such as tax incentives and cheap labour.

- Improvements in technology have made the world market very accessible:
  - Companies have seen dramatic changes in the way in which they communicate. The growth of the Internet, e-mail, video conferencing and mobile phones means that communication is available between companies and their staff, 24 hours a day, seven days a week. This makes world trade far more open and reduces the barriers built by time zones.
  - Travel both for staff and goods is quicker and cheaper. This creates savings for companies in terms of time and money and makes the world a smaller place. Developing infrastructure is also opening up new markets for trade to occur and allowing opportunities for customers to travel abroad, sampling different cultures and a widening range of goods and services.
  - Improvements in transport have made it easier for companies to get their products to the customer quickly, cheaply and with minimal damage.

Transport improvements have been a vital factor in globalisation

Coca Cola is a worldwide brand

- Consumer behaviour has changed. Consumers now accept global products. Across the world, many of us drink the same brands, wear the same clothing brands, watch the same movies and play the same games. While national/ethnic/cultural differences do still occur, companies are better able to produce a product or service that they can sell globally. This mass production opens up further opportunities to gain economies of scale and either increase profit margins or drive down price.

Why might companies choose to go transnational?

In general, companies develop into transnational operations for the following reasons:

- Selling a product on the world market means increasing market size, with the potential of greater profits.

- The domestic market may have been saturated, with further expansion only possible in a global market.

- New markets may have emerged that the company wishes to take advantage of, e.g. Internet and mobile phone companies have seen the potential for global branding.

- Sites abroad may offer incentives to reduce production costs, including cheaper skilled labour, raw materials and government incentives.

- Expanding into new markets may offer companies the opportunity to diversify. This may allow them to spread their risk both across products and national markets. Products and economies may experience high and low points and TNCs may be in a better position to smooth out these fluctuations than companies that produce a limited range of goods and services or sell to a limited market.

- Companies may decide to pursue higher profit margins through longer production runs and other economies of scale.

- Some companies may be keen to seek additional status through developing globally.

Ultimately, companies that develop their operations globally are aiming to minimise their costs and maximise their revenue. This may result in them choosing to site their manufacturing plants where costs are low and sell in markets where prices are high.

TASK 2

Big Corporation manufactures chocolate bars. Its home base is in Europe, and it sells 67 per cent of its chocolate bars in the USA and Europe. Its chocolate bars are high quality and contain a minimum of 75 per cent cocoa solids. Recently, the company has faced growing competition, and, in order to maintain profit margins, it is investigating changing the production of its best selling chocolate bar to another site. Three sites have been chosen as possible locations:

	Country A	Country B	Country C
Site	Europe	Africa	Africa
Population	67 million	135 million	187 million
Average income	US$12,000 p.a.	US$3,000 p.a.	US$1,200 p.a.
Unemployment	4%	7%	13%
Main industry	Finance Light engineering	Food processing Mining	Agriculture
Literacy level	99%	78%	34%
Main export	Banking Electronic equipment Electrical goods	Semi-processed food Tin	Foodstuffs
Other information	Booming economy A lot of high tech industry	Intermediate economy Recently discovered tin Small chocolate making industry set up	Developing economy Main crop is cocoa

In groups, choose one of the three sites for the new production plant. Prepare a presentation to the board of Big Corporation, explaining your decision.

Global branding

'A **global brand** is a brand where people around the world share the same vision of that brand' – John Hegarty, Bartle, Bogle Hegarty (BBC for Business video *Branding – the Marketing Advantage*).

Is globalisation good or bad?

There are many sides to the argument of whether or not globalisation has gone too far or not far enough. TNCs have become some of the most powerful economic and political entities in the world economy. Many TNCs have more economic power than the countries in which they locate production sites. The combined revenue of Ford and General Motors exceeds the combined gross domestic product of all sub-Saharan Africa. This gives TNCs the power to influence the economic, trade and political policies of countries with little accountability to anyone other than their shareholders. They also have the power to develop world trade and create vast investment flows.

TNCs are now able to produce global brands. A bottle of Coca Cola, a Ford car, a McDonald's burger are recognisable products throughout the world. But the global branding goes further than simply the product itself. Company logos, advertising campaigns and pricing strategies are all consistent across the global market. As a consumer, you may watch an advert for a global product and not be able to understand the language, but you will be familiar with the style and approach of the advert. The marketing team in a TNC must ensure that it carefully balances the drive for global branding with the need to meet the likes and dislikes of the local consumer.

Globalisation should allow consumers to enjoy the widest possible range of goods and services on the world market, but some believe that global branding is reducing our choice and allowing TNCs to dominate.

An advertisement for Volkswagen Golf from a Russian magazine

Arguments for TNCs	Arguments against TNCs
TNCs generate 70 per cent of world trade. They are therefore key to our living standards and help to provide a wide range of goods and services.	TNCs are often more powerful than the host country. This gives them the opportunity to dictate terms when choosing a site, including wage levels, government grants and working conditions.
Companies that are able to produce a more standardised product can enjoy the benefits of economies of scale. These cost savings can be passed on to the consumer in the form of lower prices.	TNCs have operations throughout the world but most of them have their head office based in the northern, industrialised world. More than half of the TNCs come from just five countries: France, Germany, the Netherlands, Japan and the United States. While they may generate income for their host countries, profits return to the company and its shareholders.
Competition (in a world market) forces companies to be efficient. Consumers may gain through lower prices, improved quality and new products being launched.	TNCs are constantly seeking to reduce costs. This may mean closing down and/or moving plants to minimise outgoings. When a TNC leaves a country, the effect can be very damaging to the economy.
Countries that host TNCs gain employment, income generation and may see their balance of payments improve.	TNCs are accountable only to their shareholders. Governments that seek change in trade and economic policies may have to do this with the cooperation of TNCs.
	Seeking to minimise costs may cause bad publicity for the TNC, e.g. Nike was severely criticised for the 'sweatshop' conditions in many of its Asian plants.

TASK 3

Using information from the article, plus any other relevant researched data, write a 400-word letter to the editor of the Business News section, either supporting or opposing any future plans for other car manufacturers to enter the UK.

Honda to create 1,000 UK jobs

Honda yesterday lifted the motor industry gloom with the announcement of plans to recruit another thousand workers for a second car assembly plant it is building at Swindon.

The expansion could provide a lifeline to the 10,000 Rover workers who face job cuts following BMW's decision to sell Rover.

BMW chairman Joachim Milberg is meeting Trade and Industry Secretary Stephen Byers today to discuss BMW's potential involvement in government plans to regenerate the West Midlands.

'The planned sale of Rover and Land Rover is no retreat from the UK but a reorientation of BMW in the UK. The group will remain an essential economic factor in the UK,' Dr Milberg said.

Honda is looking for 120 skilled engineers immediately and will be in the market for almost 900 in the summer in the run-up to the opening of the new assembly hall next year when the total workforce on the site will be around 4,000.

There is a marked contrast between the two companies. Honda has not received a penny in either state or local aid towards the Swindon development while more than £3 billion was pumped into Rover to keep it on the road.

A Honda spokesman said: 'It's our policy not to ask for financial assistance because we don't want to be beholden in any shape or form to a national government.'

A TALE OF TWO UK CAR COMPANIES		
	Rover	Honda
Employees	28,000	3,000
Output	390,000 (inc Land Rover)	150,000
Vehicles per employee	30 (Longbridge)	64
State aid	£3 billion	Nil
Euro ranking	30th (Longbridge)	10th

Honda, which followed Nissan and Toyota to Britain, has invested around £600m building a 150,000-a-year car assembly and engine plant at Swindon, producing the Accord and Civic ranges.

It is spending another £450m to increase output by 100,000 in the second plant which is expected to house the 1.3 litre Honda Logo.

The Japanese company says its UK operations are profitable but it has been pressing privately for British entry into the euro while making it clear that the Swindon expansion does not depend on the abolition of sterling. Honda says: 'We are thriving in Britain.'

It is still producing around 20,000 engines for Rover cars but is likely to lose the contract as the new owners rationalise the business. The Rover 400 and 600 models are based on Honda designs.

Source: *The Daily Telegraph*, 23 March 2000.

Irn Bru remains a 'local' brand

Is there a place for the small, local company?

The growth of TNCs over the past 20 years has seen some small companies closing down. Where TNCs are able to use their power and size to reduce costs, they have had the opportunity to drive down prices and force their smaller competitors out of the market. But does this mean that global brands will soon be our only choice on the product market?

TNCs cannot afford to ignore local needs and wants. The ice cream manufacturer Haagen-Dazs, for example, works locally to adapt its brand to suit individual countries' tastes, taking account of national influences.

Not all companies seek to become TNCs. AG Barr, which produces the soft drink Irn Bru, made a decision to remain local. Companies may decide to stay local because of trade barriers, lack of appropriate staff, language barriers and transport problems.

KEY TERMS

Brand – the unique identity that a company creates for a product or service.

Economies of scale – the factors that allow unit costs to fall as a result of the size of the firm.

Global brand – a brand that is recognised around the world. People will share the same vision of the brand.

Globalisation – the process by which companies operate across the globe, choosing to locate in many countries and sell a global product in a range of world markets.

Marketing – the combination of decisions that a business makes about a product's price, promotion and the place it is sold.

Trade barriers – methods used to stop free trade occurring. Trade barriers may include tariffs, quotas and administrative controls.

Transnational corporation (TNC) – a company which operates in several countries.

Factfile

Ford Motor Company

Vehicle unit sales (1997):

USA	4,016,000
Outside USA	2,927,000
Total	6,943,000
Sales:	US$153,627million
Shareholders:	74,000
Growth rate (1997):	4.2%
Employees:	400,000

Operates in over 200 countries including Brazil, India, Thailand, Vietnam and Belarus.

Factfile

India

GDP (1998):
US$1.689 trillion

GDP growth (1998):
5.4%

Main industries: textiles, chemicals, food processing, steel, cement, mining, petroleum, machinery.

Export partners (1997):

USA	19%
Hong Kong	6%
UK	6%
Japan	6%
Germany	5%
Population (1999 est.):	1,000,848,550
0–14 years	34%
15–64 years	61%
65+	5%

67% work in agriculture

Source: www.geographic.org

Questions

1 What reasons might Ford Motor Company have for:
  a setting up a production plant in India
  b selling Ford Motor cars in India?
2 Why might the Indian government be keen for Ford Motor Company to produce cars in India?
3 Imagine you are a government adviser in discussion with managers of Ford about the possibility of the company locating a production plant in India. Using the evidence from the factfiles, plus any other data you are able to research, write a report, outlining the benefits to Ford of locating in India. You may wish to include incentives that you think your government might offer Ford.
4 What problems do you think Ford Motors might face when:
  a locating a production site in India
  b selling Ford cars in India?

Extension

Research how powerful TNCs are compared to host countries in terms of:
a revenue (GDP)
b share of trade and investment
c political processes.

THEME 2

Marketing

UNIT 10

Marketing objectives and the marketing plan

This unit is about the importance of marketing to a business, how a business decides its marketing goals and how it goes about planning its marketing.

At the end of the unit, students should be able to:

- explain why marketing has become important

- identify the different elements of the marketing mix

- explore the possible marketing objectives of different businesses

- calculate and know the significance of market share

- draw up a marketing plan.

Why is marketing important?

Henry Ford, the founder of the Ford motor car corporation and the 'inventor' of mass production of cars, is famous for saying to customers about his cars: 'You can have any colour as long as it is black'.

This was very true in the 1920s and 1930s. People were faced with a limited choice of products and had limited incomes for buying products like the motor car. For many people in the first 50 years of the twentieth century, just owning a car was a huge desire. There was little competition between companies and very limited choice between products. The cars really sold themselves.

Today's customers have the income to buy a vast range of goods and services and are faced with a huge choice between different companies' products. Businesses therefore must market their products. **Marketing** is the process in a business of identifying customer needs and satisfying those needs at a profit in such a way that the customer will buy the product again and again. In the competitive world of the global economy it is marketing that allows businesses to:

- go out and create new customers

- find out what customers want

- produce products that meet the customers' needs

- inform customers about their products

- persuade customers to buy their products

- earn enough revenue to meet the costs of production

- get the product to the customer

- make sure that the customer is happy with the product and buys it again.

All the different activities of marketing described above are known as the **marketing mix**. To make it easy to remember the range of activities, they are often summarised as the 4Ps:

- **Product** – researching and developing the product

- **Promotion** – advertising and promotion to persuade consumers to buy

- **Price** – setting the right price to sell profitably

- **Place** – making sure the product is available to buy at the right place and time.

Product

Promotion

Price

Place

The 4 Ps

TASK 1

Working in a small group, prepare a presentation to give to the class on the subject, 'What is marketing?'.

Here are some suggestions to help you put your presentation together.

a Decide upon a well-known product that you buy regularly, e.g. CDs, jeans, burgers, etc. Take a large sheet of flipchart paper and in the centre draw a sketch of your product.

b Around the sketch of your product divide the paper into four quarters and write in each one of the 4 Ps.

c 'Brainstorm' all the methods of marketing that you know are used to sell your chosen product. Record them on the flipchart in the appropriate section of the 4 Ps.

d Display your sheet and then choose one of the group to tell the rest of your class about how your chosen product is marketed.

Marketing objectives

Because marketing is so important to a business, most businesses will set themselves objectives – targets or goals – to aim at so that their business continues to develop and grow. Here are some **marketing objectives** that businesses might set:

- A local greengrocer might set a target of increasing its sales of organic fruit and vegetables. This might be by encouraging existing customers to buy more organic food.

- A DIY superstore might set a target of increasing its weekly sales totals in comparison to local competitors. This might be by opening for longer hours at the weekend.

- The owner of a restaurant in a seaside resort might set a target of moving into a new aspect of business by opening a separate takeaway service which can be supplied from the restaurant's kitchens.

- The managers of a large soap and detergent maker might set a target of launching a new soap powder for selling in eastern Europe where they haven't operated before.

The greengrocer is interested in selling more of a new product to existing customers. The DIY superstore is interested in selling more of its existing products to its existing customers. The restaurant owner is interested in selling more of an existing product to new, takeaway customers. The detergent manufacturer is interested in selling more of a new product to new customers. For all these developments, marketing will be essential for the goal to be achieved.

TASK 2

Can the Olympics put the spring back in Nike's step?

These should be golden days for Nike. Sales are higher than ever. New training shoes and running shirts are flying off production lines. The company's list of sponsorship sports people includes Michael Jordan and Tiger Woods. In the Olympics in Sydney, Nike's trademark swoosh logos are worn by the entire Australian team as well as a clutch of athletics stars including Michael Johnson.

But Nike is struggling to fight its way out of a two-year doldrum in sales revenue, growing only by 2 per cent in the last year. Once it was cool to wear Nike shoes and parade them around the shopping mall. But the company has been attacked for too much reliance in production on cheap labour in the Third World.

To get out of its slowdown, Nike has a number of plans. One is to continue its international expansion in up to 110 countries worldwide. A second one is to find out new sporting trends – building on its success with Tiger Woods in the sport of golf. A third is to move into women's sportswear, a market which it has not yet exploited. The company has also recently agreed to follow the United Nations guidelines on labour exploitation, for example by not employing any workers under 18 years of age.

Tiger Woods

Source: Adapted from *The Independent*, 13 September 2000.

a Explain why Nike's 'sales are higher than ever' and yet its revenue grew by only 2 per cent in the past year.

b What objectives is Nike setting to help it boost its sales revenue?

c Do you think Nike will be successful in regaining its growth in sales revenue? Give your reasons.

Market share

Businesses will have a number of ways of measuring the success of their marketing. For a profit-making company the level of sales revenue and the resulting level of profits will be vital. But businesses will also be interested in their **market share**.

This is the share of the total market that their product's sales capture. It is calculated by the following formula:

$$\text{Market share} = \frac{\text{Total sales of the company's product}}{\text{Total sales in the market as a whole}} \times 100\%$$

A rising market share will mean that the product is doing well in comparison to rivals and that the marketing is working well. A falling market share means that the product is not competing well against rivals and that the marketing may need to be improved.

Organisations such as local authorities or charities which are not producing for profits will be just as interested in marketing their services but will have different targets. Charities, for example, will be interested in meeting the needs of those they help by maximising the revenue they gain, while keeping their costs low. They will want to make sure that any marketing does this effectively. Local authorities will measure the success of the services they market by the satisfaction of their customers – council tax payers. They may do regular surveys of local residents to find out if they feel services are improving and use these as a measure of success.

TASK 3

Below are figures for the number of cash withdrawals from the major high street banks in 1995 and 1999.

Bank	Number (millions) 1995	1999
Abbey National	92	184
Bank of Scotland	44	68
Barclays	235	273
HSBC Bank (formerly Midland)	179	261
Lloyds TSB	300	334
NatWest	217	297
Royal Bank of Scotland	75	148
Clydesdale Bank	38	39
Co-operative Bank	7	14
Yorkshire Bank	37	36

Source: *The Observer*, 9 July 2000.

a Assuming these companies make up the whole market for high street customers in banking, calculate the market share of each company in 1995 and 1999.

b Has the total number of cash withdrawals grown between 1995 and 1999? Explain why your answer may have happened.

c i Which company is the market leader in 1995 and 1999?

ii Which company has seen its market share grow by the largest amount between 1995 and 1999?

iii Which company has lost most market share between 1995 and 1999?

TASK 4

You are a greengrocer who owns three outlets in different parts of a large city. Your shops are called The Vegetable Garden. You have set yourself a business target of increasing your sales of organic fruit and vegetables by 25 per cent over the next 12 months.
You have set aside a £20,000 budget to help you do this.

a Draw up a marketing plan showing how you intend increasing your organic vegetable sales. Cover as many aspects of the marketing mix as you feel appropriate, but keep to your £20,000 budget.

b What outside factors over the next 12 months might mean that you will not be able to meet your targets?

The marketing plan

Having set marketing objectives a business will need a **marketing plan** to help it achieve its goals. It will form an important part of the business plan for a business. It may contain the following information:

- the expected size of demand
- the target market
- its main competitors
- the price/price range to be charged
- any special offers available
- how the product will be promoted
- how the product will be distributed
- how much the business will spend on marketing the product.

Not all businesses, especially small businesses, will have a detailed marketing plan but their business plan will include many of these elements, as the success of the marketing of a product will be central to the success of the product.

Below is a summary of a possible marketing plan for the DIY superstore identified in the last section.

DIY superstore marketing plan	
Marketing strategy:	To open longer at weekends, from 10.00 am to 8.00 pm, rather than 6.00 pm at present
Target increase in sales:	10% increase per week at weekends
Target market:	Existing customers, especially those who work in the week and rely on weekend visits
Competitors:	B&Q open from 10.00 am to 8.00 pm Homebase open from 10.00 am to 6.00 pm Focus open from 10.00 am to 7.00 pm
Promotion of increased opening – advertising:	Through national TV advertising and national newspaper advertising. Target weekend programmes and newspapers
Promotion of increased opening – other sales promotions:	Special offers available only between 5.00 pm and 8.00 pm on Saturday and Sunday. Use of in-store promotions on the increased opening hours
Marketing budget:	£0.5 million for first six months, then review progress

KEY TERMS

Marketing – the process in a business of identifying customer needs and satisfying those needs at a profit.

Marketing mix – the different activities involved in marketing, often summarised as the 4Ps – product, pricing, promotion and place.

Marketing objectives – the targets that a business might set in relation to new and existing markets and products.

Marketing plan – a plan that shows how a business hopes to achieve its marketing objectives and which forms an important part of the business plan.

Market share – the share of the total market that a product's sales capture, often used as a measure of the success of a product.

Place – part of the marketing mix; involves making sure the product is available to buy at the right places, in the right quantity and at the right time.

Price – part of the marketing mix; involves setting the right price to sell profitably and changing price as the market changes.

Product – part of the marketing mix; involves researching and developing a product to meet the customers' needs.

Promotion – part of the marketing mix; the advertising and promotion of a product to persuade consumers to buy.

The success of Pritt Stick

In 1973, Henkel launched a revolutionary new product in the UK. It was a solid glue stick that was cleaner, quicker and easier to use than liquid glues. Pritt Stick is now the most used adhesive in homes, schools and offices. The stick adhesive market has grown from nothing to over £17 million in the UK alone and Pritt Stick has a 75 per cent market share.

Pritt Stick was a new invention in a well-established market. The makers of Pritt Stick decided to adopt a snowball marketing strategy – they targeted children in the early 1970s who have now grown up into adults, parents, teachers and office workers. This helped to make Pritt Stick a very well recognised brand by the 1990s.

For a long time Henkel did not change the product in any way. Only recently has it brought in other products in the range such as a correction roller. Advertising has been an important

marketing tool for Pritt Stick. Mr Pritt, a cartoon character, was introduced in 1983 and has appeared ever since. In 1998 he was re-launched in a computer-generated form. He is aimed to appeal to children at school and their parents, the main part of the Pritt Stick market.

Campaigns have been run on TV, on posters, in cinemas, in the press and on the underground.

Sponsorship has also been important. In 1998 Pritt Stick sponsored Art Attack, a children's ITV programme, and more recently, Comic Relief Red Nose Day. There is even a Pritt Stick hot-air balloon for trade fairs. Mr Pritt is also used on many promotions in retail outlets that sell Pritt.

The distribution of the product is complex and very important. The company has three major distribution channels. It sells through many medium and small stationers and newsagents. It sells to schools, where price is an important factor and where it often gives free samples to new primary school children. And it sells to companies where it offers reductions for bulk purchases – one free carton of small Pritts for every two cartons of large Pritts.

The company's marketing has allowed Pritt Stick to become an established and dominant product in its market.

Source: Adapted from www.mbapublishing.co.uk/cd/casestudies/henkel.

Q Questions

1 What were the main marketing objectives of Henkel when it first developed Pritt Stick?
2 Explain what is meant by the phrase 'Pritt Stick has a 75 per cent market share'.
3 The company used different parts of the marketing mix in selling its product.
   a Identify each one and explain what it did in each case.
   b Which elements do you feel have been most important for Henkel?
4 Why would the company decide to:
   a sponsor *Art Attack*?
   b sponsor Comic Relief Red Nose Day?
   c give free samples to new primary school children?
   d give a free box of Pritt Sticks to companies that bought two large boxes?
5 What evidence is there that Pritt Stick has been a success?

E Extension

1 a Explain what Henkel's snowball strategy meant.
   b What type of products would suit this type of strategy?
2 Identify the key elements of the marketing plan that have been used to make Pritt Stick a success.

Market research

This unit is about how businesses find out what their customers want them to provide. It also shows how they can use research to improve the goods and services that they do provide.

At the end of the unit, students should be able to:

- identify the information that market research can provide

- understand the difference between desk research and field research

- evaluate the different methods of market research that businesses use

- analyse the use that businesses make of market research.

What is market research?

Market research is the process of collecting, presenting and analysing information about a particular product or service. It will provide a business with important information such as:

- what type of customer will buy the product
- the price consumers are expected to pay
- how often consumers will buy the product
- the features of a product that customers particularly like
- the style of packaging that customers like
- what customers don't like about a product.

Whether a business is small or large, it needs to know what customers want before it starts to operate or produce a new product. Methods of market research are generally grouped into those that are desk based and those that are field based.

Desk research

Desk research uses **secondary data**, that is, data which has already been collected by someone else. This might be:

- government statistics and publications containing information collected on a national basis like the *Annual Abstract of Statistics*
- trade journals and newspapers which will contain a wealth of background data about the market and what competitors are doing
- information from competitors such as their product brochures and price lists
- secondary data already within the business such as sales data or previous customer surveys
- information from the Internet that may include information about competitors or the views of customers.

Field research

Field research involves collecting **primary data**, that is, data from a new source. Owners of a small business could ask friends, existing customers, relatives or neighbours for their opinions. They could visit the shops, showrooms or factories where products are sold. They could carry out their own small-scale survey of as many of their customers as possible.

A large business has thousands of customers and could not possibly contact them all. When carrying out a survey it is likely to get in touch with only a **sample**. A sample is not just any small group of consumers – it will be scientifically chosen. The sample may be a **random sample**. For example, a leaflet is posted through the letterbox of every 10th house along the street, or every 50th person on the electoral register is asked to complete a survey questionnaire. Samples can also be subdivided according to age, income, interests, etc. in order to get representation from across different groups. This is known as a **stratified sample**.

TASK 1

Marvin Sobers is hoping to use some of his redundancy money and his knowledge of music from working as a DJ in local clubs to set up a shop called Marvin's Music.

Over the past few months, friends have made various comments to Marvin.

> I like CDs in a shop to be arranged in alphabetical order rather than according to type of music.

> I'd like a music store which is open until 8 pm most evenings and until 10pm on Fridays.

> I want to be able to buy T-shirts, videos and blank tapes in a music shop.

> I never pay more than £12.99 for a chart CD. I look round all the stores and buy where it is cheapest.

If Marvin was able to collect this sort of information from a large number of potential customers, he would have a very accurate idea of his target market. But he needs some help.

a Devise a questionnaire which Marvin could use to carry out a small-scale survey of his likely customers.

b Try out the questionnaire with a small number of your class. Which questions were effective? Which would you change?

c How many people should Martin aim to include in his sample? Explain your recommendation.

Methods of market research

A business has a variety of market research methods which can be used. It may instead choose to pay a specialist market research agency to carry out market research on its behalf.

Questionnaires are sets of questions which are designed to find out consumers' buying habits and opinions. The most usual way to ensure that the questions are effective is to provide only a limited number of possible answers to choose from.

For example, a question such as:

> Do you use the bus service from Stockport to Manchester?

will give only yes/no answers which will add very little to existing knowledge about the customer. A more specific question is needed such as:

> How often do you use the service from Stockport to Manchester?
> ☐ Daily
> ☐ Weekly
> ☐ 1–3 times a month
> ☐ Less than once a month
> ☐ Never

This will help the bus company work out the proportion of its customers who use the bus service on a regular basis. Providing a selection of tick-box answers also helps the business analyse the answers more quickly and accurately. For example, asking:

> Why do you use the bus service?

might lead to answers such as:

> Because it is cheaper/Because buses run more often/ Because it is more convenient.

These might be time consuming and difficult to classify. Therefore, asking a similar question but with a series of answers provided will allow the bus company to pinpoint the most common reason why customers use the bus service. For example:

> For which of the following reasons do you use the bus service?
> ☐ Good value transport
> ☐ Regular service
> ☐ Stops close to my home/destination
> ☐ Provides an alternative to the car
> ☐ Moves through traffic quickly
> ☐ Other – please specify _____

When large-scale questionnaires are used they will be analysed by computer. Questionnaires are sometimes distributed by post to the chosen sample of consumers, probably with a reply-paid envelope or special offer to encourage its return. The response rate from postal questionnaires, however, may be as low as 12 per cent.

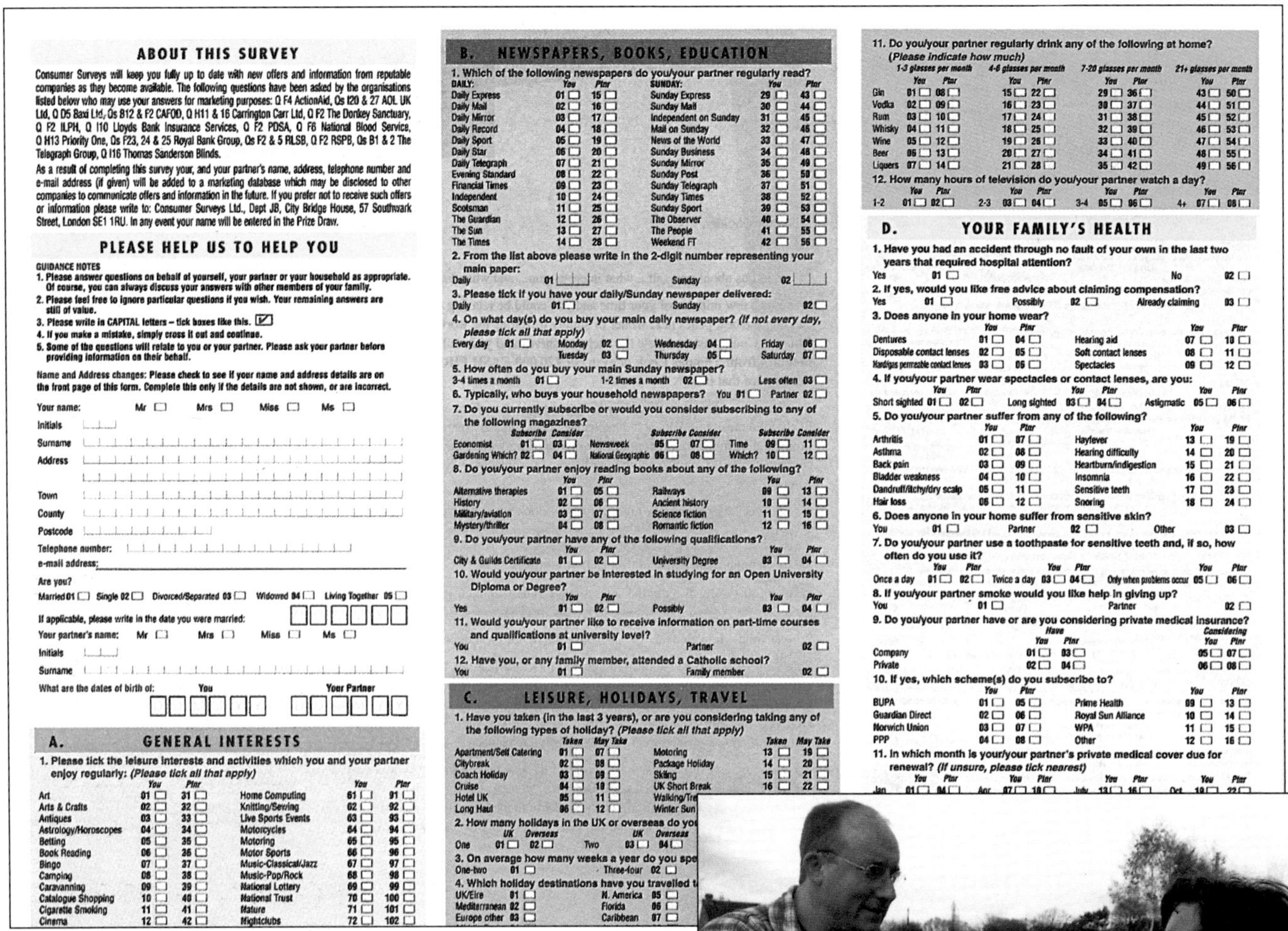

ABOUT THIS SURVEY

Consumer Surveys will keep you fully up to date with new offers and information from reputable companies as they become available. The following questions have been asked by the organisations listed below who may use your answers for marketing purposes: Q F4 ActionAid, Qs I20 & 27 AOL UK Ltd, Q D5 Baxi Ltd, Qs B12 & F2 CAFOD, Q H11 & 16 Carrington Carr Ltd, Q F2 The Donkey Sanctuary, Q F2 ILPH, Q I10 Lloyds Bank Insurance Services, Q F2 PDSA, Q F6 National Blood Service, Q H13 Priority One, Qs F23, 24 & 25 Royal Bank Group, Qs F2 & 5 RLSB, Q F2 RSPB, Qs B1 & 2 The Telegraph Group, Q I16 Thomas Sanderson Blinds.

As a result of completing this survey your, and your partner's name, address, telephone number and e-mail address (if given) will be added to a marketing database which may be disclosed to other companies to communicate offers and information in the future. If you prefer not to receive such offers or information please write to: Consumer Surveys Ltd., Dept JB, City Bridge House, 57 Southwark Street, London SE1 1RU. In any event your name will be entered in the Prize Draw.

PLEASE HELP US TO HELP YOU

GUIDANCE NOTES

1. **Please answer questions on behalf of yourself, your partner or your household as appropriate. Of course, you can always discuss your answers with other members of your family.**
2. **Please feel free to ignore particular questions if you wish. Your remaining answers are still of value.**
3. **Please write in CAPITAL letters – tick boxes like this.** ☑
4. **If you make a mistake, simply cross it out and continue.**
5. **Some of the questions will relate to you or your partner. Please ask your partner before providing information on their behalf.**

Name and Address changes: Please check to see if your name and address details are on the front page of this form. Complete this only if the details are not shown, or are incorrect.

Your name: Mr ☐ Mrs ☐ Miss ☐ Ms ☐

Initials ☐☐

Surname ☐☐☐☐☐☐☐☐☐☐☐☐☐☐☐☐☐☐☐☐

Address ☐☐☐☐☐☐☐☐☐☐☐☐☐☐☐☐☐☐☐☐

☐☐☐☐☐☐☐☐☐☐☐☐☐☐☐☐☐☐☐☐

Town ☐☐☐☐☐☐☐☐☐☐☐☐☐☐☐☐☐☐☐☐

County ☐☐☐☐☐☐☐☐☐☐☐☐☐☐☐☐☐☐☐☐

Postcode ☐☐☐☐☐☐☐☐

Telephone number: ☐☐☐☐☐☐☐☐☐☐☐☐☐☐

e-mail address: ____________________

Are you?

Married 01 ☐ Single 02 ☐ Divorced/Separated 03 ☐ Widowed 04 ☐ Living Together 05 ☐

If applicable, please write in the date you were married: ☐☐☐☐☐☐

Your partner's name: Mr ☐ Mrs ☐ Miss ☐ Ms ☐

Initials ☐☐

Surname ☐☐☐☐☐☐☐☐☐☐☐☐☐☐☐☐☐☐☐☐

What are the dates of birth of: You ☐☐☐☐☐☐ Your Partner ☐☐☐☐☐☐

A. GENERAL INTERESTS

1. Please tick the leisure interests and activities which you and your partner enjoy regularly: *(Please tick all that apply)*

	You	Ptnr		You	Ptnr
Art	01 ☐	31 ☐	Home Computing	61 ☐	91 ☐
Arts & Crafts	02 ☐	32 ☐	Knitting/Sewing	62 ☐	92 ☐
Antiques	03 ☐	33 ☐	Live Sports Events	63 ☐	93 ☐
Astrology/Horoscopes	04 ☐	34 ☐	Motorcycles	64 ☐	94 ☐
Betting	05 ☐	35 ☐	Motoring	65 ☐	95 ☐
Book Reading	06 ☐	36 ☐	Motor Sports	66 ☐	96 ☐
Bingo	07 ☐	37 ☐	Music-Classical/Jazz	67 ☐	97 ☐
Camping	08 ☐	38 ☐	Music-Pop/Rock	68 ☐	98 ☐
Caravanning	09 ☐	39 ☐	National Lottery	69 ☐	99 ☐
Catalogue Shopping	10 ☐	40 ☐	National Trust	70 ☐	100 ☐
Cigarette Smoking	11 ☐	41 ☐	Nature	71 ☐	101 ☐
Cinema	12 ☐	42 ☐	Nightclubs	72 ☐	102 ☐

B. NEWSPAPERS, BOOKS, EDUCATION

1. Which of the following newspapers do you/your partner regularly read?

DAILY:	You	Ptnr	SUNDAY:	You	Ptnr
Daily Express	01 ☐	15 ☐	Sunday Express	29 ☐	43 ☐
Daily Mail	02 ☐	16 ☐	Sunday Mail	30 ☐	44 ☐
Daily Mirror	03 ☐	17 ☐	Independent on Sunday	31 ☐	45 ☐
Daily Record	04 ☐	18 ☐	Mail on Sunday	32 ☐	46 ☐
Daily Sport	05 ☐	19 ☐	News of the World	33 ☐	47 ☐
Daily Star	06 ☐	20 ☐	Sunday Business	34 ☐	48 ☐
Daily Telegraph	07 ☐	21 ☐	Sunday Mirror	35 ☐	49 ☐
Evening Standard	08 ☐	22 ☐	Sunday Post	36 ☐	50 ☐
Financial Times	09 ☐	23 ☐	Sunday Telegraph	37 ☐	51 ☐
Independent	10 ☐	24 ☐	Sunday Times	38 ☐	52 ☐
Scotsman	11 ☐	25 ☐	Sunday Sport	39 ☐	53 ☐
The Guardian	12 ☐	26 ☐	The Observer	40 ☐	54 ☐
The Sun	13 ☐	27 ☐	The People	41 ☐	55 ☐
The Times	14 ☐	28 ☐	Weekend FT	42 ☐	56 ☐

2. From the list above please write in the 2-digit number representing your main paper:

Daily 01 ☐☐ Sunday 02 ☐☐

3. Please tick if you have your daily/Sunday newspaper delivered:

Daily 01 ☐ Sunday 02 ☐

4. On what day(s) do you buy your main daily newspaper? *(If not every day, please tick all that apply)*

Every day 01 ☐ Monday 02 ☐ Tuesday 03 ☐ Wednesday 04 ☐ Thursday 05 ☐ Friday 06 ☐ Saturday 07 ☐

5. How often do you buy your main Sunday newspaper?

3-4 times a month 01 ☐ 1-2 times a month 02 ☐ Less often 03 ☐

6. Typically, who buys your household newspapers? You 01 ☐ Partner 02 ☐

7. Do you currently subscribe or would you consider subscribing to any of the following magazines?

	Subscribe	Consider		Subscribe	Consider		Subscribe	Consider
Economist	01 ☐	03 ☐	Newsweek	05 ☐	07 ☐	Time	09 ☐	11 ☐
Gardening Which?	02 ☐	04 ☐	National Geographic	06 ☐	08 ☐	Which?	10 ☐	12 ☐

8. Do you/your partner enjoy reading books about any of the following?

	You	Ptnr		You	Ptnr
Alternative therapies	01 ☐	05 ☐	Railways	09 ☐	13 ☐
History	02 ☐	06 ☐	Ancient history	10 ☐	14 ☐
Military/aviation	03 ☐	07 ☐	Science fiction	11 ☐	15 ☐
Mystery/thriller	04 ☐	08 ☐	Romantic fiction	12 ☐	16 ☐

9. Do you/your partner have any of the following qualifications?

	You	Ptnr		You	Ptnr
City & Guilds Certificate	01 ☐	02 ☐	University Degree	03 ☐	04 ☐

10. Would you/your partner be interested in studying for an Open University Diploma or Degree?

	You	Ptnr		You	Ptnr
Yes	01 ☐	02 ☐	Possibly	03 ☐	04 ☐

11. Would you/your partner like to receive information on part-time courses and qualifications at university level?

You 01 ☐ Partner 02 ☐

12. Have you, or any family member, attended a Catholic school?

You 01 ☐ Family member 02 ☐

C. LEISURE, HOLIDAYS, TRAVEL

1. Have you taken (in the last 3 years), or are you considering taking any of the following types of holiday? *(Please tick all that apply)*

	Taken	May Take		Taken	May Take
Apartment/Self Catering	01 ☐	07 ☐	Motoring	13 ☐	19 ☐
Citybreak	02 ☐	08 ☐	Package Holiday	14 ☐	20 ☐
Coach Holiday	03 ☐	09 ☐	Skiing	15 ☐	21 ☐
Cruise	04 ☐	10 ☐	UK Short Break	16 ☐	22 ☐
Hotel UK	05 ☐	11 ☐	Walking/Tre		
Long Haul	06 ☐	12 ☐	Winter Sun		

2. How many holidays in the UK or overseas do yo

	UK	Overseas		UK	Overseas
One	01 ☐	02 ☐	Two	03 ☐	04 ☐

3. On average how many weeks a year do you spe

One-two 01 ☐ Three-four 02 ☐

4. Which holiday destinations have you travelled t

UK/Eire	01 ☐	N. America	05 ☐
Mediterranean	02 ☐	Florida	06 ☐
Europe other	03 ☐	Caribbean	07 ☐

11. Do you/your partner regularly drink any of the following at home? *(Please indicate how much)*

	1-3 glasses per month		4-6 glasses per month		7-20 glasses per month		21+ glasses per month	
	You	Ptnr	You	Ptnr	You	Ptnr	You	Ptnr
Gin	01 ☐	08 ☐	15 ☐	22 ☐	29 ☐	36 ☐	43 ☐	50 ☐
Vodka	02 ☐	09 ☐	16 ☐	23 ☐	30 ☐	37 ☐	44 ☐	51 ☐
Rum	03 ☐	10 ☐	17 ☐	24 ☐	31 ☐	38 ☐	45 ☐	52 ☐
Whisky	04 ☐	11 ☐	18 ☐	25 ☐	32 ☐	39 ☐	46 ☐	53 ☐
Wine	05 ☐	12 ☐	19 ☐	26 ☐	33 ☐	40 ☐	47 ☐	54 ☐
Beer	06 ☐	13 ☐	20 ☐	27 ☐	34 ☐	41 ☐	48 ☐	55 ☐
Liquers	07 ☐	14 ☐	21 ☐	28 ☐	35 ☐	42 ☐	49 ☐	56 ☐

12. How many hours of television do you/your partner watch a day?

	You	Ptnr		You	Ptnr		You	Ptnr		You	Ptnr
1-2	01 ☐	02 ☐	2-3	03 ☐	04 ☐	3-4	05 ☐	06 ☐	4+	07 ☐	08 ☐

D. YOUR FAMILY'S HEALTH

1. Have you had an accident through no fault of your own in the last two years that required hospital attention?

Yes 01 ☐ No 02 ☐

2. If yes, would you like free advice about claiming compensation?

Yes 01 ☐ Possibly 02 ☐ Already claiming 03 ☐

3. Does anyone in your home wear?

	You	Ptnr		You	Ptnr
Dentures	01 ☐	04 ☐	Hearing aid	07 ☐	10 ☐
Disposable contact lenses	02 ☐	05 ☐	Soft contact lenses	08 ☐	11 ☐
Hard/gas permeable contact lenses	03 ☐	06 ☐	Spectacles	09 ☐	12 ☐

4. If you/your partner wear spectacles or contact lenses, are you:

	You	Ptnr		You	Ptnr		You	Ptnr
Short sighted	01 ☐	02 ☐	Long sighted	03 ☐	04 ☐	Astigmatic	05 ☐	06 ☐

5. Do you/your partner suffer from any of the following?

	You	Ptnr		You	Ptnr
Arthritis	01 ☐	07 ☐	Hayfever	13 ☐	19 ☐
Asthma	02 ☐	08 ☐	Hearing difficulty	14 ☐	20 ☐
Back pain	03 ☐	09 ☐	Heartburn/indigestion	15 ☐	21 ☐
Bladder weakness	04 ☐	10 ☐	Insomnia	16 ☐	22 ☐
Dandruff/itchy/dry scalp	05 ☐	11 ☐	Sensitive teeth	17 ☐	23 ☐
Hair loss	06 ☐	12 ☐	Snoring	18 ☐	24 ☐

6. Does anyone in your home suffer from sensitive skin?

You 01 ☐ Partner 02 ☐ Other 03 ☐

7. Do you/your partner use a toothpaste for sensitive teeth and, if so, how often do you use it?

	You	Ptnr		You	Ptnr		You	Ptnr
Once a day	01 ☐	02 ☐	Twice a day	03 ☐	04 ☐	Only when problems occur	05 ☐	06 ☐

8. If you/your partner smoke would you like help in giving up?

You 01 ☐ Partner 02 ☐

9. Do you/your partner have or are you considering private medical insurance?

	Have		Considering	
	You	Ptnr	You	Ptnr
Company	01 ☐	03 ☐	05 ☐	07 ☐
Private	02 ☐	04 ☐	06 ☐	08 ☐

10. If yes, which scheme(s) do you subscribe to?

	You	Ptnr		You	Ptnr
BUPA	01 ☐	05 ☐	Prime Health	09 ☐	13 ☐
Guardian Direct	02 ☐	06 ☐	Royal Sun Alliance	10 ☐	14 ☐
Norwich Union	03 ☐	07 ☐	WPA	11 ☐	15 ☐
PPP	04 ☐	08 ☐	Other	12 ☐	16 ☐

11. In which month is your/your partner's private medical cover due for renewal? *(If unsure, please tick nearest)*

	You	Ptnr		You	Ptnr		You	Ptnr		You	Ptnr
Jan	01 ☐	04 ☐	Apr	07 ☐	10 ☐	July	13 ☐	16 ☐	Oct	19 ☐	22 ☐

A questionnaire

A more time consuming method of market research, but one which might provide a better response rate and more detailed responses, is the **interview**. This might be carried out on the street or door to door by a skilled market researcher. Questionnaires will often form the basis of the interview. A cheaper alternative is the telephone survey when a wider number of customers can be contacted quickly.

If a business would like to test out new ideas or campaigns on a representative group of consumers, then it may use a **focus group** or **consumer panel**. The focus group will contain a cross-section of customers who give feedback on a new product idea or promotion. Focus groups are now also used by central and local government to find out how people feel about public services. A consumer panel will consist of consumers who will be using the product or service over a period of time and may keep a diary recording their thoughts about the product.

Electronic research is also being used by many businesses. When customers buy products through electronic point of sale (EPOS) tills the sale is recorded and can be analysed to find out trends in purchases. When this is tied to a loyalty card system like Sainsbury's Reward Card, the company can find out what its most regular customers are or are not buying and aim promotions at them. The **Internet** also provides research information through customer comments on web sites and through direct ordering online.

Large businesses may also have the resources to be able to **test market** their product. This means manufacturing the product but only advertising and selling it in one area of the country, usually one which is served by a regional TV or radio station. The benefit of this type of research is that it shows consumers making actual buying decisions rather than just saying what they might do in a questionnaire or interview.

TASK 2

The background data given below has been obtained from questionnaires completed by 1,000 consumers who recently purchased double glazing.

a As an employee of the market research agency which carried out the survey, write a short report to the double glazing firm describing the most important range of consumers interested in buying its product. Your report should be word processed and in report format.

b How will this information help the double glazing firm?

c What other market research information might the firm also need to consider?

■ **Age**

Below 20	21-30	31-40	41-50	over 50
259	117	402	129	93

■ **Sex**

M	F
361	639

■ **Income**

up to £10,000	above £10,000 but less than £20,000	above £20,000
276	697	27

■ **Housing**

Terraced	Semi-detached	Detached	Bungalow
62	528	347	63

■ **Number of bedrooms**

1	2	3	4	more than 4
82	83	439	335	61

■ **Number of years at current address**

Less than 1	Between 1 and 5	More than 5
359	462	179

■ **Council Tax Band**

A	B	C	D	Above D
42	321	417	195	25

■ **Number of cars per household**

0	1	2	More than 2
26	817	103	54

■ **Number of people in household**

1	2	3	4	More than 4
254	159	396	152	39

■ **Credit cards held**

None	Barclaycard	Access	American Express	Storecards
276	173	130	58	363

■ **Maximum education level**

Up to A Level	Up to First Degree	Up to Higher Degree
751	204	45

TASK 3

A chocolate manufacturer is considering the national launch of a new chocolate bar. It has hired a market research agency to carry out research on its behalf. The agency has offered the company a number of different methods which could be used, with their likely costs:

Survey 1:	A national survey involving face-to-face interviews with a stratified sample of 1,000 consumers	£25,000
Survey 2:	A national telephone survey of 2,000 consumers chosen at random from telephone directories	£12,000
Survey 3:	Five focus group meetings with regular consumers of chocolate	£10,000

a Explain the likely advantages and disadvantages of each method of research presented.

b If the company has a maximum budget of £25,000 for this research, which method would you recommend? Give reasons for your answer.

How market research is used

The results from market research must be used to justify the money and time spent on the research.

Once the information has been collected, then it has to be:

- collated and presented – using a variety of tables, graphs and charts to help understanding

- analysed – to understand what the data tells the business; there might need to be further statistical analysis at this stage to help decide how reliable the data is

- recommendations made – the business should say what should be done as a result of the findings.

The main benefit of market research will be to provide a business with more definite information about what is happening in the market as an aid to decision making. This will help to reduce the risks of, for example, launching a new product or redesigning a successful one.

However, any research will have limitations. People may not tell the truth or may change their mind. Markets change very quickly. The size of the sample will always be small and there may be bias in the way the survey was carried out.

TASK 4

Sheffield is not the first place you would associate with a raving music scene, but Sheffield's place in the pop music industry was enough to secure it Britain's first National Centre for Popular Music.

The £15 million centre opened in March 1999 amid great publicity. Market research indicated that it would attract about 400,000 visitors a year. But a year after opening visitor numbers had reached only 100,000 and the Centre had debts of £1 million. Some 20 out of 50 staff lost their jobs.

The company Coopers & Lybrand had produced the market research forecast of 400,000 visitors per year. The Centre had accepted what they had been told. But there was doubt that a visitor attraction in Sheffield would be as attractive as, say, one in York. Market research for other Lottery funded visitor centres has also proved inaccurate. Companies research how many people live within an hour's drive but do not take into account that people living in Manchester do not often drive to Sheffield.

Source: *The Times,* 4 February 2000.

a What type of market research do you think Coopers & Lybrand carried out for the Popular Music Centre?

b Why do you think the number of visitors has been less than forecast by the survey?

c Was market research necessary before the Centre opened? Explain your answer.

Below is a Parcelforce Survey which the company has been sending by post to customers about its service.

PARCEL-FORCE WORLDWIDE

CUSTOMER SURVEY

Mr Chambers
9 Egerton Road
Stockport
Cheshire
SK3 8SR

NT/00003598

1. Was your parcel;   *(please tick only one box)*

   a) delivered directly to your household? ☐   d) left with a neighbour? ☐
   b) delivered to another address directed by you? ☐   e) left at your address? ☐
   c) returned to the depot and collected by you? ☐   f) none of the above? ☐

   | | Yes | No |
   2. Did you receive a card from us stating what we had done with the parcel? ☐ ☐

   | | N/A | Yes | No |
   3. If you telephoned our depot about a recent delivery were you satisfied with the service you received when you rang? ☐ ☐ ☐

   | | Very Satisfied | Fairly Satisfied | Fairly Dissatisfied | Very Dissatisfied |
   4. Overall, how satisfied were you with our service? ☐ ☐ ☐ ☐

   Is there anything particularly good or bad you would like to mention about Parcelforce Worldwide?

   ....
   ....
   ....
   ....
   ....

   You may like us to contact you to discuss your comments - if so, please provide your daytime phone number: ....

   Thank you for your time - please return this questionnaire in the freepost envelope provided

---

Q Questions

1 From the information provided, why is Parcelforce carrying out this particular questionnaire survey?

2 Is this an example of desk or field research? Explain your answer.

3 How is the sample for this survey chosen?

4 Look at the questions that are asked in the survey.

   a Why does the company use a range of tick-boxes for responses?

   b What information is the company hoping to get from the final question?

5 What methods of research might Parcelforce have used other than a postal questionnaire?

E Extension

1 Would you expect Parcelforce to get a good response to this questionnaire? Explain your answer.

2 Choose one other method of market research that Parcelforce might have used and explain its advantages and disadvantages in comparison with a postal survey.

The marketing mix – product

The product as part of the marketing mix

It was shown in Unit 10 that when planning the marketing of its products a business has to make decisions about the 4 Ps – **product**, **promotion**, **price** and **place**. Decisions about product are usually the first decision that a business makes. The later decisions about price, promotion and place are then strongly influenced by the product being sold. Products come in many forms:

This unit is about how a business identifies and develops the products and services that consumers wish to purchase.

At the end of the unit, students should be able to:

- draw up and interpret a product life cycle for categories of products

- understand the process of product development

- explain how a business might differentiate its product

- identify the target market for a range of goods and services

- carry out a market segmentation exercise for well-known products.

Consumer single-use goods | Consumer durables | Consumer services

Producer single-use goods | Capital goods | Producer services

Public goods | Public capital | Public services

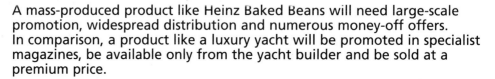

A mass-produced product like Heinz Baked Beans will need large-scale promotion, widespread distribution and numerous money-off offers. In comparison, a product like a luxury yacht will be promoted in specialist magazines, be available only from the yacht builder and be sold at a premium price.

Product life cycle

Although there are many differences between products, many follow a *product life cycle* similar to that of a person.

A product passes through four stages:

• *Birth* – during this period the business spends a lot of money designing the product. It may try out the product, either as a one-off prototype or by **test marketing** it. This involves producing and selling the product in one geographical area, e.g. the North East. Changes to the product may be made as a result of these tests. This period covers also the launch of the product on to the market. Many products that are developed do not get beyond this stage.

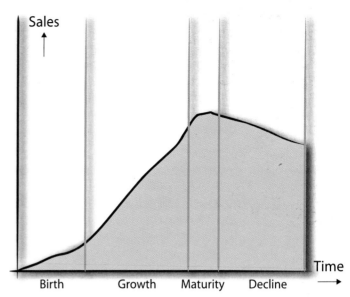

Product life cycle

• *Growth* – during this period the product will be placed on sale nationally. If it is a success sales will start to increase rapidly as people are attracted to a new product. Businesses may also offer the product at a low 'introductory' price to encourage new purchases.

• *Maturity* – this stage is one where the product continues to be bought by a steady number of customers. Many of their purchases may be repeat ones – the same product being bought again and again by loyal consumers. The maturity stage is often the longest in practice and many successful products stay in this stage, e.g. Coca Cola, Mars Bars, Big Macs, Sellotape, Guinness.

• *Decline* – at this stage sales of the product are falling. It may have gone out of fashion or have been replaced because of changes in technology or taste. Businesses decide to stop production if the decline is not halted.

A large business will try to make the maturity stage last as long as possible because of the high costs the business has had to meet in the birth and growth stages. A product often does not make a profit until maturity. The business will find ways of extending a product's life. This might be by:

• producing a 'new' or 'improved' version of the same product
• finding new uses for the product
• finding new markets for the product
• using advertising campaigns to remind people about the product
• producing spin-offs from the product.

TASK 1

a Sketch a possible product life cycle for the following products, showing how the cycle might differ between the products:
  i a single that reaches number 1 in the charts after 2 weeks and stays there for 3 weeks
  ii a new washing powder
  iii a Harry Potter novel
  iv a jumbo jet from Boeing.
b Choose two products you buy regularly that you think are mature products. For each product identify:
  i ways in which the life of that product has been extended by the producers
  ii new ways in which further extension might be possible.

Product development

This is the process of developing and introducing new products. Businesses need to do this in order to replace old ones that are near to the end of their life or to keep up with changes in taste or technology.

Product development is often carried out by a business's **research and development (R&D)** department. This is a team of researchers, engineers and designers who try to turn ideas into marketable products. A large firm will need to continue developing new products even when it has successful ones. It will be trying to improve its products so that more are sold over a longer period of time. It will need to do this to keep up with competitors.

One way of improving a product is to carry out a **value analysis**. This means taking the product apart and asking a whole range of questions. Some are shown on this page.

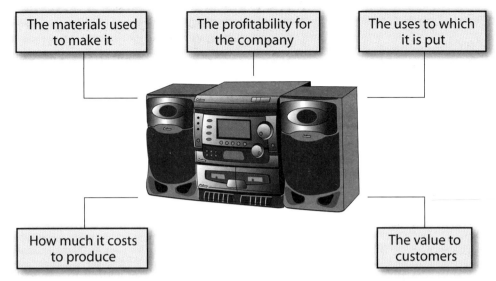

The materials used to make it

The profitability for the company

The uses to which it is put

How much it costs to produce

The value to customers

The factors in a value analysis

A business may come up with a number of decisions as a result of a value analysis:

- To use cheaper materials in order to cut costs.
- To promote new uses for the product.
- To seek new customers for the product.
- To use new techniques in making the product.
- To change the look of the product.

Businesses may also compare their products with the ones that are most successful in the market. This is known as **benchmarking**. They would look at their competitors' products in order to find out why they are successful, and then use that information to improve their own product.

TASK 2

Product development at British Aerospace

One of the most significant civil aviation projects since Boeing launched the 747 'Jumbo' jet in the late 1960s is the Airbus A3XX. It involves British Aerospace working with a French company Airbus Industrie and five other European aerospace companies. They aim to develop a larger plane than the Jumbo (to carry 550 passengers) but one which is cheaper to run and maintain. It must also be able to operate from existing airports without the need to alter the stands where aircraft park. It will have four aisles – two on the main deck and two on the top deck – and maximum comfort for passengers, including a gym. The development is likely to cost US $8billion, with the first aircraft in service in 2004. New manufacturing processes are being developed to help build such large planes. Computer technology is being pushed to help bring together all the designers and engineers working on the project across Europe.

Source: Adapted from www.bized.ac.uk/compfact/bae.

a Why do you think British Aerospace wants to be involved in developing the A3XX?

b Explain why so many companies would need to be involved in this product development.

c What advantages might the A3XX have over Boeing's Jumbo jet?

Making the product different

If a small business is to survive competition from larger firms, it is important that there is something special about its product or service. This is called **product differentiation** and it involves a business providing something for customers that is different from what is available elsewhere.

A business can choose to differentiate its product in several ways:

- *Branding* involves providing the product or service with a recognisable name and image. A good strong brand name encourages customers to buy the product again and again and is very valuable to a business.

- *Quality* can give a small business especially an advantage over a larger business. If a company uses better quality materials or can provide a service which exactly matches its customer's requirements, then it can keep its place in the market alongside mass-produced, lower quality products.

- *Availability* can make a particular product or service attractive to customers. A small organisation might be able to ensure that its product is always in stock or be able to provide a rapid response time to an order.
A service may be available 24 hours a day or to meet an individual need.

- *After-sales service* provided with a personal touch by well-qualified staff may make a product more attractive from one business than from a larger competitor.

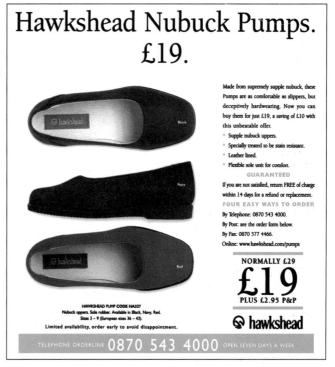

Hawkshead Nubuck Pumps. £19.

Made from supremely supple nubuck, these Pumps are as comfortable as slippers, but deceptively hardwearing. Now you can buy them for just £19, a saving of £10 with this unbeatable offer.

- Supple nubuck uppers.
- Specially treated to be stain resistant.
- Leather lined.
- Flexible sole unit for comfort.

GUARANTEED
If you are not satisfied, return FREE of charge within 14 days for a refund or replacement.

FOUR EASY WAYS TO ORDER
By Telephone: 0870 543 4000.
By Post: see the order form below.
By Fax: 0870 577 4466.
Online: www.hawkshead.com/pumps

NORMALLY £29
£19
PLUS £2.95 P&P

HAWKSHEAD PUMP CODE HA327
Nubuck uppers. Sole rubber. Available in Black, Navy, Red.
Sizes 3 – 9 (European sizes 36 – 43).
Limited availability, order early to avoid disappointment.

hawkshead

TELEPHONE ORDERLINE **0870 543 4000** OPEN SEVEN DAYS A WEEK

TASK 3

Richard Reed, Jon Wright and Adam Balon founded Innocent in April 1999 to deliver the only natural drinks range to the UK consumer. Richard Reed says: 'We began thinking about making fruit drinks and decided that we would be the food and drink company that doesn't compromise and makes only 100 per cent natural products. Everybody told us 'You need sugar and water' but it took time to discover those are just for a manufacturer's convenience …. We called the brand Innocent because the product is unadulterated.'

They test marketed their Fruit Smoothie drinks at a London Jazz festival. After only 12 months' trading, Innocent supply some 500 retail outlets including leading high street cafés such as Coffee Republic. The current product range includes the Fruit Smoothie, Thickie, made with yoghurt, and the soon to arrive Veggie made with fresh vegetable juice.

Source: Adapted from *The Independent,* 17 May 2000; and Shell-Livewire web site, July 2000.

a How did the founders of Innocent differentiate their product?

b Have they been successful in doing this?

c Why does the company now sell three different products?

Identifying the target market

Most people wanting to set up a business will have a good idea of the type of product or service they intend to sell. But it will also be important for the business to identify the **target market** for their product, that is to find out at which specific consumers the product or service is to be aimed. This will help the business change its products if necessary to match the needs of its customers better.

Each of the following people is setting up or expanding his or her business. Before they can do this they need to establish the profile of their consumers.

	Business idea	Possible customer profile
	Jo has been making dried flower arrangements for her friends for years but now wants to turn her hobby into a small business.	40+ age group Married with older family Lower to middle earning groups House/flat owners Interest in gardening/flowers
	Bob who runs Westminster Cabs is wondering whether to expand his taxi fleet to include a larger 'people carrier' that is also adapted for disabled use.	Disabled children or adults Groups/clubs Large families without own transport Urban residents
	Chris has worked for a small building firm as a painter/decorator for a few years. He now wants to set up on his own offering a more specialist service offering high-quality room 'make-overs'	30–50 age group Single or married but with no children House/flat owners Medium to high earners Interest in house style/decorating
	Annette owns a local dry cleaning shop. She knows that a competitor has recently closed. She wonders whether to add an evening 'home collect and return' service to her normal over the counter one.	Single or married working people Professional occupations Medium to higher earning groups Live in locality for delivery

The cases above give some examples of the way in which businesses can build up a customer profile. The profile shows the characteristics of customers which make them behave in certain ways. These characteristics might include:

- their income
- their age and sex
- their interests and lifestyle
- their occupation
- their marital status and family size
- where they live.

TASK 4

Draw up possible consumer profiles for the following business ideas:

a Ushma has worked as a care manager in nursing homes for 10 years but has decided to set up an agency to provide nurses and nursing care in the north of Wales.

b Ilana runs Blooming Babies Nursery in south-east Essex which provides childcare for babies and nursery education for children aged 3–5.

c Polly has a giftware shop in a popular tourist attraction in Devon and is thinking of expanding into selling guidebooks, maps and souvenir books by buying the shop next door

The above all relate to consumers. But some businesses supply their goods and services direct to other businesses. Their customer profile may include factors like size, turnover, location, number of employees and length of existence.

Segmenting the market

Larger businesses will have a wide range of products selling to a wide range of consumers. They will not develop just one consumer profile but will need several. When a business **segments its market** it divides its customers into smaller groups and may well produce a range of products to meet the needs of each of those groups. In this way it hopes to sell more.

There are a number of ways a business might segment its market:

- By age and sex. Many products or services are aimed at a particular age group, e.g. Saga holidays for the over 50s. Many are also aimed at one sex or the other – aftershave for men, perfume for women. Some also combine sex and age – Tammy selling clothes to young girls; Etam to women.

- By occupation and income. This is often known as socio-economic segmentation. A very common set of groups is used by the advertising industry for this purpose.

Classification	Who is included
A	Higher managerial, administrative and professional
B	Middle management, administrative or professional
C1	Supervisory or clerical, junior management
C2	Skilled manual workers
D	Semi-skilled and unskilled manual workers
E	State pensioners, students, casual workers, unemployed

- By geographical area. People in different regions of the UK and Europe have different tastes, preferences and lifestyles. For example, washing machines sold in Mediterranean countries have far lower spin speeds than those sold in northern Europe because the washing is much more likely to dry in the open air.

TASK 5

Boots the Chemist has seven major product and service categories that they sell. These are:
- medical products such as prescription drugs
- over-the-counter health products such as vitamins
- beauty products such as cosmetics and hair care
- baby products such as toys, nappies and food
- gifts such as stationery, home gifts, greetings cards
- photographic – cameras, films and developing films
- food such as sandwiches and crisps.

In a group, choose one of these categories and identify possible ways that Boots could segment the market for the particular product grouping.

Present your ideas to the class.

The Solero ice cream success story

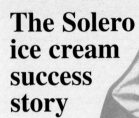

Most new products hit the market place in a blaze of advertising and publicity. Wall's Solero was different. It arrived in retail freezer cabinets in June 1994 almost unannounced. Yet by August it was the UK's third fastest selling hand-held ice cream. Wall's were delighted by its success and decided that in 1995 it would be launched throughout Europe and supported by a £3 million marketing budget in the UK.

The Solero story started with a marketing decision to tackle the adult refreshment sector of the ice cream market. The goal was to repeat the success of Magnum in the indulgence sector. Research indicated that an opportunity existed for a premium quality product targeting 20–35-year-olds, which offered both refreshment and indulgence. As the brand mapping diagram shows, Solero was to open up a new segment of the market.

An initial meeting was arranged in March 1993 to bring together product development, marketing and production staff. After their discussions, a product developer said, 'While you're all here, what you think of this?' They were given a square, orange-coloured lolly on a stick. A couple of licks of the exotic fruit coating, and the discovery of dairy ice cream inside, convinced them that the right product had been found before they had even started looking.

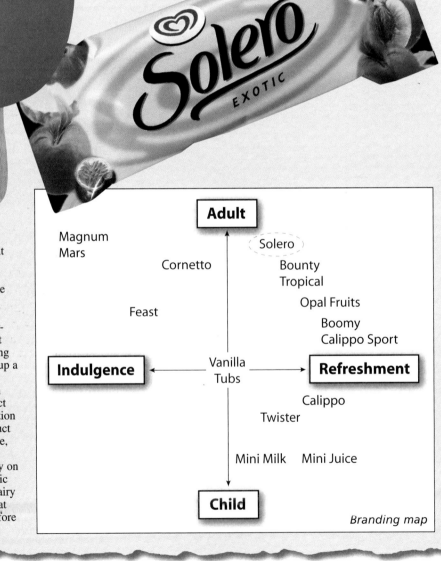

Branding map

The product's shape, taste and size were refined during the summer, using qualitative research. The whole product concept was then researched in Germany, Italy, Holland and Portugal in November 1993, to see how well it might perform as a Europe-wide brand. The results were so encouraging that the Birds Eye Wall's board decided to rush the project forward for a 1994 test launch in Britain.

Meanwhile an appropriate brand name was sought that could be pronounced and registered throughout Europe. The final choice was between two: Oasis and Solero. The Solero name was not available in Belgium, but its association with the sun and its exceptional pronounceability made it the winner. (In Belgium, you will have to ask for Soledo.)

At the same time, the packaging design had been decided upon and the price set at 80p – between Opal Fruits at 65p and Magnum at 90p. The product was ready for launch.

As June 1994 approached it was still not certain whether the factory would be able to produce this new style of ice cream in sufficient numbers. So it was decided that no advertising would run until it was clear that production could keep up with demand. This was fortunate, because although factory output proved buoyant, an exceptionally hot July sent demand rocketing for all refreshment products.

The market share graph shows Solero's rise to a 20 per cent sector share in its first, rushed season. Pleasingly for Birds Eye Wall's, it hit the share held by Mars Opal Fruits

brand and – surprisingly – Mars ice cream. Most important of all, however, Solero achieved its target of expanding the market for ice cream. One quarter of Solero buyers were not previously ice cream impulse buyers at all.

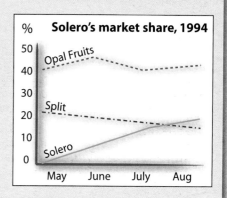

Source: www.bized.ac.uk/compact/unilever

Q Questions

1 Which market segment was Solero aimed at? Use evidence from the case study to illustrate your answer.

2 Which departments in Wall's were involved in developing Solero?

3 How was market research used to influence the Solero product?

4 How did Wall's decide upon a price for the Solero?

5 Was the launch of the Solero a success? What evidence is there to show this?

E Extension

1 Explain what the brand mapping diagram shows about:

   a the type of product that Solero is

   b the type of customer that Solero is aimed at.

2 Why do you think there are no products listed in the Indulgence/Child sector of the brand mapping diagram?

3 How do you think Mars might have responded to the launch of Solero?

This unit is about the ways in which a business persuades its customers to buy its products through the use of advertising and other methods of promotion.

At the end of the unit, students should be able to:

- identify the different ways in which a product can be promoted

- distinguish between advertising and other methods of promotion and merchandising

- analyse the way packaging is used to promote products

- compare different methods of sales promotion

- choose appropriate methods of advertising for small and large businesses

- identify the advantages and disadvantages of different advertising media

- explain why good public relations is important for a business.

Promoting a product or service

Through market research, a business can find out who its customers are likely to be. Through product development, it can develop a product that should meet the needs of its target customers. It will then feel more confident to go ahead with the launch of the product. Promotion is the next important part of a business's marketing strategy.

Promotion is about getting the message to the customer so that the customer reacts by buying the product. Promotion techniques can be grouped under five headings:

- personal selling
- packaging and merchandising
- sales promotions
- advertising
- public relations.

Personal selling

This is an important method of promotion for small businesses as it involves communicating face to face with the customer. This allows the owner to respond to individual questions about the product and to show how the product may meet the customer's needs.

A large business may use personal selling to promote its products to other businesses especially. The business will have a team of sales representatives who make personal contact, demonstrate the product and take orders.

Exhibitions such as the Motor Show and the Clothes Show Live and trade fairs for businesses are important events that give businesses a chance to promote their products directly to their personal and trade customers.

Personal selling is also a way of distributing the product and will be looked at again in Unit 15.

TASK 1

In a survey by the Exhibition Industry Federation buyers were asked why they visited trade exhibitions.

- 89 per cent said that the opportunity to make face-to-face contacts was important
- 87 per cent said that demonstrations of products was important
- 77 per cent said that the ability to compare products was important.

Source: *The Essential Marketing Sourcebook* by Ros Jay, FT/Prentice Hall; 1998.

a What does this survey show about the importance of exhibitions as a way of promoting a business's product?

b Your business has developed a new type of food mixer and has hired a space at the BBC's Food and Drink Show at the Birmingham National Exhibition Centre. Working in pairs, think of five ways in which you might promote your product during the show. Compare your methods with those of other pairs in your class.

Packaging and merchandising

Packaging refers to the way in which the product or service is presented to the consumer.

TASK 2

Collect three empty packages of products that you or your family buy regularly, e.g. a cereal box, a crisp packet, a tin of baked beans.

Look carefully at the packaging and labels on the products. For each one, try to answer the following questions:

a What variety of information is included on the packaging? Why is this information included?

b How is each business using the packaging to promote the product?

c Could a different type of packaging be used for any of the products you chose? Suggest some alternatives.

d Of the three packages, which is most effective in marketing the product? Give your reasons.

Most often the term refers to the physical appearance of the package in which a product is placed. The packaging serves three purposes:

- It protects the product from damage.
- It decorates and promotes the product to make it attractive to consumers.
- It allows information about the product to be displayed.

It is the successful combination of these three features that helps to promote the product. Through its packaging a business will try to create a strong brand image. This means creating a name and look for the product which is easily recognised and remembered by customers. When they next want to buy this product they can recognise the packaging quickly because it includes a familiar product name or **logo**. A logo is a symbol which is recognised as the product or company.

Some well-known logos

In addition to how the product is packaged, the way it is displayed is also important. In supermarkets, where there are many similar products being sold, a good display with posters, special shelving, good lighting, etc. will make a particular product stand out. Many companies tell shops how their product should be displayed. These point-of-sale displays and promotions are known as **merchandising**.

Sales promotions

Sales promotions are the ways in which businesses provide incentives for people to buy their products. They are used to bring about a quick increase in sales in the hope that once consumers have bought the product they will carry on purchasing it long term.

As markets have become more competitive, so the use of sales promotions has increased. Here are some examples:

Loyalty cards encourage customers to return to the same shop time after time

- Money-off coupons or offers may be printed in newspapers or sent through the post or appear on the product itself. Sometimes free samples of a product may be distributed or offered in a supermarket or at a special event.

- Free gifts are included with many products, especially magazines, as an incentive to buy. They are a reward for purchasing the product but they might also be used to promote further the image and name of the product, e.g. through free pencils, key rings, mugs etc.

- 'Buy one, get one free' offers – or similar incentives – are now very common in supermarkets as competition between the major retailers increases. They are usually found on regularly purchased consumer products, but are now spreading to services. For example, many airlines offer two seats for the price of one on off-peak flights and many theme parks offer free children's tickets if two adults pay the entrance fee.

- Loyalty cards have developed in the past five years as a way for companies to reward regular customers by giving them either refunds after building up points gained from purchases or by giving money-off offers only to those holding the loyalty cards. Many retail chains now have loyalty cards – from supermarkets to clothes retailers to petrol stations.

- Competitions are an important promotional tool for some products. The competitions offered by newspapers have been especially influential on sales, although the impact of the National Lottery has reduced the use of competitions generally.

TASK 3

a What type of sales promotion does this Sainsbury's advertisement use?

b Why might Sainsbury's want to use this type of sales promotion to help sell its food?

c Why do you think Sainsbury's has included the pasta recipe in its advertising?

Advertising

Advertising is the process of communicating information about the product or service to as many potential customers in the target market as possible. The aim of advertising is to increase sales. Every advertisement will try to do two things:

- Inform consumers about the product.
- Persuade consumers to buy the product.

But advertising must not be misleading. Unit 8 showed that there are legal controls on what and how businesses can advertise.

Small businesses

A business can make use of a wide range of **advertising media** in order to get its message across. These are the different advertising channels that exist. A small business such as a sole trader will use methods of advertising which suit its small market and small budget. One of the following may be used:

- Word of mouth – customers telling other consumers how good a service or product is. This is free for the business, but obviously the owner has no control over what is said. An alternative could be a firm telephoning its regular customers to tell them about a special offer.
- Local newspapers or local radio – this will reach a larger number of readers or listeners who live close to the business, but would be a relatively expensive method for a small business if the advertising is used regularly.
- Commercial directories – like *Yellow Pages* or the *Thomson Directory*. These go into everyone's home and have a longer 'life' than newspaper advertising. As adverts are placed into categories those using the directories at least have some intention of buying. However, any page contains many rival advertisements so that a business's message may not get through.
- Delivering leaflets – this is a relatively cheap form of advertising which has the potential to be organised so that a greater success rate can be achieved. This can be done by targeting consumers in particular locations or with specific interests.
- Web sites – it is relatively inexpensive for small businesses to develop their own web sites in order to promote the business or take orders. There is no guarantee, however, that those accessing the site will be in a position to buy products. They may just be browsing the Net.
- Specialist magazines – although this method may be expensive as the magazines will charge a national rate, the benefits are that the business is reaching the target market who are interested in the product on sale.

TASK 4

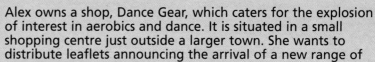

Alex owns a shop, Dance Gear, which caters for the explosion of interest in aerobics and dance. It is situated in a small shopping centre just outside a larger town. She wants to distribute leaflets announcing the arrival of a new range of dancewear that she has just bought from a supplier. She seeks some advice from her local small business adviser about the best ways to distribute the leaflets. The adviser gives her two options:

- Distribute the leaflets to the houses in the area around where the shop is situated and at random to other roads in the town.
- Visit local dance studios and leisure centres at times when classes are taking place and distribute the leaflets by leaving them under car windscreen wipers.

  Alex has only a limited budget for her promotion and so has to choose between these methods.

a What information should Alex include on her leaflet? Explain why she should include it.

b Design and desktop publish an appropriate leaflet for Dance Gear. Why is the presentation of the leaflet important?

c Which method of distribution should Alex include? Explain the advantages and disadvantages of both methods and why you made your choice.

Large businesses

A large business can make use of a wider range of advertising media including those which operate nationally or globally, e.g. national newspapers, magazines, television, cinemas, national independent radio, and the Internet. Such media will reach a large number of consumers but will only be within the reach of the large advertising budgets that large companies have. They must prove cost effective, that is, the increase in sales revenue from extra customers should outweigh the high costs of the advertising.

THERE'S MUCH MORE TO MAZDA THAN MEETS THE EYE.

A large business will have a plan for its advertising. For each of its products it may carry out an **advertising campaign**. This is a plan for advertising a product or service over a period of time and using a variety of media. Many campaigns will focus on certain times of the year. For example, holiday companies will produce brochures, posters and advertising on TV around the Christmas period. Store advertising, is often linked to the summer or winter sales. Other advertising campaigns focus upon new or improved products and will lead up to the launch of the product.

An advertising campaign to sell a new car model may include advertising slots on TV and radio, newspaper and magazine advertising, brochures and billboard posters. National advertising can use the following range of media. With each method there are a number of advantages and disadvantages.

Media	Advantages	Disadvantages
TV	Adverts can be shown several times in one day or week Advertising slots can be booked for specific times Certain programmes can now be sponsored Rates vary according to the time of day	TV advertising is expensive to produce and to run Consumers may not watch the advert or may fast-forward through them on video taped programmes
Radio	Adverts can be played several times in one day or week Advertising slots can be booked for specific times Lower rates than TV advertising and cheaper to produce Impact of spoken voice sometimes greater than visual impact	Limited range of stations to choose from Smaller number of potential consumers than TV Listeners may switch stations when the adverts come on
Newspapers	Adverts reach a large number of consumers Adverts can be displayed in a large number of fonts or styles	Adverts are static and may lack impact Adverts may not be read by the intended consumer
Magazines	Adverts can reach a large number of your target consumers Adverts can be displayed in a large number of fonts or styles	Adverts are static and may lack impact The best pages in magazines are very expensive There will be a lot of competing advertising in specialist magazines
Posters/billboards	The size of a billboard can have a great impact This type of space is relatively cheap, and yet can have national coverage	Many people may not notice the poster They need to be changed regularly or they will lose their impact
Direct mail	Use of Royal Mail to ensure national coverage Can target consumers exactly through mailing lists Produces a better response rate in terms of follow up purchases	Very expensive if used on a national scale Will not help to persuade those who are not regular customers May be treated as 'junk' mail
Internet	Potential coverage is very wide Each company can control how its products are presented through its own web site Can employ specialist companies to produce and keep up-to-date, good quality web sites	Many browsers may not be interested in purchasing Adverts may be ignored or 'clicked' off by browsers Consumers are still reluctant to make purchases through web sites

A large business which intends to use national advertising media will probably employ an **advertising agency**. This is a specialist business which makes commercials, posters, newspaper advertisements, etc. They may use a 'storyboard' approach to designing a TV or cinema advertisement, that is, a series of pictures that show how the advertisement moves along. The storyboard would be discussed with the business and shown to potential customers before the finished advertisement is produced and shown.

TASK 5

Wall's has ice cream market licked despite clouds

Despite June 2000 having seen the worst weather for ice cream sales on record, Naomie Ditzler, the face on the Wall's Magnum bars posters, is having a profound impact on the company's profits.

'Last year we sold around 88 million bars,' said Simon Stevens of Wall's. 'This year we reckon we will sell more than 150 million bars, up nearly 80 per cent on last year.'

The impact of the poster campaign, showing the model chomping through a Magnum bar, is thought to have been largely responsible for this rise in sales. The rise is surprising, given June 2000's dreadful weather. Surveys have shown that the Magnum series of posters scored third in consumer awareness after campaigns by One 2 One mobile phones and Lucozade featuring Lara Croft.

Wall's sees Magnum as a 'power' brand which can compete with products like KitKat and Walker's Crisps. It has dramatically increased its Magnum marketing spend from £2.5 million in 1999 to £7 million this year.

Source: Adapted from *The Observer,* 30 July 2000.

a Why would Wall's have expected demand for Magnum to fall in June 2000?

b What impact has the Magnum poster campaign had?

c What are the advantages to companies like Wall's, One 2 One and Lucozade in using poster campaigns?

d What other methods might Wall's be using to promote Magnum?

Public relations

Public relations (PR) is the way in which companies try to promote their own image to particular groups. These groups might be shareholders, customers, the public as a whole or their own employees. They might do this in a number of ways:

- Through **sponsorship** of major sporting, artistic or other events. This might range from Boots sponsoring the Body Zone in the Millennium Dome and Carling sponsoring the football premiership to a local paper sponsoring a town carnival or a local business sponsoring the town's football team.

- Through being involved in **campaigns** which show that the company is socially responsible. For example, the Co-operative Bank refuses to lend money to businesses that operate in 'unethical' ways. Many businesses have adopted 'green' policies which show they are environmentally friendly. Many companies donate time and money to national fund raising such as Comic Relief's Red Nose Day and the BBC's Children in Need.

- Through the use of press conferences and press releases to inform the media about what the company is doing or to respond to any negative publicity it may have received.

- Through the use of their own business web site which can provide both information about the business and its products and publicity for the business.

Larger companies and other organisations like charities and pressure groups may well employ a public relations agency to advise them on their activities and to provide the publicity that the companies want.

TASK 6

McDonald's announces global Olympic sponsorship for 2002 and 2004

McDonald's today announced its worldwide sponsorship of the Olympic Games for the 2001–2004 quadrennium, continuing the company's long-standing commitment to the international Olympic movement. The agreement extends McDonald's exclusive global Olympic marketing rights in the restaurant and food service category through the 2002 Winter Olympic Games in Salt Lake City, USA and the 2004 Summer Olympic Games in Athens, Greece.

'We're extremely proud to support the Olympic movement and the very important ideals and values it represents,' said Jack Greenberg, Chairman and Chief Executive Officer of McDonald's Corporation.

'As a top global sponsor, we are uniquely capable of bringing the fun and excitement of the world's premier sporting event to 43 million customers every day.'

McDonald's participation in The Olympic Partner Programme (TOP) includes the right to use the Olympic Rings in McDonald's marketing efforts, sponsorship of all the 199 National Olympic Teams around the world and status as the Official Restaurant Partner of the XVIII Winter Olympic Games and the XXVII Olympiad. McDonald's will help feed the world's athletes and Olympic spectators in Salt Lake City and Athens, as it did in Atlanta in 1996 and Nagano in 1998, and is preparing to do in Sydney this September. Financial terms of the deal were not disclosed.

Source: McDonald's press release, 6 June 2000.

a Why would McDonald's want to be a sponsor of the Olympic Games?

b How would a customer of McDonald's know that the company is an Olympic sponsor?

c What might be the disadvantages for McDonald's of this type of promotional activity?

KEY TERMS

Advertising agency – **an organisation that devises and runs advertising campaigns for businesses and other organisations.**

Advertising campaign – **a plan to advertise a product or service over a period of time using a variety of advertising media.**

Advertising media – **the ways in which advertisements can be shown, e.g. by using TV, magazines or the Internet.**

Logos – **a symbol, words or picture by which a particular company is recognised, e.g. McDonald's Golden Arches.**

Loyalty cards – **discount schemes run by companies which reward regular customers with points or special offers.**

Merchandising – **point-of-sale displays and sales promotions.**

Packaging – **the way in which a product is protected and promoted on the shelf.**

Personal selling – **marketing a product through communicating directly with the customer, e.g. by telephone selling.**

Public relations (PR) – **methods of promoting the image of a business rather than promoting a product.**

Sales promotion – **the methods a business uses to try to attract the customers to buy its product.**

Sponsorship – **providing financial support for an event or a community activity in order to promote the image of a company. A form of public relations.**

Quick Lamb

Lamb consumption within Great Britain is suffering from a long-term decline. We are now consuming just over 6 kg each per annum, down from 7.5 kg in the early 1990s. As a result of the reduction in grants to farmers and more lamb being exported, lamb is now one of the most expensive meats to buy. Consumer research about lamb showed that:

- over 70 per cent of lamb is eaten by consumers aged 45+
- today's consumers want quick meals that take no more than 30 minutes to prepare
- 90 per cent of meat buyers like lamb because of its taste and flavour
- lamb is not versatile enough to be used in a variety of dishes
- consumers do not feel that lamb gives value for money – due to the high price and too much fatty waste on the plate.

Because of the decline in sales, the Meat and Livestock Commission (MLC), which promotes British Meat, decided to start a major advertising campaign for lamb. It decided upon a target audience of younger consumers aged 25–45 and for whom free time was limited. It decided upon the following marketing strategy:

- Establish a new range of boneless lamb cuts which were quick to cook.
- Introduce a new brand to assist in marketing this new range.
- Have an advertising campaign to raise awareness of the range, and encourage trial of the new lamb cuts.

The MLC used consumer focus groups drawn from its target market to help it to choose which lamb cuts were preferred and the name for the brand – 'Quick Lamb'. A logo was also chosen – 'succulent boneless cuts' – to go with the campaign.

The advertising campaign was called 'Women Behaving Badly' and highlighted the convenience of the new lamb cuts for young women preparing for a night out. Over a four-week period it was shown on ITV, Channel 4 and Channel 5 and selected satellite stations. To back up this campaign there were a number of other promotions:

- a press pack containing Quick Lamb recipes sent to women's magazines
- a telephone hotline for readers to request a recipe booklet
- point-of-sale merchandising in large supermarkets and butchers
- radio interviews with Denise Lewis, Olympic heptathelete, promoting Quick Lamb
- several Internet pages including recipe information.

The results of the campaign were positive. Research showed that:
- the commercial was seen by 88 per cent of housewives with children
- Quick Lamb was mentioned in 42 publications reaching over 4 million readers
- Quick Lamb was talked about on 26 regional radio stations reaching 3 million listeners
- leading supermarkets and independent butchers were very positive about the in-store merchandising.

Most importantly, sales in the month after the launch showed a 21 per cent increase in boneless lamb cuts.

Source: Adapted from www.bized.ac.uk/compfact/mlc

Q Questions

1 Explain with an example each of the following terms used in the case study:
   a target audience
   b focus group
   c brand
   d point-of-sale merchandising.

2 What were the reasons for the decline in lamb sales since the early 1990s?

3 Why was the Quick Lamb brand chosen as the centre of the campaign to promote lamb sales?

4 Why do you think the Meat and Livestock Commission used TV advertising as a major part of its Quick Lamb campaign?

5 Was the campaign a success? What evidence is there to back up your answer?

E Extension

1 Why did the Meat and Livestock Commission choose radio, magazines and the Internet to back up its TV campaign?

2 Compare the use of TV advertising with point-of-sale merchandising for a product such as lamb.

3 This campaign for lamb took place in 1998/9. The web address of the British Meat promotional campaign is www.britishmeat.org.uk. Use the Internet to research the present marketing campaigns for British meat, including lamb.

The marketing mix – price

This unit is about how a business determines and sets the price for its product and how price can be used as a marketing tool by a business.

At the end of the unit, students should be able to:

- understand that there is a range of ways that a business can set a price

- distinguish between cost-based and market-based pricing

- carry out simple cost-based pricing exercises

- compare full-cost pricing with contribution-cost pricing

- identify and compare a number of market-orientated pricing strategies

- explain how price discrimination works.

Setting a price

Any business hopes to make a profit. The owner has to try to set a price for the product or service that allows him or her to do this.

Setting a price is not as easy as it sounds. If the price is too high, no one will buy. If the price is lower, it is possible that all the product will be sold and a profit will be made. However, if the price is too low the money earned, or revenue, will not be enough to cover the costs of buying the replacement materials.

There are various ways in which a business can work out what price to charge. It may have used market research to ask likely customers what price they would be prepared to pay. Unless the new business is very specialised, other business competitors will be offering similar products or services and their price can provide a starting point. This is called **market-led pricing** because the business has followed the example set by other businesses in the market.

Sometimes, particularly with a sole trader, business is specialised, and the owner has to work out the price for himself or herself. Where this is the case, it is likely that every job will be different and an individual price will need to be worked out for each job. This is called **one-off pricing** because no two jobs are the same.

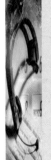

Tracy's hair salon is in a small row of shops on the outskirts of Bolton. Tracy knows her prices have to be competitive. She has a few friends in the trade with shops in similar neighbourhoods and they keep in touch over prices. On her day off, Tracy also looks at the prices town centre firms charge. She has to keep her prices much lower than those in the town because her facilities are not as good. Tracy's customers are quick to tell her if they think her prices are too high. This is known as market-led pricing.

Norrie works for a kitchen and bathroom fitter. At weekends and in the evenings he works for himself because he is saving up to buy a house. His private customers find out about him by word of mouth. Norrie has no standard price because each house and each customer are different. The size, age and shape of the house will affect how long the kitchen or bathroom takes him to fit. He has to give each of his customers an individual price which means he has to know his trade thoroughly as customers expect the estimate to be accurate. This is known as one-off pricing.

Cost-plus pricing is the most usual method of calculating the price.
The owner works out all the costs involved in selling either the product or service and adds on either a flat rate amount or a percentage increase in order to arrive at the selling price. This is often known as a **mark-up**.
In working out costs, the owner might divide the costs into two categories.
Fixed costs are those which have to be paid whether any product is made or service provided. Fixed costs include things like rent, rates and insurance.
Variable costs are those which change depending on the quantity of product made or service provided. Variable costs include things like raw materials, parts and packaging.

TASK 1

Alec Clegg is setting up his own business, Ace Window Cleaning. His previous employer is too old to carry on and many of the existing customers have told Alec that he can clean their windows. His experience of this type of work helps him to work out the likely costs. He separates the costs into fixed costs – those which he has to pay whether he cleans any windows or not – and variable costs

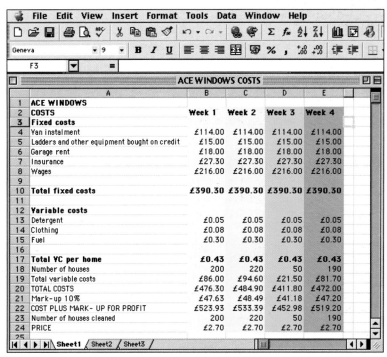

	A	B	C	D	E
1	**ACE WINDOWS**				
2	**COSTS**	Week 1	Week 2	Week 3	Week 4
3	**Fixed costs**				
4	Van instalment	£114.00	£114.00	£114.00	£114.00
5	Ladders and other equipment bought on credit	£15.00	£15.00	£15.00	£15.00
6	Garage rent	£18.00	£18.00	£18.00	£18.00
7	Insurance	£27.30	£27.30	£27.30	£27.30
8	Wages	£216.00	£216.00	£216.00	£216.00
9					
10	**Total fixed costs**	**£390.30**	**£390.30**	**£390.30**	**£390.30**
11					
12	**Variable costs**				
13	Detergent	£0.05	£0.05	£0.05	£0.05
14	Clothing	£0.08	£0.08	£0.08	£0.08
15	Fuel	£0.30	£0.30	£0.30	£0.30
16					
17	**Total VC per home**	**£0.43**	**£0.43**	**£0.43**	**£0.43**
18	Number of houses	200	220	50	190
19	Total variable costs	£86.00	£94.60	£21.50	£81.70
20	TOTAL COSTS	£476.30	£484.90	£411.80	£472.00
21	Mark-up 10%	£47.63	£48.49	£41.18	£47.20
22	COST PLUS MARK- UP FOR PROFIT	£523.93	£533.39	£452.98	£519.20
23	Number of houses cleaned	200	220	50	190
24	PRICE	£2.70	£2.70	£2.70	£2.70
25					

– those which depend on the number of houses he works on. He decides to add on 10 per cent for profit, and with a weekly round of 200 houses, sets his price at £2.70. Look at his spreadsheet above.

Alec has been careful to include all his costs and to set his wage at the amount he received as an employee. He has used the cost-plus method of setting his price.

This is what happens during Ace Window's first four weeks:

Week 1 goes according to Alec's plans.

Week 2 is even better and Alec is feeling very cheerful. He manages to clean windows at 220 houses.

Week 3 is a disaster. There is torrential rain for three days and Alec is unable to clean any windows. The rain continues as showers over the next two days and only 50 houses are covered.

Week 4 brings a slight improvement in the weather although the showers slow Alec down and only 190 houses are covered.

a Alec has set his price at £2.70. What is Alec's total revenue in each of the four weeks? (*Hint:* Number of houses cleaned x price.)

b Work out the difference between Alec's total revenue and his total costs for each of the four weeks.

c Over the four-week period, which is the greater, total revenue or total cost?

d What would you suggest to Alec he could do to improve the situation?

Cost-orientated pricing

Small businesses usually produce a narrow range of products and will use relatively simple methods of costing and pricing for their products. Larger businesses will be producing a range of products, all of which will be expected to contribute to the profits of the company. When a large business launches a new product it has to set a price which enables it to make a profit in the long run, that is over the months or years of the product's life. Very few products make a profit immediately because of their enormous development and production costs.

There are two main approaches which a business can take towards its cost of production (**cost-orientated pricing**).

- It can decide that every penny of the costs of developing, making and selling should be included in the price of the product. This is known as **full-cost pricing** and covers both fixed and variable costs of production.

- It can decide that it wants the price of its product to cover only the variable costs, such as raw materials, in full and merely to make a contribution to the fixed costs – this is known as **contribution-cost pricing**. Such a decision can be valid only for the short term, e.g. when a product is launched and is new to the market. In the long run a product's price must cover the fixed costs of its production as well as the variable costs.

Market-orientated pricing

A small business is likely to have to choose a price that is market-led because it has no real power in the market place. However, a large business does have more influence over the market and can use its price as a way of influencing customer behaviour. This is known as **market-orientated pricing**. There are a number of pricing strategies that can be used if a business has some control over its market.

- **Market penetration**. This involves deliberately charging a lower price than a competitor. In the airline industry, BA set up a low-price airline called Go in order to undercut other no-frills airlines such as easyJet and Virgin Atlantic. The aim of market penetration pricing is for a business to get its products bought by as many customers as possible in the shortest time possible. This will get the business a strong foothold in the market and it may drive some of its competitors out of business.

- **Market skimming**. This involves charging more than its competitors, choosing to compete on the grounds of quality, luxury and reliability. Market skimming strategy creams off the most profitable part of the market. Bang and Olufsen compete at the luxury end of the hi-fi market. Products are sold through upmarket retailers and their emphasis is on quality and appearance. Businesses might also use this strategy when launching a new product which they know will be in demand, in order to make as much profit as possible while the product is popular. New computer consoles like PlayStation 2 are sold at a high price when launched and prices are then reduced when the initial 'must have' demand falls.

- **Loss leaders**. Businesses deliberately sell certain products at a low price and therefore at a loss. They do this in order to attract customers to buy other products at the same time from which they will make more profit. In any supermarket there will be 'special offers' to attract customers into the store, where they will also buy many full-price goods.

- **Discounting**. Businesses will offer lower prices to certain groups of customer, to people buying in bulk or at certain times of the year during sales. Often in the building supply industry there will be one price for domestic customers and a lower price for 'trade' customers, that is professional builders, electricians, etc. In these cases, it is the volume of sales that makes it worthwhile for the business to cut its price.

TASK 2

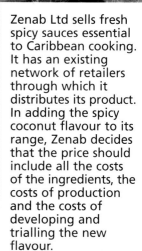

Zenab Ltd sells fresh spicy sauces essential to Caribbean cooking. It has an existing network of retailers through which it distributes its product. In adding the spicy coconut flavour to its range, Zenab decides that the price should include all the costs of the ingredients, the costs of production and the costs of developing and trialling the new flavour.

Super Software plc has a substantial share of the business software market through its successful suite of translation programs. Super Software is anxious to diversify into the home computer market. It has therefore decided to keep the price of its new school software packages low and base the price only on the direct costs of production. The heavy fixed costs, particularly those relating to research and development, will be covered by increasing the price of its existing products instead.

a Identify the two different pricing methods of Zenab and Super Software.

b Explain how each of these methods work in relation to the two examples given.

TASK 3

Centrica targets 3m BT customers

Centrica, a company which owns British Gas as well as the roadside assistance organisation the AA, will shortly launch its telecommunication strategy in a bid to get 3 million of British Telecom's 28.5 million fixed-line telephone customers.

The new telecoms service will offer customers 25 per cent discounts when compared with BT. The service will be offered through Centrica's British Gas subsidiary and will be added to a range of 'home services' it already offers, from gas and electricity supply to central heating and home insurance.

Its strategy is to target the higher income customers in order to gain as much revenue as possible from telecoms. It will aim to capture customers whose bills are above the average £230 per year by offering low cost calls to those changing from BT. Centrica has already been successful at winning customers by offering lower prices than competitors in the electricity business. It now has 3 million electricity customers won from regional electricity suppliers. Now it is moving in on BT.

Source: Adapted from *The Observer*, 3 September 2000.

a What type of pricing strategy do you think Centrica will be using when it moves into the telecoms market? Explain your answer.

b Why does Centrica want to enter the telecoms market?

c Why does Centrica think it will be successful with this strategy?

d How might BT respond?

TASK 4

The Best in Home Reference
Yours for only £4.99 (+p&p)

a What type of pricing strategy is the advertisement illustrating?

b Why would the publisher Dorling Kindersley be willing to sell the dictionary for £4.99?

Price discrimination

Unit 12 introduced the idea of market segmentation. Market segments are smaller groups of consumers with specific needs. By segmenting its market and meeting the needs of different groups of consumers, a business will be able to increase its total sales. More profit can be made if a business can charge these different groups of consumers different prices for the same product or the same service. This is known as **price discrimination**.

It is most successfully used in relation to time and place. Many services, e.g. transport, leisure facilities, holidays and telephone calls, are priced differently according to the time at which the service is purchased. A good example of price discrimination is the peak and off-peak rates charged for mobile telephone calls. Other services, such as theatre tickets, are priced differently according to place. Customers will pay more to see a performance of *Phantom of the Opera* if they sit in the front stalls than if they sit in the back stalls. In transport, many passengers travelling on the same plane or train will have paid different prices for the same trip.

TASK 5

The P&O ferry fares chart shows that a range of prices are charged for an identical journey from Portsmouth to Cherbourg and Le Havre in France. Most of the prices are based on the cost of a vehicle together with a number of passengers. Two of the reasons for the price differences are the type of vehicle and the number of passengers making the journey.

a The chart is an example of price discrimination according to time. Describe this example and explain why it is possible for the company to charge different prices at different times.

b The chart also shows another form of price discrimination other than one based upon the time when people travel. How else is this price discrimination carried out?

c Why is it in this company's interests to be able to charge different customers different prices?

P&O Ferry Prices — P&O PORTSMOUTH

2000 FARES VEHICLES & VEHICLE PASSENGERS

The prices quoted are based on travel from Portsmouth to Cherbourg, Le Havre and Bilbao in the applicable period. For a quotation, please telephone our Call Centre with full details of your travel plans, and our staff will be happy to assist. To make things easier for you we have removed long lists of fares and simply published a selection of starting prices.

		2 Jan-22 Mar '00	23 Mar-13 July '00	14 July-20 Aug'00
SINGLE	For a Car & up to 2 Passengers*	FROM £95	FROM £125	FROM £170
	For a Car & up to 9 Passengers*	FROM £100	FROM £130	FROM £175
5 DAY RETURN	For a Car & up to 2 Passengers*	FROM £90	FROM £140	FROM £190
	For a Car & up to 9 Passengers*	FROM £100	FROM £150	FROM £200
10 DAY RETURN	For a Car & up to 2 Passengers*	FROM £120	FROM £190	FROM £255
	For a Car & up to 9 Passengers*	FROM £130	FROM £200	FROM £270
STANDARD RETURN	For a Car & up to 2 Passengers*	FROM £190	FROM £245	FROM £335
	For a Car & up to 9 Passengers*	FROM £200	FROM £260	FROM £350
MOTORCYCLE RETURN	For the Rider & Passengers	FROM £50	FROM £70	FROM £110
CARAVAN RETURN	For vehicles up to 6m long & 1.83m high	FROM £72	FROM £100	FROM £100
FOOT PASSENGER RETURN	Per Person	FROM £40	FROM £50	FROM £60

KEY TERMS

Contribution-cost pricing – a method of determining the price in which the price makes a contribution to the fixed costs of production but does not cover them.

Cost-orientated pricing – a strategy for determining the price which takes account of the costs of production.

Cost-plus pricing – setting the unit price by working out the total costs for the number of products or service units produced, adding a mark-up, and then dividing by the number of units of products or services.

Discounting – offering lower prices to certain groups of customers, at certain times of year or for bulk purchase, in order to encourage sales.

Full-cost pricing – a method of determining the price of a product based on the total cost of production.

Loss leaders – products that are sold below cost price in order to encourage consumers to buy other products being sold by the business.

Mark-up – the amount, usually a percentage, that a business will add to cost price in order to determine the price charged. The mark-up will ensure that a profit is made.

Market-led pricing – setting the price of a good or service at a level similar to that of other similar products.

Market-orientated pricing – the way a large business uses the price of a product to influence customer behaviour.

Market penetration – obtaining a large share of the market.

Market skimming – selling to the most profitable customers in the market.

One-off pricing – setting an individual price for each good or service.

Price discrimination – charging a range of prices for the same good or service, e.g. because the same product or service is sold at different times or to people of a different age.

Tariffic choices – competition for mobile phone customers

There are more than 23 million mobile phones in use in the UK. There is also a bewildering array of phone tariffs to choose from – more than 140 were analysed by a recent article in the consumer magazine *Which?*.

There are four main mobile phone networks: BT Cellnet, One 2 One, Orange and Vodafone. But there are also tariffs offered by other companies known as indirect service providers. They are provided through one of the four networks. For example, the Virgin tariff operates through the One 2 One network as does the Carphone Warehouse's tariff. These indirect tariffs are often the cheapest.

There are three broad types of tariff offered by these companies:

- Prepay or 'Pay as you go' – customers pay in advance for the mobile phone (around £40) and pay for calls in advance by buying vouchers of between £5 and £75. There is no separate connection fee, contract charge or monthly bill. However, the charges per minute tend to be more expensive than other tariffs.

- Conventional – the mobile phones are heavily subsidised and sometimes cost nothing. Customers have to sign an annual contract and may have to pay a one-off connection fee, about £35. Customers pay a line rental per month but the charges for calls are lower and some free call-time is included.

- All-inclusive – these are based on the conventional tariff but customers pay for the phone, a year's charges, connection charges, line rental and some inclusive call-time in advance. They are sold as a package starting from around £100.
  After 12 months the customer will switch to the conventional package or can cancel the contract and look for another deal.

The pre-pay tariffs tend to be cheapest for people who use their mobile phones for social use. Conventional tariffs tend to be popular with more regular users, especially business users. All-inclusive tariffs are the least popular because of the big initial outlay – but may turn out cheaper than the conventional tariff over the course of a year.

The main networks offer different rates for daytime, evening and weekend calls:

Network	Time	Charge
One 2 One	Daytime	10p
	Evening	2p
	Weekend	2p
Orange	Daytime	25p
	Evening	5p
	Weekend	5p
Vodafone	Daytime	35p
	Evening	5p
	Weekend	2p

But there are also many variations depending upon, for example, whether customers are phoning other mobiles or land lines and how much call time has been purchased in advance.

Source: Adapted from *Which?*, 20 September 2000.

Q Questions

1 What type of pricing polices do you think the mobile phone companies are following? Explain your answer with reference to the case study.

2 Recommend for the following consumers which type of tariff might be best if they choose to buy a mobile phone:

   a a student wanting a set to phone friends and family

   b a delivery company wanting to keep in touch with its drivers

   c a self-employed builder wanting to telephone customers and suppliers.

3 Why might Virgin want to undercut the other companies in offering its Virgin tariff for mobile phone users?

4 a What type of price discrimination is illustrated in the call charges shown in the case study?

   b Why would the networks want to use this type of discrimination?

E Extension

1 Explain at which market segment each of the three types of tariff might be aimed by the large networks.

2 What other competitors might these mobile phone companies have in the telecoms market? Research the rival tariffs that might also be available for consumers.

The marketing mix – place

This unit is about how a business makes sure that its products reach the consumers who wish to buy them in sufficient quantity, at the right time and at the right quality.

At the end of this unit, students should be able to:

- identify different channels of distribution

- compare the benefits and disadvantages of direct selling and mail order

- evaluate the role of wholesalers and retailers

- carry out a retail survey

- assess how businesses choose their methods of distribution

- identify the advantages and disadvantages of franchising

Getting the product to the customer

The fourth P of the marketing mix is placement, or place, and is more commonly known as **distribution**. This is the process of getting goods and services from producers to consumers. This might be farm suppliers delivering feed to farmers, or farmers delivering milk to dairies or dairies delivering milk to supermarkets or door to door through the milkman/woman. All of these involve distributing the product between one stage and the next.

At first sight, it seems as though for a business there is only one way to get a product or service to the customer and that is through a shop. However, in practice there is a variety of ways, some of which involve direct contact with the customer and some which do not. For example, some hairdressers are mobile and take their service direct to the customer's home. Others provide their service through a salon.

For businesses which make things rather than providing a service there are four broad methods that might be used to distribute their products. These methods are known as **channels of distribution**. The goods might be supplied through **mail order**, through **direct sales** to the customer, through **retailers** or via a **wholesaler** and **retailers**. These are shown in the diagram.

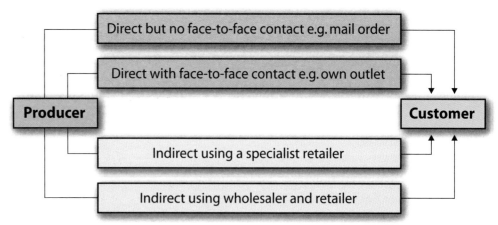

Channels of distribution

TASK 1

a Identify the various channels of distribution that are used for the following products or services.

   i bread **ii** newspapers **iii** motor cars **iv** railway tickets.

b Choose one of the products and identify any major changes in distribution that have been taking place over the past five years.

In the last few years new technology has had a major effect on the distribution of some products and many services. This has been because of the development of new ways of interacting between producer and customer via the telephone, e.g. home banking; the TV, e.g. TV-selling; and the Internet, e.g. dotcom companies like Amazon selling books.

Direct selling

Selling direct usually means getting the product or service to the customer without using any of the middle stages. The two main ways of doing this are either through a factory shop or by selling door to door.

Selling from the factory is only likely to be a very small part of a large organisation's distribution arrangements and is usually for slightly damaged goods or those which are no longer produced. However, this area has been growing recently through the creation of a number of factory outlet shops grouped together in a restored mill or factory.

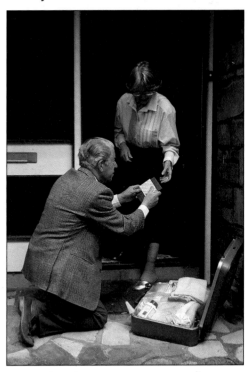

Many small businesses in arts and crafts, e.g. pottery, jewellery, lace and embroidery, sell their goods from their workshop. This is not only cheaper for the business but can also be attractive to consumers as they can see the goods being made.

One or two large organisations have successfully sold door to door, for example Avon cosmetics, Betterware household goods and some of the double glazing companies. Some organisations have started to sell direct in new ways, for example telephone banking and Internet selling of services.

Door-to-door selling requires the company to employ agents to carry out the selling on its behalf. Agents are used mainly to sell services to the public. They receive a basic wage and commission, that is a percentage of the price, from the company for any sales they make on its behalf.

TASK 2

Andrew Cohen was running a chain of curtain shops in 1983 when he first spotted Betterware, an ailing door-to-door sales company founded in the 1920s. 'Everybody over 50 I spoke to said 'Oh yes, they are the brush people who sell door to door.' Betterware's success has been helped along by changes in Britain's high street. Hardware stores have all but disappeared. Britons spend only an average of £32 per household each year on direct sales. The French spend £48 and the Germans more than £100.

The advantage of direct selling is its low cost base in contrast with the large store groups. Betterware's secret is that it manufactures nothing itself and employs only 200 people directly. It sells its products, most of which cost under £5, through an army of 10,000 salespeople, mainly part-timers, who deliver the Betterware catalogue door-to-door and return a few days later to pick up orders. Customers pay by cash or cheque when orders are delivered.

Source: *The Sunday Times.*

a The article says that 'Betterware's success has been helped along by changes in Britain's high street'. Explain how these changes have helped Betterware to increase its sales.

b Betterware is a low cost business. Why are its costs so low?

c Find out which other businesses sell door to door in your area. Are any of them successful? If so, why?

Mail order

Many small businesses only supply by mail order because having a shop or other outlet where people buy goods and services is expensive. Mail order means that goods and services are supplied by post. Customers order the goods and services either by completing an order form or by placing their order by telephone. This keeps costs low as expensive premises in prime business areas are not needed.

Some large organisations also supply only by mail order while others supply items by post as an extra service to their customers. Some companies, e.g. W H Smith, set up separate subsidiaries as book or record clubs to which consumers subscribe by post. Some organisations have been commercially successful in supplying a range of goods by mail order. They are often known as 'catalogues', e.g. Littlewoods, Freemans, Kays. Some consumers like to buy in this way because it enables them to spread the payments for their goods; others because they can shop from their armchair and the goods are available on sale or return.

Much of the selling by dotcom companies on the Internet is by mail order – with the catalogue displayed on screen but with the added advantages that products can be seen moving or can be listened to. Also orders can be made and confirmed instantly. But the goods still have to be delivered by traditional methods.

Next has a successful mail order business in addition to its high street shops.

TASK 3

Companies abandon the 'dotcom'

The glory days of online sales being the key to a successful business could be over. Some companies are choosing to drop the dotcom suffix from their names because the image is becoming soured. Dotcom is beginning to mean never making money and making lots of people redundant.

A natural health products company, Thinknatural, has dropped the dotcom from its name and decided to concentrate on selling its products through more traditional methods such as catalogues. Carol Dukes, the chief executive, said that while the company was keeping its web site, it was no longer appropriate to keep dotcom on its logo. 'Once you have a warehouse of products and a means of shipping it out, an order is an order,' she said. Ms Dukes added that 75 per cent of the population still did not use the Internet regularly to buy goods. After its high profile launch the company has been expanding in more traditional areas by sending out more catalogues and advertising particular products.

Source: Adapted from *The Independent*.

1 What is meant by dotcom selling?
2 Why has Thinknatural decided to drop dotcom from its name?
3 What are the advantages for Thinknatural of selling through catalogues rather than through the Internet?
4 Do you agree that 'the glory days of online sales are over'? Give your reasons.

Wholesalers

Wholesalers buy in bulk from manufacturers. They often specialise in one type of product, such as electrical goods or building supplies, and sell to the trade, that is, to shops or other small businesses. They offer an important service especially to small businesses.

Wholesalers do the following:

- They buy in large quantities and sell in smaller quantities. This is called breaking bulk. The service allows the small business to get some benefit from buying in quantities larger than the individual consumer does.
- They buy new products enabling the small business to examine them before committing themselves to stocking them.
- They often supply goods to the trade on credit.
- They deliver goods produced by large businesses to small business outlets. For many large organisations the use of wholesalers enables them to supply small businesses. It would be uneconomic for a large manufacturer to make individual small-scale deliveries to a large number of small businesses, but a wholesaler provides this crucial service.

A more recent alternative to a wholesaler is a cash and carry store. Prices may be lower than at a conventional wholesalers but, as the name suggests, it is unlikely to offer credit and the goods must be taken away from the store by the purchaser.

A cash and carry outlet

TASK 4

Magazine wars

Currently magazines are distributed via a regional wholesaler network, but this is now under threat from Tesco. It wants to sign up with the wholesaler W H Smith News as the only distributor to its 658 stores. Safeway is also keen to follow Tesco's lead.

Publishers of magazines are afraid that this will threaten small retailers who rely on the regional wholesalers. If Tesco and other supermarkets are no longer part of the regional network, then regional wholesalers will find it uneconomic to deliver to small retailers alone. Many customers will then not be able to buy the specialist magazines they want. Publishers fear that small retailers will be excluded from a supply chain that is geared to large supermarkets.

In response Tesco claims that the new system of distribution will benefit everyone as supply of magazines will be spread more equally across the country.

Source: Adapted from *The Observer,* 3 September 2000.

a How are magazines distributed at present?

b Why do Tesco and Safeway want a new method of distribution?

c How might consumers benefit or suffer from the new method?

d Why do magazine publishers oppose the new method?

Retailers

Many large organisations have their own outlets for their goods and services and these are often, although not always, the only outlet through which these goods and services are supplied. Having their own outlets means they are more able to control the prices of the goods they sell. It also ensures direct contact with the consumers and enables tighter control on manufacturing and stockholding. Car showrooms are good examples as are the branches of banks and public houses managed by breweries.

However, in the mass consumer market the large retailers have become the dominant force in distribution. Both large and small food producers rely on the likes of ASDA, Tesco, Sainsbury's and Safeway to purchase and sell their goods. Clothes manufacturers are equally reliant on Next, Gap or Marks & Spencer. Many of these companies have also diversified (see Unit 18) into selling new products previously only sold through company-owned outlets, such as petrol, insurance and banking, and even motor cars.

Many small retailers would like the advantages from which a large organisation like Safeway can benefit, e.g. large-scale advertising, buying in bulk and obtaining discounts. Some small retailers therefore get together to form a **voluntary chain** through which they can act as a large organisation. Spar and Mace are both groups of small grocers. Unichem is a group of independent pharmacists.

TASK 5

Carry out a retail survey

To do this you will need to visit a shopping centre or shopping mall.

Your teacher may well organise this for your class. It is usually best to work in pairs or groups of three or four in carrying out the research, but you will need to write up your findings independently.

Choose a row of about 20 shops in the shopping centre or mall. Collect the following information about each shop:

1 What is the shop called?

2 What type of products does the shop sell?

3 How large is the shop? You can count the number of 'shop fronts' that it covers.

4 From your knowledge or through asking people who work in the shop, is the shop:

  a part of a local chain of shops

  b part of a national chain of shops

  c an independent retailer?

5 What type of service does the shop provide? Is it:

  a self-service with check-outs

  b self-service with sales assistants

  c service by sales assistants

  d automated service?

6 Briefly describe and comment upon the advertising and other methods of promotion that the shop uses to attract people into it.

Using ICT, produce a report of your findings about the 20 shops.

a Collate the results of your survey in tables.

b Present the results by using bar charts or pie charts as illustrations.

c Write a summary of your findings about the shopping centre or mall.

d Do you think that the shopping centre is successful at attracting customers? Give your reasons.

Choice of channel of distribution

Choosing the right **channel of distribution** will depend very much on a range of factors:

- The type of customer – where the customer is another business, a sales force engaged in personal selling is likely to be the chosen channel.

- The type of product – a fragile or perishable product is likely to go straight from the producer to the consumer cutting out any middlemen.

- The size of the business – a small business will benefit from the range of outlets that a wholesaler can supply; a large business may be able to afford to carry out its own distribution or it may own its own outlets

The table shows some of the advantages and disadvantages of the ways in which a business might provide goods and services to the consumer.

Method	Advantages	Disadvantages
Own outlet or shop	Customer knows location and can become loyal Premises can help to convey the image of the business Control over how goods are sold	High overheads for prime business location Expensive to run individual stores
Mail order, including Internet selling	Low cost premises Goods can be dispatched from warehouse Final price less than shops	No face-to-face contact with consumer Possible high level of returns from dissatisfied customers
Door-to-door sales	Direct contact with the consumer Captive audience	Cost of travelling to the consumer Expensive to employ sales people
Direct sales, including telesales	Ensures that the goods reach the customer Direct contact with customer	Relies on a sales force Resistance to hard sell Resistance to buying goods from home
Wholesaler	Provides reputable outlet for the product Allows a range of goods to be sold to small outlets without direct contact May benefit from other services which the wholesaler provides	No direct contact with the customer Wholesalers charge for their services and take a cut of the profit

TASK 6

First at the door

Dougald Hine is one of an unlikely band of 130 students from British universities selling children's books, homework manuals and CD-ROMs to families on the doorsteps of their homes.

Kingfisher, the children's book publisher, now sells some of its books solely through door-to-door salespeople and has found that it sells more copies that way. Parents like being able to look at the books in their own living room before making up their minds whether they will buy.

'We get these books in front of thousands of prospective buyers every week, whereas people do not walk into bookshops as readily,' says Duncan Battishill, district sales manager for Southwestern Company, the firm behind the scheme. If a family agrees to buy, the sales person returns and spends time showing the family how to get the most out of the books.

Source: Adapted from *Guardian Education*, 1 August 2000.

a Why do you think door-to-door selling is successful for children's books?

b What disadvantages might there be to this method?

c What other method of selling books is mentioned in the article? What are its advantages and disadvantages?

d Identify and explain two other ways in which children's books might be sold.

Franchising

A franchise is the right to sell a good or service produced by a large, possibly multinational business, on the payment of a fee plus a percentage of the profits. The small business has to agree to receive all raw materials and components from the **franchisor** and to follow the rules set out for the operation of the franchise. The small business buying the franchise is called the **franchisee**.

The system allows a small business to trade in a well-known product for a minimal outlay. Some of the risk associated with setting up on your own is therefore removed. It is often easier for franchisees to obtain finance because of the association with a large well-known product or service. Examples of franchise opportunities are Kentucky Fried Chicken, Prontaprint and The Body Shop.

Prontaprint
■ DIGITAL DESIGN PRINT COPY

The large organisation, the franchisor, also benefits from this arrangement. The franchise system allows the large organisation to sell its products direct to the consumer without the expense of opening its own retail outlet. The franchisor meets the costs of providing services such as research and development, promotion, administrative backup and communication within the network but the stock and equipment are owned by the franchisee. The franchisor also benefits from the proportion of income it receives from the franchisee who is likely to be better motivated than an employee and therefore more likely to make a profit.

The main disadvantage to the franchisor of operating a business in this way is that it has only limited control over the franchisee. The franchisor, therefore, has to make sure that it only grants a franchise after the franchisee has undergone tests and interviews to ensure suitability.

TASK 7

There are 710 franchisors in Britain operating through 39,760 franchisees. Many well-known names are franchisors: Body Shop, Kentucky Fried Chicken, Holiday Inn hotels, Swinton Insurance, Thorntons chocolates, Fatty Arbuckles restaurants and most of the fast food giants such as McDonald's, Burger King and Wimpy.

Martin Dancy and Josephine Giles started their own small business eight years ago. They originally launched Oscar, their own brand of pet food and sold it to supermarkets. They found that this restricted the amount of money they could make. They considered setting up their own shop but decided that the overheads would be too high. They now sell through more than 100 franchisees. Their new business is Oscar Pet Foods home delivery service. They make up pet food to their own recipes and it is sold to the franchisees who operate on a door-to-door sales basis. This enables them to achieve nationwide sales whilst keeping costs to a minimum. Launching their franchise cost £250,000 and they now sell each franchise for £7,500. They provide the franchisee with a tried and tested business system, training on animal nutrition and drawing up contracts, advertising and the opportunity to take part in franchise exhibitions.

Source: Adapted from *The Sunday Times*, 1 September 1996

a What are the benefits to the franchisor of operating a franchise?

b What sorts of services do franchisors provide to their franchisees?

c How do these help the franchisor to control the quality of service offered?

d Why did Martin Dancy and Josephine Giles become a franchisor? What benefits has this given them?

KEY TERMS

Channels of distribution – the many ways in which goods and services can move from manufacturer to customer.

Direct selling – getting the product or service to the customer without using any middlemen.

Distribution – the process of getting goods and services from producers to consumers.

Franchise – giving a business the right to sell a good or service produced by a larger business, on the payment of a fee plus a percentage of the profits.

Franchisee – the smaller business which buys the franchise.

Franchisor – the company that sells the franchise.

Mail order – supplying goods and services by post after the customer has used a catalogue to choose the products he or she wants.

Wholesalers – organisations which buy in bulk from manufacturers and break down the quantities to supply to retailers.

The closure of C&A

C&A, the clothing retailers, was founded in 1841, 43 years before Marks & Spencer, by two Dutch brothers, Clemens and August Brenninkmeyer. They opened their first C&A (after their initials) store in the Netherlands. The store expanded to Britain in 1922 and grew to become a major feature of the high street, selling decent quality clothing at cheap prices. Its main market was budget-conscious shoppers who found M&S too expensive.

Over the past 10 years the clothing market has changed. Supermarkets led by Tesco and Asda have moved increasingly into clothing. A new wave of discount clothes stores have emerged including New Look, Matalan, Peacocks and Primark. These shops have attracted shoppers with more fashionable clothes than C&A but at cheaper prices. There has also been the growth of more stylish brands such as Gap, Next and French Connection. C&A has been suffering a long slow decline.

In 1994 C&A still controlled 4.4 per cent of the British clothing market but by 2000 this had fallen to 1.9 per cent. The company has made losses of £250 million in the last five years. Given the poor performance of the company, some shop closures were predicted. But in June 2000 the Brenninkmeyer family, which still owns the company, announced that all 109 stores in Britain would close, with the loss of up to 4,800 jobs. For the staff the sudden closure came as a great shock as the family-run private business has always been seen as a good employer.

The Brenninkmeyers are closing only in the UK. They will now concentrate on developing C&A in other main European markets such as Germany, France and Spain and in new markets like the Czech Republic and Mexico.

Source: Adapted from *Which?*, 20 September 2000.

Q Questions

1 What type of business was C&A?
2 What type of customer did C&A try to target?
3 Identify and explain the changes in clothing retailing which caused the decline in C&A in this country in the 1990s.
4 Why would supermarkets like Asda be interested in expanding their sales of clothing?
5 What might be the impact on a town of a large shop like C&A closing? What other businesses might be affected?

E Extension

1 Analyse why C&A is more successful selling in France and Germany than in the UK.
2 What other changes are taking place in clothing retailing? Use the Internet to research other clothing companies such as Marks & Spencer, Next and Gap to find out the latest trends in the industry. Produce a short report which analyses the likely future trends.

THEME 3

Production

Organising production

This unit is about the different ways in which businesses organise the production of goods.

At the end of the unit, students should be able to:

- define production and the chain of production

- understand how a product or a service is developed

- explain the need for patents and copyright and the process involved in setting them up

- explain what is meant by job, batch and flow production, using relevant examples

- decide when small- and large-scale production is appropriate

- explain what is meant by subcontracting and why large companies may choose to use subcontractors.

Production

Manufacturing firms exist to make a product. During the process of **production** they aim to add value so that the product sells at a higher price than the combined raw material costs. The service sector is no different in that the service provided should offer value added to the purchaser of the service.

In order to produce a good or service, factors of production will need to be used. The four factors of production are:

- land
- labour
- capital
- enterprise.

These are covered in more detail in Unit 1.

Chain of production

There are many stages in the production process starting with the raw material and ending with the finished product that the consumer buys. In Unit 1, the stages of production were defined as primary, secondary and tertiary. It is also possible to trace the chain of production as a flow chart. For example, the **chain of production** for a loaf of bread might be:

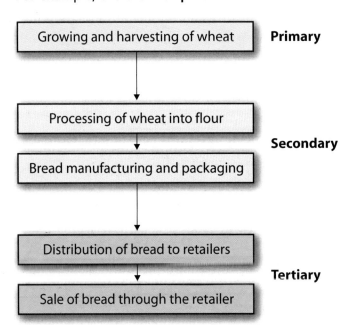

| Growing and harvesting of wheat | **Primary** |

| Processing of wheat into flour | |
| Bread manufacturing and packaging | **Secondary** |

| Distribution of bread to retailers | |
| Sale of bread through the retailer | **Tertiary** |

TASK 1

Draw a flow chart showing the possible chain of production for each of the following products:

a a china plate

b a woollen jumper

c a newspaper

d a CD

e a tyre

f a chicken tikka ready meal.

Product development

All companies need to find the right good or service (product) to sell. For some, this may mean developing a new product to sell in the market, for others it may mean legally copying a product that is already on the market.

The first aspect of **product development** is to find a product that will sell. Just because something is new on the market does not mean that it will automatically sell. A small firm has to be even more careful in product development as it may not have the financial backing to cushion any failures.

New products on the local market can come from inventions, reading trade papers, adapting ideas from abroad, etc. Any idea(s) then needs to be tested. Which is the best one? If you have only one investor can you convince other investors to join in? Will it meet a changing market? A good way to test out the idea is to draw up a list of questions and grade the answer, e.g. a minus score for a bad answer and a plus for a good answer.

The questions that should be asked of any new idea should include the following:

- Is the market dominated by any local companies?
- Is the production process without problems, e.g. do you need to learn new skills, do you have the necessary expertise?
- Are there good distribution facilities, e.g. do you have outlets through which you can sell the item?
- Do you have a suitable sales force?
- Have you got the right image for the item?
- Have you got reliable/available suppliers?
- Does your idea rely on any seasonal variations, e.g. hot summers?
- Are you confident about the market, e.g. size, loyalty?
- Are you fully aware of the characteristics of your buyer?

It is estimated that most new products fail (the failure rate is around 90 per cent) because companies rush into new projects only on the basis of a hunch. Small firms may find the bank's business adviser will ask probing questions about their idea when they apply for a business loan to finance the new project.

Sunny Delight, launched in 1997, is an example of an extremely successful new product – it achieved sales of £80 million in its first year, and at one point was outselling bottled Coca-Cola

If the idea is a new one it may be protected legally from competition by one of the following:

- A **patent** – this will provide a 20 year monopoly but costs around £1,500 for the UK and another £1,000 for each additional country in which you require protection.

- A registered design – if your new product has a distinctive visual appearance you may be able to register the design for around £100.

- A registered trademark – this does not protect other firms from copying the product but it does stop them from using the name of the product. Often, the name becomes an important marketing advantage in large-scale production but this may not be a useful form of protection for the small-scale producer.

marbles™

The TM sign shows that this product name is a registered trademark

- **Copyright** – protects an idea rather than a product which has a tangible design or external appearance. It is important to keep all records of the product dated and if possible validated to prove the idea is yours and when it was created.

TASK 2

New kiwi fruit developed in New Zealand

The kiwi fruit is green and hairy – right? Well it is, unless that is, it is not hairy and it is golden. Get ready for the new kiwi – New Zealand's answer to its rivals, who have been stealing the kiwi-eating market from under their noses.

The new golden hairless kiwi has been developed by New Zealand international marketing company Zespri. Guus Van der Clay, Zespri's regional manager for Europe, says: 'The interesting part of this new fruit is of course the inside, and that is a difficult point for a consumer because he is looking at the outside, and the outside is still brown but a little bit less hairy than the normal kiwi fruit. But it is in taste, absolutely completely different.'

'The development costs were high. Marketing a new product, particularly at a time of the year when the fruit basket is already full because we have the summer fruits from south Europe, and this one with the particular taste palate it has – with a bit of a mango taste and melon – it is not easy to bring a product like that on to the market.'

'So what we did was quite a lot of consumer research, and that told us that the more we introduced it as a completely new food, the better our chances would be.' 'There are many consumers who do not like the slightly sour taste of the green, and they are consumers we are looking for.'

Source: Adapted from an interview on the BBC World Service, 18 August 2000.

a What factors would you consider to help you decide whether this product will be a success or a failure?

b How might Zespri ensure that its product competes successfully on the market?

c Design a campaign that you think Zespri could use to successfully launch the new kiwi fruit.

Organising production

Small companies are able to take advantage of their size by specialising and using shorter production runs. Because of this, smaller companies are often more suited to **craft production** and production in sectors where demand is changeable. Larger companies are often more suited to longer production runs. Small companies are more likely to use job or craft production where the product is based upon a 'one-off' or a small-scale order e.g. custom-made clothes. Such production is often highly labour intensive due to the skilled workforce and the inability to invest in machinery due to the changing nature of the product.

Small companies may choose to specialise in producing and selling a service rather than a good. The product development of a service is intrinsically no different from that of a good. A service must also meet the needs of a customer and small-scale production may again be best able to meet the specialised area of the service market, e.g. a local radio station.

Small-scale production

Firms that are involved in small-scale production find that there are advantages and disadvantages to the process (see table below).

Benefits of small-scale production	Disadvantages of small-scale production
The decisions in a small-scale operation can be made far more quickly and therefore the business is more responsive to changes in the market. Large-scale production often suffers from long chains of command and bureaucratic decision making processes.	The division of labour will be small, therefore production may not be as efficient as possible. Economies of scale will be less possible. Unit costs will be higher.
Personal supervision of the production process ensures that work will proceed with maximum speed.	The personal abilities of the owners affect the scale of business, e.g. ill health, lack of sound financial expertise. Small firms often lack specialist management skills.
If the firm is under the control of a small number of owners, the service offered may be of a higher quality. Small-scale producers offer greater flexibility to work longer hours, undertake special requests and deal with problems on the spot.	Often small-scale production is undertaken by companies with unlimited liability. In this situation, the owner(s) is responsible for the debts of the business.
Small-scale production involves smaller numbers of employees and hence there is a more personal working relationship between the employees and the employer. This may help the efficiency of production and creates a more loyal workforce.	The impact on the market and the customer will be limited because of the small scale of the output.
	Small-scale companies are less likely to be able to make use of new technology in production.

Large-scale production

There are three basic methods of production for a large firm.

- **Job production** is where a single product is produced from start to finish as a result of an individual customer order. Although this may appear to suit small-scale production it can also operate on large-scale production plants such as the manufacture of a ship or aircraft. This type of production often requires very skilled labour and therefore a labour intensive production process.

- **Batch production** is where the production process is divided into product areas. Each product is made in a batch or set. Once a batch has been made the next one can be started. Most manufacturing occurs through batch production, e.g. a biscuit manufacturer may do batch production of different biscuit types to suit different customers.

- **Flow production** is where a product is passed through a production line where different stages of the process occur before moving on to the next stage. It differs from batch production in that each stage of production does not have to wait for a completed batch to be passed on. It is often called mass production and can be seen in the motor car industry.

As with small firms, large firms will survive only if they have chosen the method of production that has greater benefits than disadvantages. Many of the benefits of small-scale production are disadvantages in large-scale production, as seen in the table below.

Benefits	Disadvantages
Average costs are reduced as the company is able to take advantage of economies of scale (see Unit 18).	The product lacks individuality. Production lines will run off standard products that may not meet individual needs.
Production lines can be set up to take advantage of automation and technology. This allows computer-controlled production with less human error and longer production runs.	The costs of setting up a production line are often very high. Companies will invest only if they are confident that there will be a return on their investment.
Production lines should be able to produce products of a standard quality.	Staff working on the production line may find their job boring and repetitive. This can lead to error, high staff absence and turnover and lower productivity.
Automated production lines can be more flexible as the market changes. Lines can be shut down at quiet periods, and run 24 hours a day when orders are high.	If one part of the production line breaks down, it can cause serious bottlenecks and may lead to customers not receiving goods on time.
Staff are able to specialise. This may lead to increased output as staff become skilled in a particular area and allows the company to employ staff with specialist knowledge.	There is little flexibility in the goods a specific production line can produce.

TASK 3

Here are three photographs illustrating job, batch and flow production.
For each one, explain:
a why you think that method of production suits the product being made
b what gains might   i the firm   ii the workers have, from using that form of production
c what losses might   i the firm   ii the workers have, from using that form of production.

Subcontracting

Large companies are often unable or unwilling to produce specialised components or services. It may be far too costly in terms of machinery, labour and time to get involved in peripheral areas and in order to meet their needs, they will **subcontract** the business to small firms, e.g. Marks & Spencer subcontracts many of its clothes and pre-cooked foods to smaller suppliers. The advantage to a small company is clear in that it provides a market for production. The advantages to a company subcontracting out are:

- it is cheaper as there are no overheads
- it allows flexibility – if there is a rise in demand, more subcontractors can be used; if demand drops, there is no problem of having too many workers.

TASK 4

Horton Electronics is a company based in the Midlands. The company makes up wiring systems to customer orders and currently employs 20 staff, 18 of whom work on the production side. The company does work for 20 different companies – it acts as a subcontractor. All of its work is business to business, that is, it makes no items for sale itself: all products made are made to order through the 20 contracting companies.

The companies that contract out to Horton Electronics come from a variety of backgrounds. The products that they make wiring systems for include car alarms, surveillance equipment, generators, etc. The customer will send Horton Electronics a drawing of its wiring requirements that the company quotes a price for. If the price, supply date, etc. are acceptable, the contract will go ahead. Most of Horton Electronics' customers are regulars.

Horton Electronics also subcontracts to local small firms. It has five firms that it subcontracts work to. The work is usually specialist mechanical work, e.g. making cabinets and enclosures for the wiring systems.

a Why does Horton Electronics act as a subcontractor?

b Why does Horton Electronics subcontract work out to others?

c Is the company wise to rely totally on subcontracting? What advice might you give the company?

KEY TERMS

Batch production – **products are made in a set or batch before the next set of production occurs.**

Chain of production – **the stages of production from raw material to finished good or service.**

Copyright – **the exclusive right to use or authorise others to use literary, dramatic, musical and artistic works, sound recordings, films or radio and television broadcasts.**

Flow production – **products move on a production line where each stage of the operation is completed and the product continuously moves on to the next stage.**

Job production – **where each item produced is completed before the next is started.**

Patent – **an authority from a government giving the person to whom it is addressed the sole right of making, using and selling an invention for a certain period.**

Product development – **the first stage of the product life cycle where the product is developed, tested and altered if necessary to satisfy the firm that the product has a worthwhile future.**

Production – **the process of making something.**

Subcontract – **to use another company or person to help a business meet an order from a customer.**

Cadbury Ltd

A one-man business opened in 1824 by a young Quaker, John Cadbury, in Bull Street Birmingham was to be the foundation of Cadbury Ltd, now one of the world's largest producers of chocolate.

By 1831 the business had changed from a grocery shop and John Cadbury had become a manufacturer of drinking chocolate and cocoa. This was the start of the Cadbury manufacturing business as it is known today.

Now the leader in the UK chocolate market, Cadbury Limited is the confectionery division of Cadbury Schweppes plc, a major force in the confectionery and soft drinks international market.

It was not until the late 1950s that Fry's Chocolate Cream bars could be made by the automatic filling of the cream into the shells of chocolate. Prior to that the centres had to be deposited by hand into the metal moulds filled with chocolate.

There was a massive reorganisation in the late 1960s. The number of plants producing chocolate brands was reduced as larger automated plants were introduced.

Somerdale is a highly sophisticated factory manufacturing 14 Cadbury products most of which are 'main brands'. These are produced in over 100 different packages with many brands being made in various sizes to suit the many different chocolate eating occasions.

Operating 24 hours a day using the 11 fully automated plants with the latest control technology, the chocolate brands are produced to the highest quality standards demanded by Cadbury. Around 1,000 people are employed at Somerdale producing in excess of 50,000 tonnes of finished chocolate products every year.

Different techniques are used at Somerdale to produce the countline bars, so called because they are sold by number not weight, and other products:

- Moulding – a layer of chocolate is first set in the moulds, the filling is added and the base of the bar is sealed with a layer of chocolate. Caramel and Chocolate Cream are made by this method.
- Sheet and enrobing – the centres are squeezed out on to the conveyor in a sheet and the different ingredient layers are built up as appropriate. The sheet is then cut very precisely to size before the bars are covered with liquid chocolate in a process known as enrobing. Double Decker and Fuse are examples of brands made this way.
- Panning – the technique for making Mini Eggs, chocolate covered nuts and Tasters using large continuously revolving drums. The covering of chocolate, or in the case of Mini Eggs the sugar coating, is gradually built up around the centres over several hours.

The Cadbury famous name brands produced at Somerdale today are amongst the most popular chocolate products in the UK. Two of these still have the original Fry's name – Fry's Turkish Delight and Fry's Chocolate Cream – carrying on the Fry's tradition which stretches back over two and a half centuries.

Source: Cadbury Ltd, adapted from www.cadbury.co.uk

Chapel Chocolates

Chapel Chocolates is a family run business selling handmade Welsh chocolates, handmade truffles and a selection of other fine chocolates.

The Welsh chocolates are handmade on an old farm, situated in the heart of the West Wales countryside. They are made from the finest ingredients to secret recipes, known only to the owner and chocolate maker, Elizabeth Jones.

Chapel Chocolates started life in a converted chapel in Solva, Pembrokeshire, in 1994, moving to larger premises in Britain's smallest city, St David's, in July 1995, where it has grown into one of Wales's finest chocolate shops, selling over 100 different varieties of handmade chocolates and truffles.

For those with dietary needs, the shop holds a large selection of sugar-free chocolates and truffles suitable for diabetics and also carries a small range of organic truffles, suitable for vegans and those with dairy product intolerances.

Q Questions

1 How have Cadbury's and Chapel Chocolates organised their production methods?

2 What are the advantages and disadvantages for Cadbury's of having an automated production line?

3 How might the choice of production method have affected the two companies' pricing strategies?

4 Why are small, handmade chocolate manufacturers like Chapel Chocolates able to survive in the market?

5 In 1996, Cadbury's launched the Fuse bar. What product development might Cadbury's have done to ensure that the new bar was a success?

6 Why does Cadbury's still produce chocolate using Fry's brand?

E Extension

Many companies are now involved in computer aided manufacturing (CAM). Do some research into CAM and draw up a list of the benefits and disadvantages of CAM from the point of view of the firm, employee and customer.

Costing of production

This unit is about how businesses calculate their production costs.

At the end of the unit, students should be able to:

- define total, fixed and variable costs using examples to illustrate

- calculate average, total, fixed and variable costs

- calculate the break-even point by graph and mathematically

- interpret a break-even chart, particularly with regard to profit, loss, contribution and margin of safety

- understand the effect of changing costs and revenue on break even.

Costs of production

Any firm, regardless of size, will want to calculate the costs of production, primarily to help establish a price for its product. In order to do this, firms will have to list all their costs of production. A company can break down its costs into two distinct areas:

- **Fixed costs** – those costs that a business has to pay regardless of the level of production, e.g. salaries, rent, rates, loan repayment, etc.

- **Variable costs** – those costs that increase directly with the level of output, e.g. raw materials, power, wages, etc.

Some costs are difficult to categorise as being fixed or variable. A fuel bill, for example, may include an element that is fixed, but may also increase when the company is busy and open longer hours, producing more items.

TASK 1

Imagine that you are the sole owner of a shop where you design, make and sell clothes. Each item is individually made to meet a customer's requirements. The most recent customer has ordered a jacket from you, to be made after consultation meetings on the design.

a Write down a list of the costs you would include in the job.

b Classify the costs as fixed or variable costs.

c Were there any costs which you found difficult to classify? Explain why.

Total costs are all the costs of the business. They are calculated as:

Total costs = Fixed costs + Variable costs

Average cost or unit cost is a useful measure to a company as it helps to identify the efficiency of the firm. The lower the average cost, the more efficient the firm. In addition, the lower the average cost, the greater the opportunity to lower the selling price and undercut competitors. Average cost is calculated as:

$$\text{Average cost} = \frac{\text{Total cost}}{\text{Total output}}$$

TASK 2

Kitchens Supreme makes and fits kitchens at the luxury end of the market. It uses quality materials and all kitchens are handmade and fitted. The company has recently been concerned about its level of efficiency and has decided to look at the costs and revenue of making its basic fitted kitchen. The following information has been researched.

The company pays rent of £23,000 per year and rates of £6,000. The salaries of the management come to £62,000 per year. The cost of raw materials, power and the wages of employees needed to make and fit one kitchen comes to £12,000 and the kitchen is usually sold for £20,000.

a Work out the fixed costs of the business.

b Work out the variable costs of the business.

c Work out the total costs for the business if zero, 5, 10, 15 and 20 kitchens were made and sold.

d Calculate the average cost if zero, 10 and 20 kitchens were made and sold.

e Draw a graph to show fixed, variable and total costs you have calculated for Kitchens Supreme. (You may wish to put your calculations on a spreadsheet and create graphs from the spreadsheet.)

Break-even analysis

A management accountant might want to use the information on costs together with the sales revenue of the product in order to find out whether the product is making a profit or not. The accountant may also want to know how many units the company needs to sell in order to break even. This can be done by finding out the point at which sales revenue starts to exceed total costs.

If,

Sales revenue > Total costs, the product is making profit

Sales revenue < Total costs, the product is making a loss

Sales revenue = Total costs, the product is at break-even point.

The **break-even** point is therefore the level of output or sales of a business when the total costs of making the items equals the total revenue gained from selling them.

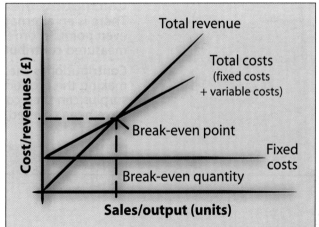

Changing costs and revenue

Companies will find that the costs and revenue that they have used to calculate break even may change over time. The effects, in general terms, are:

- where costs increase, the break-even point will rise, therefore the company will need to sell more products before it makes a profit

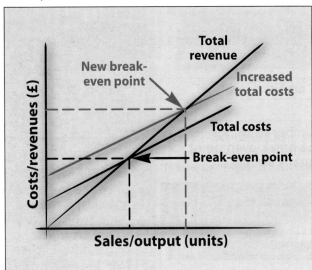

- where costs decrease, the break-even point will fall, therefore the company will need to sell fewer products before it makes a profit

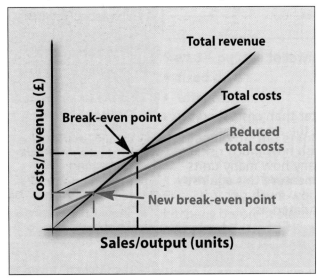

- where revenue increases, the break-even point will fall, therefore the company will need to sell fewer products before it makes a profit

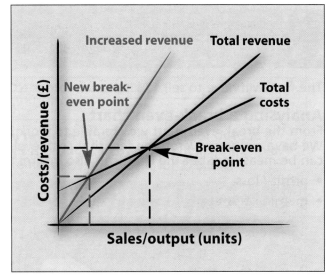

- where revenue decreases, the break-even point will rise, therefore the company will need to sell more products before it makes a profit.

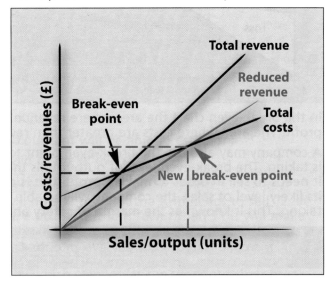

Average cost – the total cost divided by output.

Break even – the level of output for a firm where total costs equal total revenue.

Contribution – the amount left over from selling a product, once the cost of making the product has been deducted.

Fixed costs – costs which stay the same regardless of how many units are made.

Margin of safety – the difference between the actual level of output and the break-even level of output.

Total costs – the sum of all costs in a business.

Total revenue – the total amount that a business receives from selling its products over a period.

Variable costs – costs which change according to the level of output (how many goods are produced).

Geoff and Martin are brothers who jointly own a small, independent music shop called The Picture Box, in Aberdovey, Wales. They are concerned about whether or not they are selling enough DVDs and videos and if they are charging the right price.

Their business adviser has suggested that they work out their break-even point to help them review the situation. Geoff and Martin have looked at their expenses and income. They have put together the following information:

Rent	£400 per month
Rates	£40 per month
Salaries	£600 per month
Average cost of a DVD/video from the supplier	£9.00
Heat and lighting	£60 per month
Administration cost	£20 per month
Advertising	£30 per month
Average price at which a DVD/video is sold	£14

Geoff and Martin sell an average of 250 DVDs and videos per month but this will vary according to the season. Sales tend to be higher in the summer months when there are more tourists around.

Q Questions

1 Calculate the fixed and variable costs.
2 Calculate the break-even point per month, assuming maximum sales of 250. (*Hint*: This should be done by using tables to show calculations, a break-even chart and a mathematical calculation as a check.)
3 What would happen to the shop, in a month where sales fell to 180 DVDs and videos?
4 What would happen to the break-even point if:
   a they increased the selling price to £15? (knowing that sales would not fall as there is no competition nearby)
   b the rent was increased to £600 per month?

E Extension

It has been assumed throughout the unit that companies are able to calculate a precise break-even point. In reality, this is not as simple as it appears. Research and write a short report on the limitations of break-even analysis. (*Hint*: Can costs and revenue be calculated precisely? Do they rise uniformly? Are fixed costs fixed?)

The growth of businesses

How businesses grow

Many small business people are happy to keep their businesses small and if their market is small, then growth is very difficult. However, other business people do want their businesses to grow and if their markets grow, then the company can grow with the market. Many of those involved in e-commerce would fit into this category. Once a business has grown there are also major competitive reasons why it needs to continue growing – to compete with rivals in a national, European or global market place.

One of the main objectives for any business is therefore growth. Most managers would prefer to see their business achieving more than it did in the past. The ability to increase the size of a business will allow managers to organise production in a more efficient and profitable way.

Businesses can expand in a number of ways:

- **Economies of scale** – as businesses expand, they are able to take advantage of cost cutting procedures that were not available to them as a small firm. These may include hiring specialist staff, buying raw materials in bulk, mass producing and widening the range of products to reduce risk. This is covered in more detail in the next section.

- **Mergers** – where two or more companies voluntarily join together to form a single organisation. A *vertical merger* occurs where two companies at different stages of the production process join together, e.g. a travel company taking over a travel agent. A *horizontal merger* is where two companies at the same stage of production join together, e.g. one DIY store joining with another DIY store. A *conglomerate merger* is where two unrelated businesses merge together, e.g. recently the motoring organisation the AA merged with Centrica, the gas distribution company.

- **Takeover** – this is different from a merger in that the company being taken over has not wanted the two companies to join together, e.g. NatWest was recently taken over by the Royal Bank of Scotland.

- Internal growth using **ploughed back profits** – where a business retains the profit to finance growth rather than distributing it back to the partners or shareholders. This money is then used to help fund the expansion of the business through new investment in machinery, factories, offices etc.

- Market growth – an increasing population, advantageous changes in fashion, advertising campaigns, growth in overseas markets, etc. could all lead to growth in a firm's market. As a response, businesses will increase production.

TASK 1

Tops Caterers currently offers a catering service to businesses in the Birmingham area, including sandwiches, light refreshments and business lunches (hot and cold) for up to 200 people. It currently employs 28 full-time staff and 43 part-time staff. The business has developed from a three-person partnership into a limited company and has a large number of clients, many of whom are regulars from the two nearby industrial parks. Tops Caterers is considering further expansion and has decided to hire a business analyst to look at the potential for growth.

Write a report for the managers of Tops Caterers indicating to them the main ways through which the business could expand. You do not need to make any recommendations on the financing of the expansion. The report should aim to cover how the business could expand through clearly thought-out strategies that are manageable over the next three years. (Your report should be word processed.)

Economies of scale

As a business grows it is able to buy more equipment, hire more workers and move into larger premises. This is known as increasing the scale of production. As this happens, some organisations find that their unit/average costs of production begin to fall. This is known as an **economy of scale**. Businesses find that as they are able to make each unit more cheaply, they can then cut their prices below those of their smaller scale rivals and further increase their market share. Opposite is an example of how economies of scale work.

Example: Ultralite, a light bulb manufacturer, has to pay £20,000 rent per year and has variable costs of £0.20 per unit if it makes fewer than 11,000 bulbs per year. However if it makes 15,000 bulbs per year the variable costs fall to £0.18 per unit. This is because heating and lighting bills fall due to a new contract with the electricity company and special purchase arrangements for materials also begin to take effect. What has happened to the unit cost of production, assuming that there are no other costs involved?

Unit costs of production at Ultralite		
Rent (£)	20,000	20,000
Variable costs (variable cost per unit x output) (£)	2,000	2,700
Total cost (£)	22,000	22,700
Units of output	11,000	15,000
Unit cost (total cost/output)	£2.20	£1.51

This simple example shows how increasing the scale of production can have a significant effect on unit costs. By expanding its production from 11,000 units to 15,000 units Ultralite could produce each bulb for £0.69 less.

Economies of scale can arise for a number of reasons. They may be internal economies, that is, those that arise from the firm itself, or external economies, that is, those that arise outside the firm. Internal economies of scale are usually classified by the area of the operation that has caused unit costs to fall.

Types of economy of scale	Example
Production	Division of labour making the worker more skilled
	Use of computers and technology
	Bulk transportation of materials
	Mass production techniques
Marketing	Bulk buying
	Employing specialist buyers who get better deals
	Advertising costs can be spread
	Employing a specialised sales team
Financial	Easier for large firms to raise capital
	Better lending terms and lower interest rates
	Risk is spread over more products
	Greater potential finance from ploughed back profits
Managerial	More specialised management can be employed
	Overheads of administration can be spread
	Higher salaries can be offered to attract the best staff
External	Specialist labour in an area that businesses can use
	Being close to other similar businesses who can work cooperatively with each other
	Having specialist supplies and support services nearby

TASK 2

Study the following table and answer the questions that follow.

Retail sales by number of outlets, 1996		
Number of outlets	Number of businesses	Total sales turnover (%)
1	181,880	20.8
2 – 9	23,906	12.6
10 – 99	1,021	12.3
100 +	156	54.3

a What are retail businesses that have a large number of outlets around the country called? List five examples that you know of in your locality.

b Explain, using the data as evidence, whether you think economies of scale are important in the retail trade.

c Give four examples of the economies of scale that may be available to companies with more than 100 outlets that would not be available in businesses with fewer than 10 outlets.

d What benefits might small retailers have over large retailers?

Diseconomies of scale

It will not necessarily be in the interest of businesses or consumers for companies to grow and grow. As businesses continue to expand, they may reach a point where they get too big for the market in which they are operating. Their average/unit costs of production begin to rise again. This is known as **diseconomies of scale** and can be caused by a number of factors:

- A business has become so large that there is too much paperwork and bureaucracy.
- A business has become too large which leaves it insensitive to changes in the market, or too slow to react to changes.
- Communication between employees becomes poor, e.g. there are so many departments that people do not know who to deal with.
- Employees do not feel that they belong to the company and hence lose their loyalty and willingness to work. Industrial relations might get worse, leading to disputes over pay or conditions.
- Large companies are often more difficult to manage or have too many managers and not enough front-line staff.

Where businesses see their unit costs rising they may employ strategies to overcome the problem. These might include:

- splitting a business down into smaller decision making units so that communication is better
- greater investment in new technology so that unit costs can fall again
- passing more decisions down from managers to the workforce who are closer to the product and the customer
- creating specialist 'one stop shops' where all problems from customers or the workforce can be dealt with.

TASK 3

Karen had recently had a lot of problems trying to sort out a complaint with her local NHS hospital about the care her elderly mother had received during a recent illness. Every time she rang she spoke to someone different and her call was transferred from one administrator to another. She felt that she was getting nowhere as no one seemed prepared to deal with her complaint. She had considered writing in but she felt that there was more chance of speaking to the right person on the phone. After a month of making no progress over the telephone Karen decided to speak to an old school friend who she knew worked at the hospital.

Sam told Karen that she understood her problem but that she could offer her little help. 'It's like that for the staff as well,' Sam explained. 'I often get people shouting at me on the phone when I don't know who they are or who they have spoken to before. It might be that I could help them but the files I need are right at the other end of the building. Sometimes I need to see them personally to be able to help them but I'm tied to my desk. From time to time, I wonder why I bother. After all, who would know if I didn't do anything at all?'

a Identify the problems that the hospital is facing.

b Using the above case study, explain why you think that the saying 'big is better' may not always be true.

c In a group discuss Karen's problem. What suggestions might you come up with for the managers of the hospital to solve the problems mentioned above?

Monopoly and merger legislation

Imagine a situation where there was only one producer of calculators in the UK. This producer would be able to charge whatever price it liked for calculators, choose how many to make and make them whenever it decided. This sort of control of the market is possible for firms and may be harmful to the consumer, particularly if the good or service is a necessity such as food. The government has set up legislation to intervene when a single firm controls the market – a **monopoly**. The legislation covers public as well as private sector firms as many of the monopolies in the UK were created through public sector ownership, e.g. the Royal Mail.

Even if there were only a small number of producers it would still be possible for each one to have a good deal of influence over the market. Think, for example, of the control that three producers of chocolate, Cadbury's, Mars and Nestlé, have over the market in the UK. If you knew that they controlled the major market share of the snacks market:

• would you want to see a merger between any two of these three competitors and why?

• would you be concerned as a consumer and why?

• would you be concerned if you were the managers and shareholders of the business not involved in the merger?

In order to control monopolies or mergers that would influence the market significantly, governments have passed a number of laws to protect the interests of the public.

These are:

Monopolies and Restrictive Trade Practices Act (1948)

Monopolies and Mergers Act (1965)

Competition Act (1980)

Competition Act (1998)

The Acts on the previous page allow businesses to be investigated by the **Office of Fair Trading (OFT)** and for cases then to be referred to the **Competition Commission**, which will carry out an investigation to establish whether the business is exploiting its position, acting against the public interest or proposing a merger that will create or intensify a monopoly. The Secretary of State for Trade and Industry and the regulators of privatised industries such as OFTEL (telecommunications) or OFWAT (water) can also refer cases to the Competition Commission.

Sometimes, firms may act together to influence the market. For example, they may agree to keep prices high, restrict output or divide up the market so that they are not competing in a certain area and are then able to keep profits high. They are effectively creating small-scale monopolies but without merging. This is known as a **restrictive trade practice**. All practices have to be registered and agreed by the Restrictive Trade Practices Court. To be legal, the practice must benefit the public more than it harms them.

TASK 4

Below are two short case studies of mergers.
Read the information carefully and ask your teacher about anything you do not understand.

Case A
The Gillette Company and Parker Pen Holdings Limited

The Gillette company wanted to buy the Parker Pen company. Parker is a major manufacturer of writing instruments (ball point, roller ball and fountain pens) which is its sole business. Gillette has several areas of business, including the supply of writing instruments under two well-known brands, Paper Mate and Waterman.

The UK market for writing materials is worth around £225 million. Parker and Waterman supply only refillables, Paper Mate supplies mainly disposables. Market research has shown that Parker already supplies about half of the total UK sales of refillables by value and that Waterman and Paper Mate would add some 7 per cent to Parker's share. There are at least 40 brands of refillables supplied to the UK market and a wide choice of styles and finishes at all price levels.

Case B
Royal Bank of Scotland and NatWest Bank

The Royal Bank of Scotland (RBS) took over NatWest early in 2000.
This gave it just above 25 per cent of the banking market which is a trigger for investigation by the Competition Commission. RBS wanted to break into the financial services market in England, which up to now has been dominated by the big four banks – NatWest, Lloyds TSB, Barclays and HSBC. But there has been concern that banks are already making excess profits and that they are deliberately not competing very much in some parts of the market.
The takeover would also mean that between them RBS and NatWest would control 32 per cent of the small business accounts market.

a Work in a small group. You represent the Competition Commission. Discuss:
  i those points which you feel would support each merger
  ii those points which would make each merger against the public interest
  iii your overall decision as to whether or not you would allow each merger.

b Report back your ideas to the whole class.

c Produce a full individual report on one of the mergers. Use the same format as in your group discussion. Word process the report.

KEY TERMS

Competition Commission (until 1999 the Monopolies and Mergers Commission) – a body set up to investigate a monopoly or a proposed merger that will create or strengthen a monopoly. The Commission can recommend a monopoly is split or that a merger is stopped.

Diseconomies of scale – the factors that cause unit costs to rise as a business becomes too large.

Economies of scale – the factors that allow unit costs to fall as the size of a business grows. *Internal* economies of scale occur as a result of factors from within the business. *External* economies of scale occur as a result of the business being part of the wider market.

Merger – the amalgamation of two or more companies to form one new company.

Monopoly – where one supplier controls the market. By law, a monopoly is defined as any firm that has more than a 25 per cent share of the market.

Ploughed back profit – profits that are retained by a company rather than paid to shareholders or partners.

Restrictive trade practice – where two or more suppliers work together to restrict prices, output or supply.

Takeover – the acquisition of a majority shareholding in one company by another company (or individual).

The beer drinking baron from Belgium

It sounds like the perfect quiz question – who is Britain's biggest brewer? The surprising answer is Baron Paul de Keersmaeker, the chairman of a Belgian company, Interbrew.

Interbrew is a private Belgian company which produces Stella Artois and several other leading Belgian brands. Over the last six years it has been the world's fastest growing brewer. In 1995 it took over Canada's Labatt brewery at a cost of £1.3 billion and doubled its size. In 1999 it bought Whitbread's UK beer division for £400 million to get a foothold in the British market. It has expanded globally as well, owning 180 brands in a total of 23 countries from Russia to Mexico and China. Interbrew now likes to call itself 'the world's local brewer'.

In June 2000 Interbrew launched its most daring move yet, with a £2.3 billion bid for Bass, Britain's oldest and largest brewer. Bass controls a third of the UK beer market including owning UK's top selling beer brand – Carling. If the merger takes place Interbrew will become the world's second largest brewery after the American makers of Budweiser.

The company wants to become a worldwide force in the industry and is planning to float 20 per cent of its shares on the Belgian Stock Exchange. But it is having to face a review of its planned takeover of Bass by the UK's Competition Commission.

The takeover will give Interbrew a 32 per cent market share of the UK beer market as it already owns Whitbread. Its nearest competitor is Scottish & Newcastle which has 28 per cent of the market.

Interbrew argues that the UK market will be very competitive after the merger with six major brewers still operating and the strong presence of companies such as Punch Taverns which own large chains of pubs. In most EU countries the market share of the leading brewer is already higher than 32 per cent. They also claim that they manage to grow without losing sight of tradition; they keep local brands of beer going alongside the large brands.

They also have no interest in 'diversifying' outside brewing. But industry experts do not expect the takeover of Bass to go through easily. The Competition Commission turned down an earlier merger between Bass and Carlsberg which would have given a market share of 35 per cent. The watchdog Commission may well want Interbrew to sell either the Whitbread brands or some of the Bass brands before allowing the takeover to take place. The Secretary of State for Trade and Industry will make an announcement early in 2001.

Source: Adapted from *The Independent,* 28 June 2000 and 9 November 2000.

Q Questions

1 What has been the main method of growth for Interbrew in recent years? Explain your answer.
2 Why would a Belgian company want to own brands in 23 countries worldwide?
3 What is meant by the term market share. Why is it important for a business to have a large market share?
4 Why might Interbrew want to become a public limited company when it has been successful as a private limited company?
5 Present the arguments for and against the takeover of Bass by Interbrew. Do you think that the Competition Commission should allow the takeover to go ahead? Give your reasons.

E Extension

1 Why might the Competition Commission allow the takeover only if Interbrew sells some of its Whitbread or Bass brands?
2 Use the Internet to find out what the decision of the Competition Commission was in this case. You may find out on the Interbrew web site or the Department of Trade and Industry web site. Produce a short summary of the findings.

Controlling production and improving efficiency

This unit is about how companies make sure that they operate as efficiently as possible.

At the end of the unit, students should be able to:

- identify where quality control takes place

- understand the advantages of Total Quality Management

- investigate national quality schemes

- draw up and interpret stock control graphs

- explain various methods of improving efficiency

- compare methods used in the private and public sectors.

Quality control

For any business, the quality of the product being made is an important factor in maintaining market share. Small firms have to keep their product highly competitive in order to survive against the large firms and also the many small firms that may wish to capture their market. Where small firms are involved in one-off jobs or small production runs, failure to pick up on an error in quality can be extremely expensive. As a business grows and production moves to batch and flow production processes, the need to check quality is just as important. For example, workers repeating a process may become bored and make mistakes, machinery may break down and repeat hundreds of errors, mistakes may be made in the research and development stage.

If faulty goods and services reach the market, customers will become dissatisfied and will stop buying the product. Firms therefore have to establish **quality control** methods to reduce the number of faults. There are two levels of quality standard – internal quality control and external quality standards.

Internal quality control

involves the quality systems set by the company itself. Goods and services may be tested for quality at different stages of the production process:

- **Stage 1** – testing the raw materials or components. It would be impossible to make a quality product without checking the suppliers' quality. If there are too many items to check all of them, then the business can check a sample of the raw materials.

- **Stage 2** – testing the work in progress. This may also mean testing the machinery that is being used in order to ensure that the production process is operating efficiently.

- **Stage 3** – testing the final product. With mass production, samples are usually pulled out for testing and in some cases they may be tested to destruction in order to see if they meet the quality standard required by the company.

Some companies are adopting the technique of **Total Quality Management (TQM)**. Everyone, from the buyers of raw materials, through the production workers, to the office and sales staff, is made responsible for getting the quality right the first time. Not only should this help improve quality for customers, but TQM also helps to motivate the workforce as everyone is trying to achieve the same goal. The computer company, ICL, the electronics group, Bosch, and the car manufacturer Rover have all adopted a TQM approach.

TASK 1

Carillion plc is one of the UK's leading construction companies. Its building division was recently named Major Contractor of the Year and its most recently completed projects include the University of East London Docklands Campus and Dartford and Gravesham Hospital in Kent. It now has the £350 million contract for the new Government Communication Headquarters in Cheltenham, a circular building as big as Wembley Stadium.

The company is very concerned about quality. Building sites have to be managed in a way that covers all aspects of safety, quality and environmental impact. All the company's employees must get the same message. Martin Smout, managing director of Carillion, says, 'We are sharply focused on satisfying our customers' needs and expectations. That means we need to be efficient and reliable and safe in all that we do. It means that we have a quality driven agenda.'

Source: Adapted from *Business Standards*, October/November 2000.

a Why is quality so important for a construction company like Carillion?

b Identify three stages of quality control that might take place in a large building project.

c How would the large customers of Carillion make sure that the company is working to the right quality standards?

TASK 2

a Using a copy of *Yellow Pages*, identify any external quality schemes that operate for the following:
   i electricians
   ii removals
   iii plumbers.

b Choose one and research the quality standards that are expected from membership of the quality schemes that you have identified. You might do this by telephoning tradespeople or through direct contact with the national organisation.

c Produce a report for customers, explaining the quality service they should receive and what they might do if they are not happy with the service.

External quality standards

Small as well as large businesses are keen to display a badge of quality to their customers. This might be through membership of a trade association such as the Federation of Master Builders, the British Decorators' Association or ABTA, the Association of British Travel Agents. Where businesses feel confident about the quality of the product, they will offer guarantees. If a firm cannot offer a guarantee, then perhaps the provision of the good or service should be questioned. Clear guarantees may prove an added marketing bonus to the firm e.g. Austin Trumanns Steel offer a 'Touchdown Guarantee Scheme' which includes delivery dates and penalties that the firm will pay if it does not meet the agreed date.

External quality standards are set by official bodies such as the **British Standards Institute (BSI)** which was established in 1901. Goods that meet this standard carry the BSI Kitemark and are inspected regularly to ensure that they are maintaining standards. BSI not only operates standards for engineering, building, textiles and chemicals products, but it also operates in the field of units of measurement, technical terminology, training and management quality.

ISO 9000 status is an internationally agreed quality standard for business management run by the British Standards Institute. In some cases small firms may be asked to gain ISO 9000 by a larger firm from which they are subcontracting work or which they are supplying. There are now also European-wide quality standards and the BSI has also developed ISO 14001 which is a standard for environmental awareness and management for companies.

Stock control

As a business increases its scale of output it becomes even more important to maintain an efficient **stock control** system. To have the right amount of stock is vital. If there is too little (understocked), the firm may be unable to meet orders and production could be stopped. Sales may also be lost.

If there is too much stock (overstocked), the business could be tying up cash that it needs, have problems with storage and also make itself vulnerable if there is a sudden fall in demand for the stock being held.

Personnel dealing with stock control have four important decisions to make:

- What is the minimum level of stock that the business needs to hold? This might depend upon how long it takes to order new stock and upon how often there are sudden and unexpected rushes for stock.

- What is the maximum level of stock that the firm should hold? This might depend upon how much warehouse room there is for stock and the discounts that can be obtained by ordering large quantities of stock.

- What is the reorder level of stock? When stocks fall to this level a reorder is triggered so that the level of stock never falls below the minimum.

- What quantity of stock should be ordered? A reorder of stock should keep the stock level above minimum and below maximum.

Look at this stock control graph. The minimum amount of stock held is 500 units and the maximum is 1,000 units. When there are 750 units of stock, a reorder is made. In this example, it takes five days for the stock to be delivered and, when it is, the maximum level of stock is re-established.

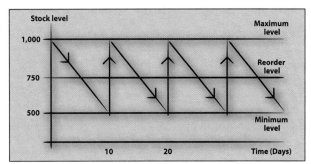

Japanese companies follow a very different method of stock control, which is beginning to influence many Western companies. Instead of holding stock at the factory, their stock is ordered on a **just in time** basis. Raw materials are ordered only as they are needed. In many Japanese plants, the suppliers of the components are often located next door to the main plant and so delivery time is minimal – in some cases, less than 10 minutes! Just in time is now widely used by companies in the UK. There is a risk, however, that if supplies are disrupted for some reason, then these businesses have no stock to fall back on and their production rates will be affected very quickly. During the petrol protests by road haulage companies in September 2000 in the UK many retailers and manufacturing companies quickly ran very low on stocks of products and supplies as they were reliant on daily or weekly deliveries to meet customer needs.

TASK 3

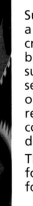

Super Cars Limited makes a small number of hand-crafted cars every year. It buys engines from a local supplier who delivers them seven days after being ordered. Here is a written record of their stock control for the first few days of the year.

This is the regular pattern for orders and deliveries for the month.

1 Jan – after the Christmas break we have a full stock of 20 engines. We are using them at a rate of one per working day.

8 Jan – reorder five engines.

15 Jan – five engines delivered.

a Draw a stock control graph for Super Cars Ltd covering a period of 30 days.

b What would happen if the suppliers had a strike in their company so that one order took 20 days to deliver? Show this on a stock control graph and explain your graph in words.

c What would happen if orders came in for 10 cars in one week rather than five? Assume that the company had not forecast this and so was still ordering five engines per week from its suppliers. Draw a stock control graph to show this and give a written explanation.

Improving efficiency in production

No company, large or small, will want to keep the same production system for years and years. It will want to try to improve the production system so that it can keep costs down, make more and hence increase profit. The need to remain competitive is an important reason for businesses to develop their production system.

In a small business, the opportunity to improve **productive efficiency** is limited but in a larger firm there is a variety of methods that can be used:

- **Work study** is where a particular job is studied by a work study engineer. Having watched the employee at work, the engineer can offer advice on better ways of doing the task which may, in turn, save both energy and time.

- **Quality circles.** It is most likely that the people who know most about the task being done and the way in which it can be improved are the workers themselves. Quality circles involve groups of workers meeting regularly to look at ways of improving how they work and what they make. There may be financial incentives for the best suggestions on how to improve efficiency. Through using quality circles a company may benefit from an improved level of productive efficiency, a motivated workforce and a saving on the cost of bringing in outside work study consultants.

- **Technological change** has been one of the biggest influences on industry in the last 30 years. Changes have occurred with **automation**, the use of information technology, improved materials and the use of robots. These have all allowed the level of production to increase without costs increasing at the same rate.

- A more negative way that businesses have been increasing their productivity in recent years has been by **downsizing**. The main focus has been to reduce labour costs by high levels of redundancies all through a business. In the UK the privatised industries such as the Lattice Group (formerly British Gas) and BT have been major downsizers, as have the banks. Both manual workers and managerial staff have suffered from downsizing. Even where jobs have been maintained or created, many have become temporary rather than permanent, or part time rather than full time.

TASK 4

Below is a table showing the number of employees made redundant in different industries in the last nine years.

UK redundancy rates per 1000 employees, 1992 – 2000				
Year	Manufacturing	Services	Other including Construction	All sectors
1992	15	8	26	11
1993	14	7	15	9
1994	11	6	16	7
1995	10	7	13	8
1996	11	6	19	8
1997	10	6	18	7
1998	12	6	10	7
1999	16	5	11	7
2000	16	5	11	7

Source: *Labour Market Statistics*, 2001, Office for National Statistics.

a Over the nine years shown here, which sector
  i has shown the most redundancies since 1992?
  ii has shown redundancies steadily decreasing since 1995?
b What do the figures show has been happening to redundancies in manufacturing? Can you explain why these changes have taken place?
c Do you think that the figures show an overall fall in employment over the past nine years? Have you got enough information?

Improving efficiency in the public sector

Recent governments have tried to make the public sector more efficient. They have tried to achieve this by making all the institutions in the public sector, e.g. schools, hospitals and prisons, more accountable for the money they receive and the way it is spent.

The difficulty of measuring performance in the public sector is that there is not always an output which can easily be measured. However, ways to encourage and measure improved performance have been adopted by NHS trusts, by local authorities and by other public sector organisations. Some examples are given below:

Increasing productivity – if output or the amount of work increases, e.g. a doctor treats more patients, then there is increased productivity. However, the idea of increased productivity would have to be questioned if this resulted in lower standards of patient care.

Improving efficiency – a simple demonstration of improved efficiency is for a department to continue to do its present level of work, or even increase its level of work from one year to the next, while maintaining or even decreasing its costs. This may be by reducing the number of people employed, as wages and salaries are the major cost in public services. Another way to measure efficiency is to compare the costs of providing services. For example, the cost of caring for a patient in one hospital for 24 hours may be compared with the cost of caring for a patient in another hospital.

Performance indicators – these are often set as targets for the organisation, a department or for individual workers. Performance is measured against the target set and if the target is reached or exceeded, a new target will be set. Sometimes the performance indicators have to be reported to a local or national audience. For example, local councils have to publish their performance against targets to the people in the local community; schools have their GCSE examination results published in the national press.

Incentives – an aspect of the need for greater efficiency in the public sector is the introduction, mainly for managers, of an element of performance related pay. Experienced teachers can now cross a threshold and receive a pay increase of £2,000 provided they show that their pupils are making satisfactory or better progress.

TASK 5

Obtain a copy of your local council's annual report.

a In a group, choose one aspect of the council's work, e.g. education, leisure services or housing. Read the section of the report that talks about this area of work.

b Identify any performance measures that are used by the council in this area.

c Has the council improved its performance in your chosen area since last year or has it worsened? You might find explanations for the changes given in the short articles which accompany the tables. Make a summary of these explanations.

d Write a short report on the main improvement or worsening of services in your chosen area and the reasons for the changes.

For British Aerospace (BAe) the production of high quality goods is vital. Safety is particularly critical with aircraft – unlike motor cars, you can't pull over to the hard shoulder if the plane gets a problem at 35,000 feet. Aircraft are built to rigorous standards laid down by the world's governments and new aircraft are extensively tested to make sure that they meet these standards.

There are many different quality control methods used by the company:

- Tests to make sure that a product works properly.
- Tests to destruction to find out the limits of a product.
- X-raying to find out if components are strong enough.
- Suppliers have to show that their quality standards are those required.

BAe also finds out if its customers are happy with quality. Surveys are used to test customer satisfaction and the results can lead to changes to the product. Recently, the company has been measuring the quality of its product against the European Foundation for Quality Management standard and found that there are a number of areas for improvement.

As well as quality BAe also looks to increase efficiency in its production. One of its major products is the Airbus and the company has been trying to reduce the overall time it takes to build and fit out the aircraft to the particular airline's requirements. The company has carried out a number of changes – to factory layout, to the production process, to the design – and has also worked closely with suppliers to speed up deliveries. The results of all this are shown below:

Airbus part	Production	Fitting out for customers
Airbus aisle	Down from 12 to 10 months	Down from 10 to 7.5 months
Body of aircraft	Down from 16 to 14 months	Down from 12 to 10 months

Source: Adapted from British Aerospace Company Facts, www.bized.ac.uk

Q Questions

1 Why is quality control so important for BAe?
2 Explain three different stages of quality control that BAe uses. Give examples of methods they use at each stage.
3 Identify from the case an example of an external quality standard. How is it used by the company?
4 How has the company tried to improve the efficiency of its production of the Airbus recently?
5 Has it been successful? Use the information in the table in the article to support your answer.

E Extension

1 Why do national governments set quality standards for aircraft production by companies like BAe?
2 How would the shareholders of the company benefit from increasing the efficiency of making the Airbus?

UNIT 20

Production and technology

The impact of new technology

The recent rapid changes in technology have had a major impact on the way that all businesses operate. Technology has led to the development of:

- new products – e.g. compact discs, mobile phones and PlayStations

- new materials – e.g. silicon chips, Lycra and genetically modified crops

- new processes in production – e.g. computer-controlled robots and just in time manufacturing

- new business operations – e.g. call centres and communication by electronic mail (e-mail)

- new businesses – like the computer software manufacturer Microsoft and Amazon.com.

Each sector of industry has been transformed by new technology. Farmers grow crops which have been developed to be more disease resistant and harvest the crops with high-tech machinery. Manufacturing companies use **computer aided design (CAD)** to produce 3D designs for their products and **computer aided manufacture (CAM)** to control the machines which make the products on the production line. They also use computers to test and monitor the quality of the product.

The application of technology has been just as significant in the service sector:

- In banks and building societies the use of cash machines, cash and credit cards, telebanking and online banking (see below) has greatly reduced the number of branches needed and the number of employees serving customers directly.

- Consumers can now book hotel rooms, holidays, train tickets and cinema tickets by credit card through the telephone or fax or through the **Internet**.

- Pupils use swipe cards at school to show that they are present and log on to the computer network for a range of lessons.

- In hospitals patients' health is monitored through computer-controlled machinery and surgeons can carry out surgery by giving instructions to a computer-controlled laser.

- The retailing sector uses bar codes and readers to speed up the supermarket check-out system as well as providing the business with information about what has been sold and to whom.

TASK 1

a Identify the major changes that have taken place in recent years because of new technology in the following industries:
   i the music industry
   ii the travel industry
   iii steel making
   iv TV and radio.
b Choose one of the above industries and produce a table similar to the one above showing the costs and benefits of the new technology for employees and customers in that industry.

New technology brings a number of benefits and costs to businesses and society. Some examples are shown in the table below.

Benefits of new technology	Costs of new technology
Increased productivity, that is, output per worker leading to higher profits for business	Capital costs of development, installation and maintenance
Improving the quality of jobs by technology removing routine and difficult tasks	Reduction in the number of jobs needed in certain industries
Reducing waste and improving the environment	Existing staff need to be retrained to keep up with the new technology
Improving people's standards of living by making high-tech goods affordable	Technology can break down or can be disrupted by energy shortages or by computer viruses
Higher incomes for those involved in developing and using new technology	Lower incomes for those involved in the old economy where technology is not being employed

Lean production

Lean production is the name given to a process which was first developed by the Toyota car company in Japan but which has since spread to many manufacturing companies in the world. It involves making maximum use of the new technology available in order continuously to improve the production of the company.

A lean production company will try to use less of everything in producing more of the product.

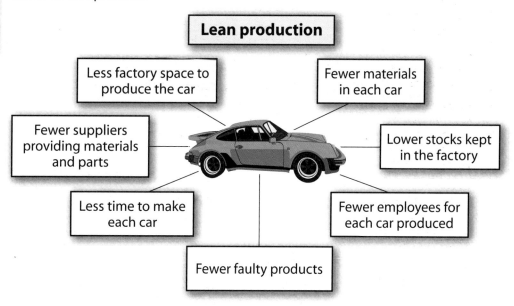

It will use less of everything by examining everything it produces and every method it uses in production and then finding ways of improving what it does. In doing this, the company may look at a competitor's product and copy what it is doing well. This is known as **benchmarking**. For the lean production company the benefits of this process are:

• increases in output but at a lower unit cost
• better quality products
• faster production
• less waste of products
• a wider range of products.

But to be successful the company has to have a flexible and well-trained workforce and the size and capital to invest heavily in new technology.

TASK 2

Jaguar's lean production

Jaguar, one of the world's most famous car manufacturers, has employed lean production methods on its Jaguar S-type production line at its Castle Bromwich factory in Birmingham. Jaguar is owned by Ford and it has been keen to introduce new manufacturing methods developed in Japan.

The company's main target has been to reduce the time taken to produce each car. To do this it has moved to team working so that all members of the workforce can be involved and give their ideas. All levels in the organisation have to be involved. An important part of the initiative was the use of control boards on computer screens all around the factory. They show how the production line is running and the daily targets, and all the employees can quickly see if problems occur.

Six key improvements were identified at Jaguar to create leaner production:

1 Not producing too many cars too soon – as these take up storage space and may get damaged. The production line is now run at the speed to meet the weekly demand.

2 Reducing the time taken to move parts around the factory on conveyor belts.

3 Not over-processing products – providing only what the customer wants.

4 Having the minimum stock needed to get the job done – too much stock uses up space and needs extra handling.

5 Improvements to the layout of the production line to cut down on wasteful movement.

6 Getting it right first time so there is no need for wasteful repairs of new cars.

Source: www.mbapublishing.co.uk/casestudies

a Why might Jaguar/Ford want to copy manufacturing methods used in Japan?

b Use the examples in this case study to explain what is meant by the term 'lean production'.

c How would technology have helped Jaguar to make the improvements that were identified?

Information and communication technology

Information and communication technology (ICT) involves the use of computers to record, process and send information. It is now a daily part of business practice in all sectors of industry. Every office desk has a personal computer (PC) which either operates independently or is linked to other PCs in the organisation by a network. Many employees also have use of smaller, more mobile laptop computers which can be carried from meeting to meeting or used on the train or at home.

PCs allow the use of a range of business software which has greatly speeded up the capturing and processing of business data. The main software applications are:

- word processing programs – which can be used to write letters, memos, reports and to produce invoices and orders

- databases – where information about customers, suppliers or competitors can be recorded, sorted and analysed

- spreadsheets – where financial information such as sales revenue, money still owed, wages and salaries can be stored and processed so that regular financial reports can be produced

- desktop publishing – which can produce high quality and well-presented reports, newsletters, brochures and other promotional material and which can incorporate pictures and video clips

TASK 3

a Find a version of Microsoft Office. There will probably be a version on your school's network or on your home computer if you have one. Make a list of the software applications that are included on this version of Microsoft Office.

b Choose one of the software applications. Look at the 'Help' information to find out more about it.

  i What are the main features of this software?

  ii For which business uses could this software be employed?

c Apple produces the iMac personal computer which uses a different operating system to Microsoft's. Many people think that this system is simpler to use than Microsoft. However, Apple has only about 10 per cent of the PC market. Explain why you think businesses have tended to buy personal computers with Microsoft rather than other operating systems.

- software such as PowerPoint which helps business people to create high quality presentations using words, graphics, sound and animation

- Other specialist applications – where software companies produce programs for specific uses, e.g. for accounting, stock control, data analysis, Clip Art, designing, wages and salaries.

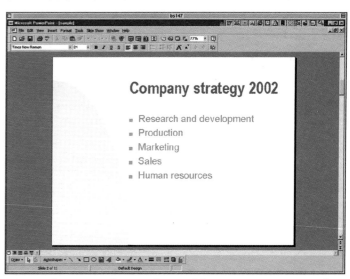

Microsoft PowerPoint can be used for company presentations

One US company, Microsoft, has produced the Microsoft Office suite of software programs which incorporate many of the above applications. The vast majority of PCs now have Microsoft software automatically loaded when they are purchased. This has led to accusations that Microsoft has a monopoly over business software. In the USA, the government has been investigating Microsoft's profits and market share and is seeking to encourage more competition.

Unit 28 shows how other applications of IT – faxes, mobile phones, e-mails – are used in businesses to improve communications with employers, suppliers and businesses.

The Internet

The Internet was developed over 20 years ago in the USA. It was first of all used by the US Defense Department to improve military communications but soon was developed by university departments around the world.

These are the main features of the Internet:

- Groups of computers are connected to other groups of computers in networks throughout the world.

- There is an agreed standard – known as the Internet Protocol – which allows all the computers to understand information sent between them.

- Each computer in the system has a unique identification name – known as a domain name.

- Large amounts of information can be accessed and sent around the Internet. Computer files, including word processed documents, databases, spreadsheets, etc. can be sent between computers or may be searched from a distance.

This means that the Internet provides people and organisations with a global means of communication as well as a source of a vast amount of information. Two facilities of the Internet are particularly important for businesses and other non-profit making organisations like government departments – **e-mail** and the **world wide web**.

E-mail (see Unit 28) is most commonly used within business organisations to help employees send memos, letters, messages, etc. to each other. But businesses can also e-mail suppliers and customers very quickly on a regular basis through the use of mailing lists set up through e-mail by themselves or by other companies. Large numbers of potential customers can therefore be contacted very easily – although people are becoming resistant to receiving a large number of e-mails in the same way that customers throw away direct mail, sometimes known as 'junk mail'.

The world wide web (commonly called the web) is the way that information in the form of text, graphics, sound and video can be displayed and shared on the Internet. One set of computers on the web acts as 'server' and serves up the information that is requested. Another set of computers acts as 'browser' and allows users to retrieve and display the information requested. The information is displayed through web pages written by using a special language. Browsers can either use 'search engines' to help them find the information they are looking for – or they may know the web address of the information. Web addresses are known as uniform resource locators, or URLs for short.

Most medium or large organisations have their own web site with their own URL. Some well-known ones are the BBC's web site, www.bbc.co.uk, the UK government's web site, www.open.gov.uk, Tesco's web site www.tesco.co.uk and the web site of the *Guardian* and *Observer* newspapers, www.guardian.co.uk.

There are three main reasons why companies maintain web sites:

- They are an important marketing and public relations tool, providing up-to-date information about new products and new developments in the company.

- Customers can look at and order products or services through the site. This is known as **online retailing**.

- Customers and other members of the public can communicate with the organisation through the site and provide feedback if requested. Many government departments and local authorities in the UK use their web site to consult individuals about their services.

A business may also operate an intranet which is an internal Internet. The users will be restricted to those directly working in the organisation and information is passed only within the organisation. This helps to maintain better security if confidential information is being communicated. However, there have been many cases where confidential data has 'leaked out' on to the Internet or where outsiders have 'hacked' into a company's confidential files. Any information held on computers is becoming very difficult to protect because of the Internet.

TASK 4

Smallest firms lag in using the Internet

Nearly all of the UK's medium-sized businesses are now using the Internet, but the smallest companies are lagging behind, according to a survey. The results showed the following:

Type of business	Already use the Internet	In the process of connecting	Plan to connect within 12 months
Medium-sized firms (51–500 employees)	70%	23%	3%
Small-sized firms (0–50 employees)	49%	20%	5%

Source: www.oftel.gov.uk.

The survey found that lack of knowledge about computer equipment and the cost of equipment were the main reasons. The cost of Internet access did not appear to be a big deterrent.

There was also a lack of understanding of the benefits of using the Internet. Some businesses surveyed said that the Internet was irrelevant to their business and there was fear about security and costs.

There was also a lower ownership of PCs among smaller businesses. Their main use of the Internet was e-mail and accessing information. Few were using the Internet for marketing or selling.

Source: *The Independent,* 30 October 2000.

a What percentage of medium-sized firms and small firms are not using the Internet?

b Explain the main reasons why many small firms are not using the Internet at present.

c What arguments would you use to persuade a small business to install and use the Internet?

E-commerce

E-commerce is the term given to the industry that has grown up around the business use of the Internet and e-mails. There are four main groups of organisations that form the basis of the e-commerce industry:

- Internet providers such as Yahoo!, AOL (America On-Line) and Freeserve provide individuals and organisations with access to the Internet and to e-mail facilities. Some charge for unlimited access, some offer free access and some charge for metered access. Because these companies have themselves to pay for use of the Internet, companies offering free access have suffered financial problems as they have not been able to attract enough advertising to pay for the service. There are also many companies which provide search engines, which design and maintain web sites, which market and promote web pages or which screen and protect users from computer viruses and unpleasant parts of the web.

- Dotcom companies such as Amazon.com which sells books and lastminute.com which sells theatre and travel tickets are companies that exist only on the Internet. At the start of the new millennium, these companies were attracting huge amounts of investment and their often young owners were very rich on paper. However, the number of customers who do all their shopping online is still relatively low and the sales revenue of these companies has been below forecasts. Over the past year a number of high profile e-commerce businesses have been taken over or stopped trading. For example, boo.com, an Internet clothes retailer, was valued at £248 million in November 1999 but was put into liquidation in May 2000.

- Established businesses have set up a separate e-commerce company for online trading. A number of financial institutions, for example, have set up their own Internet bank, including:

  Abbey National: www.cahoot.co.uk

  The Co-op Bank: www.smile.co.uk

  Prudential: www.egg.co.uk

  HFC: www.marbles.com

- There has been a trend recently for established businesses to take over some of the struggling dot.com companies rather than setting up their own operation. For example, the mail order group Great Universal Stores bought Jungle.com, an online computer retailer.

- Many medium and large organisations have their own web sites and use online shopping to add to their other trading and marketing activities.

E-commerce is a fast growing sector in which the majority of large and medium businesses are now involved in some way. In the long run it is likely to be the established companies which will form the core of the e-commerce industry rather than the new dotcom businesses. Recently, TimeWarner, a large US media company, announced that it is to merge with the Internet provider AOL. It is expected that Europe and the USA will see many more such mergers of the traditional companies with Internet companies.

TASK 5

WH Smith and Carlton unite for Internet venture

WH Smith, the retailer, and Carlton Communications, the TV and media group, have agreed a joint venture for their Internet businesses. The two companies will promote each other's web sites on their online service and will share the online revenues.

WH Smith will promote Carlton's online business in its 700 retail stores and manage all Carlton's online trade. If a Carlton customer orders a DVD or video online, WH Smith will deliver the product.

In return Carlton will use its TV, cinema screen and Internet channels to advertise the joint venture. It will sell online advertising for both companies and will allow WH Smith to sell its full range of books, CDs, DVDs and videos on Carlton's web site.

Source: *The Independent,* 22 March 2000.

a What advantages will there be for WH Smith from this joint venture?

b What advantages will there be for Carlton Communications from this joint venture?

c Can you see any problems emerging from this arrangement?

KEY TERMS

Benchmarking – **comparing your product with competitors' products and copying what they are doing well.**

Computer-aided design (CAD) – **software programes which allow designs of products to be developed.**

Computer-aided manufacture (CAM) – **where machines which make the products on a production line are controlled by computer.**

E-commerce – **the industry that has grown up around the business use of the Internet and e-mails.**

E-mail (electronic mail) – **a way of sending text and other messages to individuals and organisations via an electronic mail box.**

Information and communication technology (ICT) – **using computers to record, process and send information.**

Internet – **the network of computers worldwide that allows e-mails to be sent and which carries the world wide web.**

Lean production – **making best use of new technology and team work in order continuously to improve the production of a company.**

Online retailing – **the process of selling goods and services through the Internet.**

World wide web – **the computer-based system which allows people to send, access and receive information all around the globe.**

Amazon.com

It was in 1994 that Jeff Bezos borrowed $300,000 from his parents and began selling books over the Internet from his garage. By the end of the 1990s his company, Amazon.com, had floated on the US stock exchange and was worth over $17 billion. However, by 2001 the share value of the company had fallen dramatically.

Amazon's initial success in the USA and more recently in the UK, France and Germany was to focus on customer service. In the USA, Amazon, as well as books, sells electronics, toys, video games, software and a variety of other household products. In the UK, Amazon.co.uk sells mainly books. It can display online many more titles than any bookstore could stock. It will find any book that is asked for. It is 'open' 24 hours a day and deliveries tend to arrive when Amazon says they will.

In the USA, it has five large and highly automated distribution centres. In the UK, the centre is at Milton Keynes in the south of England, close to the warehouses of several book suppliers so that if an item is out of stock it can be found close by quickly. Amazon also sells a large number of books at a discount. Amazon is also able to build up a lot of data on its customers – what they have bought in the past – so that when a regular customer logs on, the company can make suggestions about what he or she might like to buy this time.

In 1999 sales reached $1.6 billion – but at the same time losses were $720 million, which were six times greater than 1998. Large losses continued in 2000. The company was gradually running out of cash. In early 2001 Amazon announced that it was cutting its 8,000 workforce by 15 per cent. The shares, which were once worth $400 on the US stock exchange, were down to $19. This is a blow to the owner, Bezos, and also to the Amazon workforce. The staff have been paid partly with shares in the company and have been forced to watch as the value of their shares has collapsed. To many, Jeff Bezos was seen as the king of the 'new economy' – if Amazon does not survive, the whole dotcom empire might fall.

Source: Adapted from *The Independent,* 7 June 2000, and *The Observer*, 11 February 2001.

Q Questions

1 a Why is bookselling suited to the use of the Internet?

b List four other products that are now commonly sold over the Internet.

2 What advantages did Amazon have over traditional booksellers?

3 Explain the main elements of the marketing mix that Jeff Bezos has used to develop his business.

4 Analyse why, despite sales revenue reaching $1.6 billion in 1999, the company still made such a large loss.

5 If you were an employee of Amazon, what would be your opinion of the changes in the company's fortunes over the past two years?

E Extension

1 Explain what the following phrases mean for the company:

a 'The company was gradually running out of cash.'

b 'The shares, which were once worth $400 … were down to $19'.

2 Look at the Amazon.co.uk web site. What are the key features of the business that the company is promoting? Do you think that the company will survive? Give your reasons.

THEME 4

Accounting and finance

UNIT 21

Finance for small business

This unit is about the different ways in which small businesses can raise finance.

At the end of the unit, students should be able to:

- define what is meant by a small business

- understand why small businesses need to raise finance

- explain the different sources of finance available to a small business

- explain the difference between short- and long-term sources of finance and their different uses in the business

- understand the role of government in helping to finance a small business

- explain the factors that influence the choice of finance for a small business

- apply their knowledge of finance for small businesses to a range of contexts

What is a small business?

There are many ways of deciding what size of business is a small one. Some suggested criteria are given below:

- the number of employees
- the amount of capital the business has at its disposal
- the size of the business's turnover
- the size of the business's profit
- the amount of plant and equipment.

None of the above criteria is straightforward to apply. Using the number of employees as the only criterion will make it difficult to compare, for example, a firm of painters and decorators with a computer software house. Both may have 50 employees but using the other criteria would give a different picture of which was a small and which a large business.

The Department of Employment classifies a small firm in manufacturing as one that has fewer than 200 employees whereas the Small Business Research Trust uses a measure of fewer than 24 employees. The most accepted definition is laid down by the 1981 Companies Act. This defines a small firm as one that during an accounting year does not exceed two of the following:

- a turnover of £1.4 million
- total assets of £0.7 million
- 50 employees.

Small firms are extremely important in the UK economy. In the manufacturing sector only 3 per cent of firms have more than 200 employees. This unit will concentrate on investigating how small firms are able to raise the finance to start and/or expand.

A business park – a number of small businesses are based here

Why is finance needed?

Any organisation, large or small, needs money. It might be needed to set up the business, or it might be needed to pay the bills. If the firm does well, it may need money to help it expand and move into new premises.

TASK 1

Choose a small business that you would like to set up. The list below may give you some ideas:
- café
- pet shop
- hairdressers
- sandwich shop
- gardener
- taxi firm
- jigsaw manufacturer

a Make a list of the items you would need to purchase or rent to set up the business.

b Try to make an accurate estimate of the cost for each item.

c Make a list of the items you would need to purchase or rent on a daily/weekly basis to keep the business operating.

d Try to make an accurate estimate of the cost for each item.

e Write a report, presenting your results. (You may wish to use a spreadsheet to present your costings, and a desktop publishing package to present your report.)

Generally, money is needed in the firm for three main reasons:

- Start-up. Firms often start small and have a small number of owners. This means that the finance that they are able to provide is going to be limited and they will often have to seek additional finance to cover their start-up costs including premises, machinery, raw materials, etc.

- Cash flow for day-to-day costs. The timing of payments for goods and services delivered to customers does not always match the outgoings of payments for raw materials and wages. Finance may be needed to cover those periods where the firm is short of cash. Cash flow is vital for any firm, and is covered in more detail in Unit 24.

- Expansion. Small firms may wish to expand and grow. In order to move into larger premises, open up new shops, employ more staff and purchase more equipment, the firm will need to seek finance. Some of the finance may be provided internally through ploughed back profits, but in addition, the firm may need to look externally at loans and share capital. More detail on sources of capital for larger firms is given in Unit 22.

Matthew Crick worked for 10 years for a large building company but always planned to set up his own business. With the interest in energy saving growing he made the decision to leave the building company and use his savings of £30,000 to set up a business providing loft and wall insulation for private households.

He realised however that his savings would not be enough to finance the setting up of the business. He identified and costed out the following items that he would need:

£15,000	Rent in advance for a small business unit in a local business park
£18,000	Purchase of a loft insulation and a wall insulation machine
£10,000	Buying a second-hand van for transporting his materials
£6,000	Buying insulation materials and tools
£49,000	Total start-up costs

He would therefore need £19,000 in addition to his £30,000 savings when setting up. He would also need day-to-day finance to meet costs such as petrol for the van, wages for an office assistant, his own salary, insurance, electricity, etc.

He realised that some of these items would need to be financed over a long period of time – the rent a year in advance, the machinery, the van. Some of these items would need finance over a shorter period of time – the materials, wages and salaries, other costs – and his revenue from customers could help towards these. However, without additional finance to his savings, he knew he could not operate.

It will be important for the source of finance for a particular item to match the length of time over which the item is being used and the benefits being gained. So for the rent in advance, the machinery and the van, Matthew will need either to use his savings – his capital – or to use a long-term source, e.g. a bank loan. He will be benefiting from these over a long period and therefore can pay for them over a long period. But for his materials, the wages and salary, and other regular expenses he will need short-term finance as he will need to pay these bills on a monthly basis.

What are the types of finance?

In the case study on the previous page, Matthew will need finance for setting up and operating his business. These financial needs will be for **start-up capital**, **long-term finance** and **short-term finance**.

Start-up capital is finance provided by the owners of a business; in this case it is the £30,000 of savings that Matthew is willing to use. It is permanent finance as it will need to stay in the business as long as Matthew is operating.

Long-term finance is money that is borrowed by the owners that has to be repaid but after a period of more than one year. For a sole trader like Matthew, the most likely source of this finance will be a personal loan from a bank. He will need to offer his house as collateral – that is the bank would own the house if he failed to repay the loan.

Short-term finance is money that is borrowed by the owners that has to be repaid in a period of less than one year. Matthew's most likely source of short-term finance will be credit from his suppliers of materials – he might get three months to pay for these supplies.

Unlimited liability

Many small firms are owned as either partnerships or sole traders. Their main source of capital is their savings, which may also include loans or gifts from family and friends.

In using their own savings as capital in sole traders or partnerships, entrepreneurs are accepting a risk. There is the possibility of losing not only the capital they have invested, but also any other savings and possessions that they own. This is because of unlimited liability. Just as there is no legal difference between a sole trader and his or her business, so there is no financial difference. Unlimited liability means that the owner is liable for all the debts of the business. They would gain all the profits but at the same time face the risk of all the losses.

In the case of Matthew Crick's insulation business, if he were to lose £100,000 in the first two years of running his business, not only would he be unable to pay back his trade creditors, he would be unable to pay back his bank loan. He would therefore not just lose his savings but also his house and any other possessions needed to make up the £100,000.

The same risk of unlimited liability exists with a partnership. Every member of a partnership normally has unlimited liability. Therefore if one partner makes a mistake and loses the business a lot of money, the savings and property of all the partners might be taken to pay the debts.

TASK 2

Students hit by £100m enterprise Love Bug

A young mobile phone company, studentmobiles.com, which offers students mobile phones over the Internet, is using its current national tour of university campuses to promote starting a business to undergraduates. Set up by two young graduates just six months ago, business has already grown to employ 15 people, has just linked up with Europe's largest mobile phone dealer, and has been advised by City analysts that it could be worth between £80 million and £100 million within two years.

Steven Bell (23), managing director of studentmobiles.com set up his own business after graduating from the University of Northumbria at Newcastle in 1998. Initially, he set up Bell Telecoms, a telecommunications consultancy offering a service to reduce the cost of phones. The company won a cash prize to develop the business in last year's Tyneside Shell *Live*WIRE Young Business Start-up Awards. Since winning the Shell *Live*WIRE award, sales have exceeded his expectations, and he identified a new niche market in the mobile phone industry targeting students. Steven then teamed up with George Kinghorn (28), and despite the reluctance of the banks and local enterprise agencies to back their venture, the pair managed to raise £5,000 to launch their new business last September.

Source: Shell *Live*WIRE, adapted from www.shell-livewire.org

a Why do you think Steven formed a partnership with George Kinghorn?

b What problems might emerge from taking on a partner?

c Why do you think that banks were reluctant to lend the business money?

d What is meant by 'a niche market' and why might this be important for small businesses?

Sources of loan finance

One of the advantages of large businesses is that they have a wide range of sources of finance from which to choose (Unit 22). For small businesses there is a more limited range of sources.

Trade credit

Suppliers usually allow a small business a period of time between buying materials and paying for them. Normally, this will be between one and three months. This **trade credit** is an important source of short-term finance. A small business might therefore not have to pay for its supplies until they have been used in making a product and the product has been sold. If a service is being paid for after it has been received, e.g. the work of an electrician, then this is known as an expense creditor.

There are limitations to trade credit. Any discounts which suppliers offer for prompt payment will be lost if credit is asked for. A supplier may not give credit to a new business. If a sole trader fails to pay on time, the supplier may refuse credit the next time and the business might be given a poor 'credit rating'. Other suppliers may then refuse to give the business credit.

Bank overdraft

This is where a bank allows customers to draw more from their bank account than they have deposited. It is an easily arranged source of short-term finance. The bank will decide an **overdraft** limit – the maximum that can be overdrawn. After that the business can withdraw or repay funds when it likes up to that limit. It is therefore flexible, and a business has to pay only interest on the amount overdrawn at any one time. This makes it a cheap source of finance. A small business is likely to need an overdraft to meet its day-to-day expenses when revenue is not being earned immediately.

Matthew Crick arranged an overdraft limit of £10,000 with his bank in January 2001. The bank charges 12 per cent annual interest on any sum overdrawn, or 1 per cent a month. Between January and June his account progressed as follows:

£	Jan	Feb	Mar	Apr	May	Jun
Balance at end of month	(1000)	(3000)	(4500)	(2000)	750	(2000)
Interest charged (at 1%)	10.0	30.0	45.0	20.0	–	20.0

His total interest paid over the six months was £125.00. Had he taken out a personal loan for £10,000 at 12 per cent annual interest rate, he would have paid £600 in interest in the first six months (£10,000 x 6 per cent).

For a small business like Matthew's there are risks in using an overdraft. Rates of interest can increase depending on the economic climate (Unit 7) and interest costs could cause a problem if large sums are overdrawn for a period of time. The bank can also decide at any time to reduce the limit or call in the overdraft. It is important that short-term finance like an overdraft is not used to finance long-term expenditure, e.g. on buying property or machinery.

Bank loan

This is a more certain way for a small business to borrow from a bank. A bank loan is for a specific amount for a set period of time (usually between one and three years). Therefore the business will know that it will be able to use the money over a given period. The interest rate will be either fixed for the time of the loan or variable in line with current interest rates. A fixed rate will be better at times of rising interest rates, and the business will be able to plan ahead easily.

The rate that a small business is charged for its loan is likely to be higher than that for a larger company; this is to guard the bank against the greater risk of the business being unable to pay back the loan. The borrower will also need to offer collateral against the loan. In the case of an unlimited company this might well be the business owner's house or other personal property. This could then be lost if the loan repayments are not made.

Leasing and hire purchase

To avoid having to borrow a lump sum in the form of a loan, small businesses can use **leasing** or **hire purchase** arrangements.

The leasing of equipment can have significant benefits for a business – not least because, as a 100 per cent tax-deductible expense, it is a highly tax-efficient way of acquiring equipment. In addition, leasing helps to maintain a healthy cash flow by making it less necessary for firms to borrow money and therefore leaving credit lines untouched. In addition, leasing helps to keep prices down through the establishment of a fixed cost over a given period.

When planning for future expansion, leasing overcomes budgetary constraints and allows for future equipment upgrading at any time, so as to keep pace with changing needs or in order to embrace new technology. Examples of items that small businesses may lease include: computer systems, shop fittings, close-circuit television systems, office furniture, plant and machinery, printing equipment, photocopiers, faxes and phone systems.

Instead of buying his van, or a photocopier for the office, Matthew Crick might lease them. In this way he avoids having to pay for them all at once. The leasing company keeps ownership of the van or photocopier and he pays a regular monthly sum for using the items. The leasing company also carries out repairs and maintenance, and will take back the machine when it is no longer needed, breaks down or becomes obsolete. Matthew could then take out a lease on a new machine. Leasing is expensive, but it spreads the cost of buying a vehicle or a machine over a long time period.

With hire purchase, Matthew would be paying for the item over a period of time and at the end of that period would own the vehicle or machine. He would pay a regular sum towards paying for the machine, which would include interest. Hire purchase is likely to be a more expensive source of long-term finance than a bank loan. If he falls behind in his payments, then the machine would be collected by the hire purchase company, even if the payments were nearly complete.

TASK 3

Below is a list of some of the items that a small trader setting up and running a small shop might need to purchase. There is also a list of possible sources of finance for these items.

Items purchased	Sources of finance
Stock for the shop	Own capital
The shop itself	Bank loan
A personal computer	Trade credit
Shelving and display	Overdraft
A security system	Leasing
A delivery van	Hire purchase
A checkout till	
Insurance	

1 For each of the items listed, choose a source of finance that you think would be suitable for a small business.

2 Explain why you made that choice and give one advantage and one disadvantage of the method you have chosen for a small business.

Other sources of finance

Some 80 per cent of all small businesses rely on borrowing from banks, but there are other sources of financial support. The most important alternative is the government. In recent years governments have encouraged the setting up and expansion of small businesses in order to offer people who lose their jobs an alternative source of employment.

In the 1990s most government financial support for small businesses was channelled through 82 Training and Enterprise Councils (TECs) and Local Enterprise Agencies. If a young person aged between 18 and 24 has a sound business idea, and has been out of work and claiming benefits for more than six months, he or she can seek assistance through the New Deal Initiative. He or she can meet a Business Link adviser who can determine if the idea is viable and help the individual to analyse progress.

In inner cities, enterprise zones and other areas of high unemployment, there will be certain grants and allowances for businesses that are only available in those areas. For example, if Matthew Crick was setting up in Wales he could approach the Welsh Development Agency or the Development Board for Rural Wales for help. He might get:

- reductions in rent or rates
- grants for setting up
- tax allowances for buying machinery.

He might also be able to get assistance from European Community grants, but again this will depend upon the area in which he sets up.

There is also a number of charitable organisations that try to support young entrepreneurs, e.g. the Prince's Youth Business Trust and *Live*WIRE.

It was shown earlier that a small business person may well have to offer his or her house or other property as collateral for a business loan. As an alternative the Department of Trade and Industry (DTI), part of central government, runs a Loan Guarantee Scheme which means that the government guarantees the loan for the bank rather than the individual. This should make the bank more willing to offer a loan to a small business.

TASK 4

Business idea gels for UK's top young entrepreneur

Fraser Hay (29), the owner manager of Health Scope Direct from Banff in Aberdeen, Scotland, has beaten the most diverse range of businesses from across the country that the Shell *Live*WIRE competition has ever seen. He was awarded the prestigious title of Shell *Live*WIRE Young Business Person of the Year 1998 for his seaweed based gel products. As overall winner, Fraser also walked off with a cheque for £10,000.

Fraser started Health Scope Direct in December 1996 – following help from Shell *Live*WIRE and the Prince's Scottish Youth Business Trust (PSYBT) – after an initial eight-week trial period of market testing.

He decided to set up his own business after his former job as marketing consultant introduced him to the wonders of seaweed. All of the products in the Healthcare Direct catalogue are seaweed-based – maximising its potential as an alternative healthcare product for the first time.

All the early signs of the business are very positive. Sales in March were double those forecast, while the actual closing net assets of the company at the end of March were £23,733 (a 150 per cent increase on the forecast).

By actively pursuing a policy for growth, the business is on target for a turnover in excess of £1 million within two years. The acquisition of 'beauty supply' companies will help to secure rapid future growth and enable Fraser to achieve his personal goal of owning a public limited holding company with three subsidiaries that are market leaders, all employing in excess of 100 people.

Source: Shell *Live*WIRE, adapted from www.shell-livewire.org.

a What financial support did Fraser gain when setting up Health Scope Direct?

b What help, other than financial, might Fraser have sought in his first year of business?

c Why might higher than forecast sales cause problems for the company?

d Fraser has a goal of owning a public limited company. How might this help him to expand further?

Making the choice

There will be a number of factors that a small business will need to consider when choosing finance.

What is available? There are certain types of finance that would not be available for a business with unlimited liability, e.g. share capital or **debentures** (see Unit 22).

What is the finance for? If it is for buying short-term assets like stock, or for paying creditors or employees, then it should be short-term finance, e.g. an overdraft. If it is for buying a longer-term asset, then it should be a longer-term source, e.g. a bank loan or hire purchase.

How much is needed? The larger the amount, the fewer the possible sources. Most assistance from the Small Business Service will be quite small – for larger funds a small business will have to use a bank or rely on owners' capital or retained profit (see Unit 22).

How risky is the use of finance? Some ventures will appear safer than others, e.g. finance for opening a pet shop would appear to be less risky than finance to set up a power-boat racing club. Existing businesses are likely to find extra finance more easily than new ones, if the business is operating successfully.

What is the cost of finance? If finance is available, then the price of that finance will be important, usually measured in the interest paid. The business will need to be able to meet any interest payments as well as repay any borrowing.

The Cruickshank report (2000) condemned the big four banks for exploiting smaller companies. While banks are doing more for small businesses than they were 10 years ago, many small business owners still feel that the lack of support given to them by the high street banks has driven some of them into bankruptcy.

KEY TERMS

Capital – the man-made factor of production that involves a present sacrifice in order to make more for the future. It includes machinery, vehicles, money, etc.

Debentures – long-term IOUs with a fixed interest rate issued by companies and purchased by individuals and institutions.

Hire purchase – paying for an item over a period of time to a hire purchase company; ownership does not occur until all the payments have been made.

Leasing – having use of a fixed asset in return for paying a leasing company for its use.

Long-term finance – money that is borrowed by a business for more than one year before repayment is due.

Overdraft – where an individual or company is allowed to draw more from a bank account than is deposited into the account.

Short-term finance – money that is borrowed by a business that has to be repaid within a year.

Start-up capital – money provided by the owners of the business when it is first set up.

Trade credit – the time allowed by suppliers between buying goods and paying for them; usually 30–90 days.

Camilla Ridley

Camilla Ridley started in business at the age of 23 by turning an Australian holiday into a huge profit-centre. She took over some scarves she had designed and made – and came back with orders for 2,500. Her mother lent her £7,000 and Camilla turned a profit of £20,000. Five years later, her fashion accessory lines include scarves retailing for anything up to £150, and pricey handbags. She's adding a line of posh clothing items for 1999. Big name stores in the UK, USA and Australia are established clients. Her products get strong editorial coverage in leading fashion magazines. Camilla employs two people full time in a rented workspace in London's Notting Hill, plus part-timers and contract workers.

Dee Evans and Elaine Daniels

Dee Evans was employed as a sales manager for a hotel chain. She is now one of three partners in Evans, Hughes, Baker – successful specialists in managing event venues for corporate clients. In 1993, they got their chance by a combination of networking, determination and luck. Dee had been made redundant – but so had friend and corporate client Tony Baker. In return for a partnership in the company, he invested his redundancy pay. Dee's 'best mate' Elaine Daniels (previously Hughes) left her job in a legal office to join. Dee says: 'We all took an enormous risk. We get paid in arrears. The event takes place, the client pays the venue, then the venue pays us. So no one was interested in lending us money. When Tony came along it was manna from heaven.' The company is ripe for expansion. But Dee says: 'We have to be different – there are so many other companies doing the same work.'

Madi Sharma

Madi Sharma started her Nottingham-based Original Eastern Food in 1994 with £500 savings. It makes pre-packed Asian and Afro-Caribbean dishes, turning over about £250,000. Last year it closed a deal to supply an additional £1 million worth of French cuisine convenience foods to Le Sezannais of Loughborough, and they've put Madi on the Board of the company. The growth will require a staff increase from 13 to 70, investment and bigger premises. Madi has worked as a sales and marketing manager for TSB. After she started her company, and before she looked for an overdraft, she got her father to invest £5,000. She says: 'I knew I wouldn't have got bank finance without his backing.' Original Eastern Food has used capital of £100,000, along with grants and loans from government agencies and banks. The company has won a string of awards, and trains all staff from scratch.

Joanna McKinlay

After about a year of trading, 28-year-old Joanna McKinlay's Giant Card Company is nudging the VAT threshold with a turnover nearing £50,000. She installs a 6ft high greetings card outside a house or office to celebrate special occasions. Next day she removes it, leaving no post-party litter. The well-wisher pays a daily rental of £34.99. Joanna spotted the idea while on holiday in Florida, and local Business Link advisers helped her refine it. Lloyds lent her £8,000 to buy a computer-driven cutter, secured against the house she co-owns with her domestic partner.

Source: *First Voice of Business*, February/March 1999

Have you ever...

	✓	✗
Gone to your bank for investment advice?	20%	80%
Used your bank's international trade service?	17%	83%
Used your bank to purchase insurance?	29%	71%

Have you ever been refused finance by a bank?

The pie chart shows the proportion of respondents who have and who have not been refused finance by a bank, as well as those who marked their reply as not applicable.

n/a 11%
Yes 17%
No 72%

Q Questions

1 Using the case studies, explain the different ways in which the owners raised the initial finance to start up their business.

2 Why might a bank ask a customer seeking a loan to put his or her property up against his or her business?

3 Using the evidence from the survey results, write a report outlining the positive and negative relationships between small firms and their bank.

4 Evaluate the options open to Madi Sharma to raise the finance needed to continue expanding her business.

5 Create a leaflet entitled 'Essential tips on finance and how to survive the first year' that could be given to people considering setting up their own business.

E Extension

1 Look at the last Budget and identify what has been done to help small businesses.

2 Contact your local Learning and Skills Council and research the help that they are giving small business in your local area.

UNIT 22

Finance for large business and public finance

This unit is about the different ways in which large businesses and the public sector can raise finance.

At the end of the unit, students should be able to:

- define a large business

- understand the importance of limited liability for large firms

- explain the importance of shareholders in limited liability companies

- explain the different sources of short-term and long-term finance available to large companies and the public sector

- compare sources of finance for a small and large company in the private sector

- explain the factors that influence a large company's decisions with regard to finance

- apply own knowledge of finance for large businesses to a range of contexts.

What is a large business?

In Unit 21, the definition of a small business was discussed and this gives us the basis to define what is generally accepted as a large business. A large business is defined as one that during an accounting year exceeds two of the following:

- a turnover of £1.4 million
- total assets of £0.7 million
- 50+ employees.

Companies with these characteristics are usually limited companies, often public limited companies, e.g. Marks & Spencer, ICI, Boots and HSBC.

TASK 1

Write to a company to obtain a copy of its annual report, or use the Internet to gain access to company information/annual reports. (*Hint*: try www.carol.co.uk or www.bized.ac.uk.)

a Who are the owners of the company and what proportion of the shares do they hold?

b How much capital has been invested into the company and what has the capital been used for?

c What profit did the company make in the last financial year?

d What dividend have the shareholders been paid?

e Would you want to buy shares in this company? Explain your answer.

Limited liability companies

The process of forming a **limited liability** company was outlined in Units 4 and 5. A common reason for owners forming a limited company is to raise more capital to help finance the business. By becoming a limited company a business can raise money through the issue of shares. In Unit 5 it was shown that for the owners of a sole trader or a partnership there is the risk of unlimited liability but for the shareholders of limited companies this risk is removed as they are protected by limited liability (see Unit 4).

Below are some features of the way a limited company will raise capital through shareholders:

- There must be a minimum of two shareholders but there is no maximum number. This is why many limited companies are family businesses.
- Each owner of the company puts an amount of capital into the company which is divided into shares of fixed amounts.
- If a profit is made, the shareholders will receive a dividend – a share of the profit in line with the number of shares they own.
- If a loss is made, it is the company that has to meet the debt, but the shareholders will receive no dividend. If the company cannot meet the debts, the shareholders will have to lose only the money they invested in the business in the first place.
- Finance from shares lasts as long as the business lasts. Shares of private limited companies are not sold on the Stock Exchange and can only be sold with director approval.
- To protect the interests of the shareholders a company must keep a record showing the financial position of the company at any one time. These accounts will include a balance sheet and profit and loss account (see Unit 23). The accounts must be presented to the shareholders at an AGM. They must be audited by an outside accountant – that is, checked to see that they are a true and fair view of the company's activities.
- If extra finance is required then more shares could be sold privately to existing or new shareholders.

Share capital will be an important long-term source of finance for a limited company. It will be used to finance the purchase of long-term assets like a factory or machinery, and to provide any finance needed for expansion.

Profits and dividends

The capital brought to a business by shareholders is not free. The shareholders expect to earn an income from the money they invest in the form of a dividend. This is a share of the profits of the business.

Mill Pumps Ltd produces a variety of pumps for the water companies. It is owned by six people: the two founders and four other shareholders who were invited into the business to increase the capital available. The capital structure of the business is as follows:

- 500,000 £1 shares have been issued
- Each founder owns 30 per cent of the shares – 150,000 each
- Each of the new shareholders owns 10 per cent of the shares – 50,000 each.

In 2000, Mill Pumps had a profitable year because of growth in the water industry. After tax it made a net profit of £330,000. The Board of Directors decided to retain £150,000 in the business. The rest would be paid as a dividend to the owners. The dividend which each would receive would be worked out in the following way:

Total profit for dividend	£180,000
Number of shares	500,000
Dividend per share	$\dfrac{£180,000}{500,000} = £0.36$

Each owner of Mill Pumps will receive 36p for every £1 share that he or she owns.

The two founders will receive 150,000 x £0.36 = £54,000 each.

The four new shareholders will receive 50,000 x £0.36 = £18,000 each.

If the company had made a loss they would have received no dividend. If losses continued they might lose the money they put into the business. Dividends are the rewards for the risks the owners are taking in putting their money into the business.

Going public

Both private and public limited companies are able to raise capital by selling shares to shareholders. Unlike a private limited company, a public limited company is able to sell to an unlimited number of shareholders on the Stock Exchange. To raise money from the public through issuing shares, a company will need to go through the process of 'going public' which includes the following stages:

- A prospectus must be issued which tells potential shareholders about the company and its financial record.

- Underwriters need to be arranged – these are companies that will buy up the shares if no one wants to buy them.

- A merchant bank will be needed to help organise and publicise the issue of shares.

- A choice of stock market is available:

  - for smaller companies there is the Alternative Investment Market (AIM) where it is cheaper to raise funds. The annual cost of an AIM listing is £20,000 compared to more than £100,000 on the Stock Exchange. This is still a small market.

  - for larger companies, there is a full Stock Exchange listing. This involves higher costs and more rules and regulation, but there are many more potential investors.

Shares might be offered for sale to the public at large – as happened with the BT share offer and the Railtrack privatisation. Alternatively, the shares might be bought beforehand by a merchant bank and then advertised through an Offer for Sale. Shares can then be bought from the bank (see Unit 5).

There are three groups of company that will want to sell a substantial number of shares on the stockmarkets:

- New companies that have been set up as a plc. This is quite rare, although the privatised companies such as British Airways, British Telecom, British Gas and the water companies were created as plcs.

- Companies that were formerly limited companies but want to become plcs. This is the more common type with companies looking for more shareholders in order to grow, e.g. easyJet, Orange and lastminute.com. The process is known as gaining a flotation on the stock market.

- Existing plcs which want to raise more capital from existing or new shareholders will make a rights issue. These extra shares are offered first to existing shareholders and then to others.

Whatever their reasons for wanting to raise finance through a share issue, there are costs and benefits from this method:

Costs	Benefits
The actual costs of issuing shares.	A large amount of money can be raised which is permanent capital.
The company comes into the public eye and any changes in performance are quickly noticed.	The status and reputation of the company may be raised.
Share prices go up and down however well an individual company is doing.	It is easier to borrow money; the shareholders provide increased security.
A company listed on the Stock Exchange is open to takeover by another company.	For the original owners, and for staff who own shares as a bonus, the value of their shares might well increase.

TASK 2

Liverpool to tackle flotation

LIVERPOOL Football Club is to float on the stock market within the next two seasons with a price tag of about £400 million.

The first significant soccer club flotation in three years would make Liverpool the second richest in the country behind £1 billion Manchester United and give Gerard Houllier, the Liverpool manager, further financial firepower to challenge the Manchester club's ascendancy.

Rick Parry, Liverpool chief executive, confirming the float schedule, said: 'After Granada took their stake [paying £22 million for 9.9 per cent last summer], we gave ourselves the target of getting back within the top three on the field – which we have – and getting the performance right on the commercial side. We are not there yet.'

The club last year recorded a £5 million loss on turnover of £45 million.

While Granada's acquisition valued Liverpool at £220 million, a stock market valuation is likely to be at a significant premium. Since the Granada deal, Manchester United's shares have nearly doubled to value the company at £1.06 billion. On a revenue multiple Liverpool, a club with the biggest English football brand after United, would be valued at about £400 million.

Schroders, the investment bank, has been retained to advise the club, which is 51 per cent controlled by David Moores.

Source: *The Times*, 24 March 2000,

a Why might the management of Liverpool football club want to float the company on the Stock Exchange?

b Would you advise an investor to buy shares in the company? Give reasons for your answer.

c What might be the benefits and losses to David Moores from the flotation?

Long-term sources of finance

A range of sources of loan finance has been explained in Unit 21 in relation to small businesses. As a business grows, and as it gains greater stability, so there is a greater variety of loan finance available. Larger limited companies and plcs will also find that they can arrange better terms when they borrow money – that is, the money will be cheaper to borrow.

Debentures

These are issued by plcs like shares on the Stock Exchange, but the companies pay the people who buy them a fixed rate of interest unlike a dividend which could change in value. There is also a set date for repaying the loan. Debenture holders are creditors of a company; they lend the company a fixed sum for a period of time and get paid interest in return. They are long term so would be used to finance long-term expansion.

Mortgages

These are long-term loans, usually offered by building societies and banks, which are based on property or land as security. If a business wants to buy an office block valued at £1 million it would be able to arrange a mortgage, for say £¾ million, from a building society or bank which it could pay back over a long period of time – often 25 years. The repayments would include interest as well as covering the original sum. If at any time the company fails to meet the mortgage payments, or if the company stopped trading, then the mortgage lender would gain ownership of the office block. Mortgages therefore are used to buy property which is going to be used for a period of time.

Bank loans

These are more flexible loans which can be arranged for a medium term e.g. 1–3 years, or a longer term, e.g. 3–20 years. Interest has to be paid on a regular basis. It can be either fixed for the term of the loan, or vary with the going interest rate. This type of loan is likely to be used to purchase a fixed asset which has a certain life span; the bank will usually want some security in case the repayments are not made. Banks are an important source of finance for companies, but they have been criticised in the UK for not providing sufficient long-term loans to business (see Unit 21). Larger companies can usually arrange loans more easily with banks and at a lower interest rate, than smaller ones.

Other sources of long-term loans

The traditional sources of long-term funds for business are provided by the stock market, banks and building societies but outside this group there are other schemes for helping companies to gain long-term funds.

One such source is **venture capital** where separate companies, sometimes owned by financial institutions, invest money into new and growing firms. They are often willing to support projects or ideas that are risky and which banks would be unlikely to support. The largest venture capital company is 3i – Investors in Industry – which provides half of all venture capital in the UK.

Short-term sources of finance

Businesses will need short-term sources of funds to meet their needs for working capital, that is, money to meet the day-to-day cash requirements of the business. This would include paying bills, paying wages, and paying interest on loans. In Unit 21 some of the short-term sources for small businesses were explained. For larger businesses there is a wider range of choice which includes some sources discussed earlier.

Trade credit

The larger the business, the more likely it is that it will be able to get credit from its suppliers. This is because the supplier may well be relying on sales to the company for its own well-being. Very often the supplier will be smaller than the customer. This has become especially common in the retail industry, where large shop chains can negotiate favourable trade credit with their suppliers. The benefits and disadvantages of trade credit as a source of finance were discussed in Unit 21.

Bank overdraft

As was shown in Unit 21 this is a flexible source of short-term funds. Large companies will be able to generate more cash than smaller organisations, but from time to time will need an overdraft to meet a gap between payments and receipts.

Hire purchase and leasing

Both large and small businesses (see Unit 21) are using these methods of finance, especially for the purchase of machinery and vehicles. They allow the company to spread the cost of buying such assets over a longer period of time, and therefore are a useful alternative if a business is short of funds for investment. A considerable percentage of large businesses use hire purchase to buy business assets, while it is now possible for an airline to lease planes valued at millions of pounds.

Factoring

This is where one company gets another one, known as a debt factor, to collect the money it is owed by customers. For this service the business will pay the factor a percentage commission on the value of the invoices. The advantages of factoring are that cash arrives in a business as soon as it gets new customers; it does not have to wait until bills are paid. If a customer does not pay up, it is the factor which suffers the loss.

Finance of the public sector

Many parts of the public sector are funded largely or completely by taxation, for example, the National Health Service, the police and state education. Some public sector organisations, such as the Post Office, depend heavily on income from sales and also receive government support. (See Unit 4 for more details.)

The public sector has fewer options than the private sector when it comes to managing finance. Central and local government are less likely to have the choice of whether or how to cut back on important spending.

During recession, central and local government will find that their spending will increase through areas such as social services. The problem is that at the same time, their income from taxes and rates falls. The opposite is true in periods of economic boom, but the government may be reluctant to spend its surplus or offer lower tax levels for fear of triggering inflation.

Since the 1980s the public sector has aimed to develop greater responsibility to the tax and rate payer. Budgets are more closely monitored and performance targets are set to measure efficiency. Competition has been encouraged, with some industries being privatised (see Unit 4).

TASK 3

Logans Limited

Logans Ltd is a large producer of fruit juices located in East Anglia. Logans is an independent business but competes in a market which is dominated by companies owned by large food organisations. By providing good service to its retail and restaurant customers, and a high quality product, Logans has been able to keep its market share and maintain its profits.

Logans now wants to take advantage of the more open European market. It wants to begin to sell its products in Belgium, the Netherlands and Germany as a way of testing out the European market. Good transport links with East Anglia make these countries the best to aim for.

In order to prepare itself for this expansion, Logans has identified the following financial needs:

- a new bottling plant which will produce litre-size bottles. Expected cost £½ million
- an expansion of the marketing department at an annual cost of £125,000
- new delivery vehicles for Europe at a cost of £300,000
- an increase in the amount of working capital to cover the day-to-day running costs.

The Logan family, which owns 90 per cent of the shares of the company, realises that it cannot provide the extra finance needed. It is looking to expand its financial base, but does not want to risk the independence of the company.

a How should Logans finance each of its financial needs? Explain why you have chosen this option and highlight some of the possible drawbacks that the company should be aware of.

b Write a report, as financial director of Logans, explaining the financial costs and benefits of expanding into the European market.

c What would happen to Logans' share price when the proposed expansion into Europe was announced?

TASK 4

A Bolton Metropolitan Borough Council provides these main services among others:

Education and arts:
- 129 schools for 43,500 pupils
- 21,800 school meals per day
- 19 branch libraries
- 2 museums
- Awards and grants for students

Housing:
- Maintaining 22,600 Council houses
- 2 neighbourhood renewal areas
- Advice and help for the homeless

Leisure services:
- Parks and open spaces
- 8 swimming baths
- 10 sports centres
- 7 community centres
- 7 cemeteries

Social services:
- 5 children's residential homes
- 12 homes and care centres for the elderly
- 3 day centres for people with disabilities
- 520,000 hours of home help and 211,000 home meals per year

Planning and engineering:
- Maintaining 925 km of roads and 270 bridges
- Collection of refuse
- Public health control
- Town planning
- Economic development and environmental improvement

B Bolton Metro Council Services – expenditure and income 1999 – 2000

Income	£m	Expenditure	£m
Revenue Support Grant from government	97.5	Education	124.6
Non-domestic rates	61.7	Social services	50.1
Income from charges	93.3	Housing	7.6
Council tax	51.0	Highways	12.3
Contribution from reserves	0.5	Leisure services	16.0
		Other services and levies	93.4
Total income	**303.8**	**Total expenditure**	**303.8**

Source: Bolton Metro Council Tax leaflet 1999-2000

a Using the information in section A, describe the main functions of a local authority like Bolton Metropolitan Borough Council.

b In section B, identify the two most important sources of income for Bolton Metro and the two largest areas of expenditure (ignoring 'other').

c Divide the class into five sections: Education, Social services, Housing, Leisure services and Planning and engineering. Bolton Metropolitan Borough Council has to reduce its expenditure by 10 per cent. Each group should create a presentation defending why their area should not have its budget cut and also nominating an area that they think should be cut, giving reasons why. (This could be written up as a report at the end of the presentations.)

d Compare your own local council spending levels to those of Bolton Council. How are they similar and how do they differ?

How does a large business make a choice about finance?

If a company needs to raise funds, there are a number of factors that will affect its choice.

Cost

This will be not just in terms of the interest rate that has to be paid on any loan, or the dividends on any share issued. There are also administrative costs in arranging finance.

Use of funds

As with small businesses, larger companies will need to balance the source with the use. If a company needs money for a long-term investment, e.g. the purchase of a rival company or the opening of a new factory in another region, then it will need a long-term source of funds, e.g. capital or long-term loans.

The trading position of the business

How well a private and especially a public limited company is doing is often public knowledge. A profitable or older company will find it much easier to raise finance than a loss-making or new one.

The company's balance between debt and capital

This is known as the **gearing** of a company. A business might have raised £1 million through issuing shares, and £250,000 through long-term loans. Its gearing would be 25 per cent. A business will need to make sure that its gearing is not too high. A high gear(ing) allows you to go faster, but you can face problems if there is a sudden difficulty. A low gear(ing) ensures that you go slowly, but at least allows you time to react to problems.

TASK 5

BIRCHLEY is within 50 miles of Central London. Over the past thirty years the population has grown to 75,000. It is a commuter town with a 45 minute rail link to London.

Ten years ago Birchley District Council built a leisure centre on the outskirts of town in spite of local opposition. Many residents still resent this use of public money.

Under new laws local authorities must give private firms the chance to run some local authority services.

Birchley District Council is inviting written tenders (detailed bids) from firms to manage the leisure centre. Refuse collection, street sweeping and the maintenance of parks, along with many other services, have already been privatised.

The successful tender would need to show a significant saving on the Council's management costs and guarantee an improved standard of service to the public.

Source: Southern Examining Group, 1992.

a Why might some of the residents of Birchley 'resent the use of public money' to build the leisure centre?
b Why has the council invited tenders to run the leisure centre?
c What problems might there be in allowing a private firm to run the services mentioned?

KEY TERMS

Competitive tendering – where services provided by central or local government are offered out to private firms to bid for the contract.

Debentures – long-term IOUs with a fixed interest rate issued by companies and purchased by individuals and institutions.

Dividend – a proportion of the profits paid to shareholders as a reward for contributing capital to the firm.

Factoring – selling the invoices of a company to a specialised business which will collect the money on behalf of the original company, in return for a commission.

Gearing – the balance of finance for a company between loans and shareholders' capital.

Limited liability – the responsibility for the debts of the company is limited to the amount of capital invested in the company.

Mortgages – long-term loans based upon property or land as a security.

Privatisation – also known as denationalisation. The process of returning a nationalised industry to private ownership.

Quangos (quasi non-governmental organisations) – organisations set up and financed by the government but otherwise run as independent businesses.

Shares – a share in the decision making of an organisation in return for contributing capital.

Venture capital – money invested by institutions in new or risky projects which are not usually financed through traditional methods.

Online travel firm may float

Internet travel company lastminute.com is planning to float on the stock market – at an estimated value of £400 million. The firm, which was founded only last year, may also seek a Nasdaq listing as it is poised to break into the US market. London-based lastminute.com offers cheap deals on flight and hotel booking in the UK and France, as well as gifts, auctions and entertainment.

It was launched by two former management consultants, Brent Hoberman and Martha Lane Fox. This year, it expects revenues of about £6.2 million.

The site has proved popular with people wanting bargains but without shopping around.

Now the founders are planning to launch a prospectus and are appointing Morgan Stanley Dean Witter as adviser. The site recently launched in France and plans to do so in Germany, too.

Source: BBC News Online, 17 September 1999

Overview

lastminute.com was founded by Brent Hoberman and Martha Lane Fox in 1998. The web site was launched in the UK in October 1998. Localised versions have since been launched in France in September 1999, in Germany in October 1999, and in Sweden in December 1999.

lastminute.com aims to be the global marketplace for all last-minute services and transactions. Using the Internet to match suppliers and consumers at short notice, lastminute.com works with a range of suppliers in the travel, entertainment and gift industries and is dedicated to bringing its customers attractive products and services. lastminute.com carries almost no inventory risk, selling perishable inventory for its suppliers, and, where appropriate, protects suppliers' brand names until after purchase. lastminute.com seeks to differentiate itself by generating some of the lowest prices for many travel and entertainment deals, and by packaging and delivering products and services, such as restaurant reservations, entertainment tickets and gifts, in convenient, novel and distinctive ways.

It also aims to inspire its customers to try something different. Since 1998 the company believes that it has developed a distinctive brand, which communicates spontaneity and a sense of adventure, attracting a loyal community of registered users. Recent research showed that lastminute.com is the second most recognised e-commerce retailer in the UK. At March 31, 2000 the company had approximately 1.4 million registered subscribers in Europe. Headquartered in London, with offices in Paris, Munich and Stockholm, lastminute.com currently employs around 250 people.

Source: lastminute.com Investor Relations

Q Questions

1 Imagine that you have been given the task of persuading potential shareholders to invest in lastminute.com. Write a letter of about 300 words, setting out the reasons for becoming a shareholder.

2 How did the company originally finance itself?

3 What benefits might there be in entering awards events such as 'The Company of the Year'?

4 Why did the company choose to go public?

5 Using the evidence presented, plus research on up-to-date financial statistics, explain whether or not you think that this has been a successful flotation.

6 What lessons might other dotcom companies learn from this flotation?

E Extension

There has been a recent trend for building societies to go public. This process is called 'de-mutualisation'. Find out why this is different to companies that go from private to public limited. Investigate a recent case study (both Standard Life and Nationwide were considering converting in 2000) and decide if you think that members should vote for or against the proposal to go public.

The accounts: the profit and loss account and the balance sheet

This unit is about how companies use a profit and loss account and balance sheet to monitor their financial status.

At the end of this unit, students will be able to ;

- explain who may use the financial accounts
- understand the two financial records – profit and loss account and balance sheet
- explain how profit and loss is calculated
- understand the items that make up the profit and loss account and balance sheet
- draw up a simple profit and loss account and balance sheet
- analyse the financial position of a company from its main accounts
- explain the difference between the two main accounts

Why are accounts kept?

All companies, large or small, will want to know their financial position. In a small company the owner may want to re-invest the **profits** to finance further expansion or pay himself or herself a bonus. In a larger company, profits may affect the share price and pay levels of staff. Each stakeholder group will find different parts of the accounts useful and it is only in a public limited company that the accounts are able to be viewed by people external to the business. For a plc, there will be a wide range of users:

- shareholders – who want to know what profits have been made and what their dividend is going to be
- managers – who want to see if the company is operating more efficiently from one year to the next
- employees – who want to know if their jobs are secure and if the company is doing well enough to pay them more (this group includes trade unions)
- investors – who want to know if it's worth buying shares in the company on the Stock Exchange
- creditors – who want to know if the company is in a position to pay back its debts to them
- customers – who want to see if the business is likely to survive to provide back-up service or new supplies
- the government – which will collect tax on profits made and wants to make sure that the accounts are a true record of what is happening in the company.

Each of these groups therefore has different interests in the figures in the accounts. However, there are three broad areas where they will try to make comparisons between one year and the next. To help them do this, they may well use **ratio analysis** – a ratio is a mathematical way of comparing one figure with another. The three areas that ratios are used to analyse are: profitability, liquidity and return on investment. Ratio analysis is covered in detail in Unit 25.

There are two main accounts that a company will produce to measure its financial status. These are:

- the **profit and loss account**
- the **balance sheet**.

The profit and loss account

What is profit?

Profit is the difference between the amount that a business sells its goods and services for and the costs of producing them. It is often confused with cash, especially in smaller companies.

Cash is a general term which covers an asset that the business holds allowing supplies to be bought and wages to be paid. When a business confuses this with profit, problems can emerge. If a business owner believes that cash in the till or the bank can be used to buy personal items the business can find itself short of cash to pay invoices when they appear.

An owner of a bookshop may sell 100 books at a profit of £5 per book. The revenue earned may provide income for the business, but should not be considered as final profit until all other expenses have been paid.

Most firms would agree that the larger the profit the better, but this is not true with cash.
A company would be better buying new equipment or motivating staff with bonuses rather than holding on to cash.
A company with too little cash, on the other hand, will find itself unable to pay important bills.

How is profit/loss calculated?

There are two main elements in the calculation of profit or loss:

- Revenue – this includes all the money the business receives from selling its goods or services.
- Costs – these include all the expenditure that the business incurs in producing the goods and services it sells.

Profit is calculated by subtracting costs from revenue.

Profit = Revenue – Costs

Imagine a company called Applewick Farm, which produces a mixture of arable crops and beef cattle. The farm gets its cash from selling its wheat and barley to milling companies and its beef cattle to the local market. In addition, the farm has bills to pay including supplies and wages. In 2000, the profit for Applewick Farm would be calculated as follows:

Sales revenue = Revenue from crops + Revenue from cattle
= £35,000 + £57,000
= £92,000

Costs = Supplies + Wages + Withdrawals + Electricity + Heating + Rates + Mortgage payment + Interest
= £18,000 + £24,000 + £14,400 + £4,000 + £5,200 + £8,000 + £6,000 + £2,400
= £82,000

Profit = Revenue – Costs
= £92,000 – £82,000
= £10,000

Recording profit and loss

Organisations seeking a formal way of presenting their annual trading will use a profit and loss account. For sole traders, such an account is not a legal requirement, but it is rare for a company not to produce this account as it may prove helpful when analysing the company's financial position, applying for a bank loan or filling in a tax return for the Inland Revenue.

A simple profit and loss account, for example for a sole trader, will be a table showing the sales, costs and expenses of a business over a financial year. For Applewick Farm, the financial data shown above, might be illustrated as in the account shown below.

There are two sections to this account. In the first section the direct cost of sales, that is, the costs of purchasing all the seed and animal feed necessary to produce crops and beef cattle, are deducted from the sales revenue (or turnover) to give the gross profit. In the second section the other expenses of running Applewick Farm are deducted from the gross profit. The final figure that is left is known as the net profit. This will be the amount of money which the owner would receive as a result of Applewick's trading activities for the year.

Profit and Loss Account for Applewick Farm for 2000		
	£	£
Sales revenue		92,000
less Cost of sales:		
purchase of supplies		18,000
Gross profit		**74,000**
less Expenses		
Wages	24,000	
Power	9,200	
Interest	2,400	
Mortgage	6,000	
Withdrawals	14,400	
Rates	8,000	
		64,000
Net profit		**10,000**

The profit and loss account for a larger company is more complicated. Public limited companies are legally required to publish a simplified version of their accounts. Look at the profit and loss account for Windsor Gifts Ltd, retailers of souvenirs for the tourist market.

The profit and loss account will be divided into three parts.

TASK 1

The Disney Lodge Health Studio opened in January 1997 with two owners of the partnership. By January 2001 they had attracted 1000 members, each paying £100 annual membership. They also earned £15,000 from visitors who took out day membership. The managers paid themselves salaries of £20,000, and paid £10,000 to part-time staff. The purchase of supplies cost £28,000. Electricity bills came to £2,500 per quarter, and their rent on the studio came to £8,300 which they had to pay at the start of the year. They spent £2,000 on local advertising and a further £2,500 on office expenses. Interest on an overdraft with the bank was costing them £200 monthly.

a Produce a profit and loss account for Disney Lodge Health Studios for the year of 2000.

b What was the net profit or loss for the business in 2000?

The trading account

This shows the sales revenue from the sales of gifts less the cost of those sales. The sales figure is easy to record, but the cost of sales figure is more complicated. The following information will be needed by Windsor Gifts to draw up its trading account.

Sales revenue in 2000	=	£830,000
Opening stock at start of 2000	=	£155,000
Purchases of stock during 2000	=	£430,000
Closing stock at end of 2000	=	£168,000

Its trading account will look like this:

Trading account of Windsor Gifts Ltd for the year ended 31.12.2000		
	£	£
Sales revenue		830,000
less Cost of sales		
Opening stock	155,000	
Purchases	430,000	
	585,000	
less Closing stock	–168,000	
		417,000
Gross profit		413,000

Windsor Gifts Ltd therefore made a gross profit of £413,000 from its trading activities in 2000.

The profit and loss account

The next part of the account is confusingly called the profit and loss account. This shows other income that the company has earned and other expenses that it has paid during that year. A deduction is also made for tax in this section. The profit and loss account for Windsor Gifts Ltd is shown below:

Profit and loss account of Windsor Gifts Ltd for the year ended 31.12.2000		
	£	£
Gross profit		413,000
less Expenses		
Wages and salaries	145,000	
Rent and rates	50,000	
Heating and lighting	25,000	
Telephone and postage	12,000	
Advertising	15,000	
Insurance	23,000	
Other miscellaneous	35,000	
		305,000
Profit before tax		108,000
less Corporation tax		32,000
Profit after tax		76,000

This section has shown that Windsor Gifts Ltd has made a profit after tax of £76,000 once all the deductions have been made. This is the money left with which the directors of the business have to decide what to do.

The appropriation account

Their decision is shown in the third part of the account – the appropriation account. In this section the profit is either paid out to the shareholders in the form of a dividend, or retained in the business. The appropriation account for Windsor Gifts Ltd is shown below; the Directors decided to give 60 per cent to shareholders, and retain 40 per cent.

	£
Profit after tax	76,000
Dividends paid	46,000
Retained profit	30,000

The full profit and loss account for Windsor Gifts Ltd can now be shown, built up from the three parts.

Profit and loss account of Windsor Gifts Ltd for the year ending 31.12.2000

		£	£
	Sales revenue		830,000
less	Cost of sales		417,000
	Gross profit		413,000
less	Expenses		305,000
	Profit before tax		108,000
less	Corporation tax		32,000
	Profit after tax		76,000
	Dividends paid		46,000
	Retained profit		30,000

Notice the number of different figures for profit in these accounts – gross profit, profit before tax, profit after tax, retained profit. Each figure represents a different calculation.

TASK 2

Lex Service is the leading automotive services company in the UK. Lex's activities are the distribution, contract hire and aftermarket operations for cars, trucks and lift trucks.

This is their profit and loss account.

Consolidated profit and loss account for the financial year ended 31 December 1996

	1996 £m	1995 £m
Turnover	1,564.2	1,556.9
Cost of sales	(1,326.4)	(1,328.4)
Gross profit	237.8	228.5
Net operating expenses	(200.9)	(199.1)
Operating profit	36.9	29.4
Income from interests in associated undertakings	25.0	22.8
Provision for closure and sale of business from continuing operations	–	(9.8)
Net profit on disposal of business from continuing operations	1.7	0.4
Loss on sale of fixed assets in continuing operations	(1.5)	(0.7)
Net interest payable and similar charges	(10.5)	(10.0)
Profit on ordinary activities before taxation	51.6	32.1
Taxation on profit on ordinary activities	(13.9)	(8.9)
Profit on ordinary activities after taxation	37.7	23.2
Equity minority interests	(2.0)	(2.2)
Profit for the financial year	35.7	21.0
Equity and non-equity shareholders' dividends	(18.2)	(16.0)
Retained profit for the financial year	17.5	5.0
Earnings per ordinary share	31.5p	20.4p
Dividends per ordinary share proposed and paid	16.0p	15.0p

Source: Lex Service plc, 2000

a Use the profit and loss account to explain why profit has increased.

b What might be included in the cost of sales?

c How much tax was paid by Lex Service plc in 1995 and 1996? Comment on your figures.

d Why have dividends increased from 1995 to 1996?

The balance sheet

As well as the profit and loss account, a second important record that a small business might draw up is a **balance sheet**. This shows the financial position of a business at a certain point in time. It shows sources of funds of a business and uses of those funds. Like the profit and loss account an unlimited company does not have to produce and publish a balance sheet, but it can be a useful document for owners.

A balance sheet is made up of three parts: assets, liabilities and owners' capital.

Assets are what the business owns. These might be **fixed assets** like vehicles, machinery or a factory which stay in the business for a period of time; or **current assets** like stock or cash which are held by the business for a short period of time before being used in production. A business might also have money owed to it by its customers – known as debtors – which it hopes would be paid up shortly.

Liabilities are what the business owes. These might be long-term liabilities (see Unit 21) such as loans, or current liabilities like an overdraft or money owed to creditors.

Owners' capital is the money that the owner has put into the business plus any profit that has been retained in the business.

A balance sheet, if it is calculated correctly, will always balance. In fact:

Assets = Liabilities + Owners' capital

is the way the balance will occur. Whatever a business purchases in the way of machinery, stock, etc. must be financed out of either the owners' capital or borrowing from other sources. This was shown in Unit 21.

Let us look at the balance sheet for Applewick Farm. As at 1 January 2001 the farm had the following assets and liabilities:

Fixed assets:	£	Long-term liabilities:	£
Farm buildings	125,000	Mortgage	100,000
Tractor and other vehicles	15,000	Loan for tractor	26,000
Farm machinery	15,000		
Current assets:	£	Current liabilities:	£
Stock	12,000	Creditors	11,000
Debtors	5,000		
Cash	45,000		
		Owners' capital:	£
		Capital	70,000
		Retained profit	10,000

There are two ways that a balance sheet can be set out. The traditional way is in a T shape. It is now possible to draw up the balance sheet for the farm.

Balance sheet of Applewick Farm as at 1.1.01

Fixed assets	£	Owners' capital	£
Buildings	125,000	Capital	70,000
Machinery	15,000	Retained profit	10,000
Vehicles	15,000		80,000
	155,000		
Current assets		**Long-term liabilities**	
Stock	12,000	Mortgage	100,000
Debtors	5,000	Bank loan	26,000
Cash	45,000		126,000
	62,000	**Current liabilities**	
		Creditors	11,000
	217,000		217,000

A balance of £217,000 is obtained where:

| Total assets (on left-hand side) | = | Owners' capital | + | Total liabilities (on right hand side) |

A second method of presentation is in the form of a column.
This is now the main way that balance sheets are presented.
Using the same figures as above, the vertical form would appear in the following way:

Balance sheet for Applewick Farm as at 1.1.01

	£	£	£
Fixed assets			
Building	125,000		
Machinery	15,000		
Vehicles	15,000		
			155,000
Current assets			
Stock	12,000		
Debtors	5,000		
Cash	45,000		
		62,000	
less **Current liabilities**			
Overdraft	0		
Creditors	11,000		
		11,000	
		51,000	
		206,000	
less **Long-term liabilities**			
Mortgage	100,000		
Bank loan	26,000		
		126,000	
Net assets employed		80,000	
Owners' capital			
Capital		70,000	
Retained profit		10,000	
Total capital and reserves		80,000	

In this method of presentation there is still a balance, but this time it is based on

Total assets – Total liabilities
(Net assets employed)
= Owners' capital

The balance for Applewick Farm here is £80,000.

TASK 3

When the Disney Lodge Health Studio was formed in January 1997, each of the owners had put £15,000 of their own savings into the business. By January 2001 they had seen the business grow considerably. They had installed a new gym with up-to-date fitness machines, valued at £7,000, in addition to the £28,000 worth of equipment they had originally purchased. The beauty salon had been improved with fittings costing £20,000 in 1999. A £2,000 computer system had been installed to store membership records.

They had arranged a £25,000 overdraft facility with their local bank but by January 2001 they only had an overdraft of £8,500. However, they still owed creditors £4,000 for some of their supplies. At the same time they were owed £6,000 in membership fees by their regular clients. Their stocks were valued at £5,000 and they held £2,000 in cash.

The owners had always put any net profit made back in the business. Up to January 2000, retained profit had totalled £15,700. This had helped to fund the improved equipment.

a Using either the T-shaped or vertical method of presentation, draw up a balance sheet for Disney Lodge Health Studio as at 1 January 2001. (You will need to include the 2000 net profit figure from Task 1.)

b What evidence is there to suggest that the Disney Lodge Health Studio is a successful business?

c What financial problems do you think the owners might face in the near future?

For a larger company, the structure of the balance sheet will be the same as shown above, but there will be a wider range of assets, owners' capital and liabilities. Let us look at the vertical balance sheet for Windsor Gifts Ltd, following on from its profit and loss account shown earlier in the unit.

Windsor Gifts Ltd Balance Sheet as at 31 December 2000

	£000	£000	£000
Fixed assets			
Premises		350	
Fixtures and fittings		80	
Vehicles		75	
		505	
Current assets			
Stock	168		
Debtors	120		
Cash at bank	45		
	333		
less Current liabilities			
Trade creditors	140		
Taxation owed	32		
Dividends owed	46		
	218		
Working capital		115	
Net assets employed		620	
Financed by:			
Shareholders' funds			
Ordinary share capital			
(300,000 shares at £1)	300		
Reserves	100		
Retained profit	30	430	
Long-term liabilities			
Bank loan		190	
Capital employed		620	

On this balance sheet, the use of funds is similar to a small company, but the sources of funds are different. Under current liabilities, the business can use the money it owes for tax and dividends for a short period of time before payment has to be made, as these two are paid after the end of the financial year. There is a new section called **shareholders' funds** where a record is made of what the business has raised from the shareholders/owners of the business. This is equivalent to owners' capital as discussed above. It also includes a figure for the money that the company has retained as profit in the past – known as reserves. In addition, there is the figure from the profit and loss account for retained profit. This money is used to expand the assets that the business owns, e.g. to buy more fittings for one of the gift shops.

The balance sheet for Windsor Gifts Ltd shows that the business has capital employed in it of £620,000, and working capital of £115,000. With a profit before tax of £108,000, from sales revenue of £830,000 it appears to be operating quite successfully. However, to be sure how well it is doing it would be important to compare 2000's figures with 1999's. For a public limited company the balance sheet is published for the general public. Plcs have to show this year's and last year's accounts when they are published.

TASK 4

Lex Service
Consolidated balance sheet at 31 December 1996

	1996 £m	1995 £m
Fixed assets		
Tangible assets	270.9	273.4
Investments in associated undertakings	78.3	65.8
Other investments	7.5	13.2
	356.7	352.4
Current assets		
Stocks	218.8	200.5
Debtors falling due within one year	104.1	102.7
Debtors falling due after more than one year	9.1	11.2
Cash at bank and in hand	7.3	15.4
	339.3	329.8
Creditors: amounts falling due within one year		
Bank loans and overdrafts	28.0	34.5
Creditors	266.6	225.1
	294.6	259.6
Net current assets	44.7	70.2
Total assets less current liabilities	401.4	422.6
Creditors: amounts falling due after more than one year		
Bank and other loans	67.0	85.2
Other creditors	43.0	29.1
Provisions for liabilities and charges	7.4	22.4
Net assets	284.0	285.9
Capital and reserves		
Called up share capital	29.4	29.3
Share premium account	120.4	118.6
Revaluation reserve	13.8	16.2
Profit and loss	112.9	114.6
Shareholders' funds	276.5	278.7
Equity shareholders' funds	275.5	277.7
Non-equity shareholders' funds – preference shares	1.0	1.1
Equity minority interest	7.5	7.2
	284.0	285.9

a Give two examples of
   i fixed assets
   ii current assets that Lex Service might own.

b Using the figures above, write a short report that explains to shareholders the major changes in the balance sheet between 1995 and 1996. You could word process this report and use diagrams and graphs to illustrate your points.

What is the difference between the profit and loss account and the balance sheet?

The balance sheet shows how a business has obtained and used finance over a given period of time, whereas the profit and loss account shows how well the business has been performing.

Some of the information from the profit and loss account is transferred to the balance sheet. This includes:

- retained profit, which is entered as a liability on the balance sheet
- **depreciation**, which affects the fixed assets.

Depreciation

Depreciation is the charge against a fixed asset to reflect its fall in value. Fixed assets lose value due to use, wear and tear or obsolescence (becoming out of date). In recent years, the rapid developments in new technology have meant that many assets are rejected as no longer efficient because a newer model has replaced them. Accountants work out how much an asset has depreciated and reflect this in the balance sheet and profit and loss account. This allows the company to write off the asset over time, making the accounts reflect the true value of the assets. This means that the book value of the asset will be reduced on a yearly basis.

The simplest way to calculate the depreciation charge is to use the straight line method, which is calculated as follows:

$$\text{Depreciation charge} = \frac{\text{Original cost} - \text{Scrap value}}{\text{Expected life}}$$

For example, a piece of machinery, bought for £20,000, with an expected life of 10 years and a scrap value of £4,000, will have an annual depreciation charge of:

$$\frac{£20,000 - £4,000}{10} = £1,600$$

The table below reflects the fall in value of the asset over time from its value of £20,000 when new in Year 0 to its scrap value of £4,000 in Year 10.

Year	0	1	2	3	4
Asset value	£20,000	£18,400	£16,800	£15,200	£13,600
Year	5	6	7	8	9
Asset value	£12,000	£10,400	£8,800	£7,200	£5,600
Year	10				
Asset value	£4,000				

Consolidated profit and loss account for the financial year ended 29 January 2000

	2000 Total	1999
	£m	£m
Turnover	1,425.4	1,239.1
Operating profit	180.3	157.9
Profit on disposal of business	2.4	–
Profit on disposal of fixed assets	4.1	–
Profit before interest	186.8	157.9
Net interest receivable	7.9	9.0
Profit on ordinary activities after taxation	140.2	123.9
Dividends	(76.4)	(69.1)
Profit for the year transferred to reserves	63.8	54.8
Earnings per share	38.4p	33.9p
Adjusted earnings per share (excluding exceptional items)	38.6p	32.9p
Diluted earnings per share	37.9p	33.6p

Consolidated balance sheet as at 29 January 2000

	2000 £m	1999 £m
Fixed assets	339.8	314.4
Current assets	607.3	538.7
Current liabilities		
Creditors: amounts falling due within one year	318.4	293.2
Net current assets	288.9	245.5
Total assets less current liabilities	628.7	559.9
Creditors: amounts falling due after more than one year	15.0	9.9
Provision for liabilities and charges	7.0	7.2
Net assets	606.7	542.8
Capital and reserves		
Called up share capital	37.4	37.4
Share premium account	3.7	3.7
Revaluation reserve	16.4	19.7
Other reserves	0.4	0.4
Profit and loss acount	548.8	481.6
Shareholders' funds	606.7	542.8

Source: Next plc, 2000.

Hold on to your Next trousers

Where is the nation buying its clothes now that Marks & Spencer has fallen from grace? For those not seduced by the lure of the value retailers, it seems to be Next.

Next's classic clothing with a fashionable twist has helped it to weather the retail storms which have shipwrecked larger rivals. While M&S got its knickers in a twist and Arcadia had problems with dress-down Fridays, Next has shrugged off its disastrous 1998.

Yesterday saw the company looking more frumpish than recently. Analysts were expecting like-for-like sales growth this year of 5 per cent, so when it only produced 3 per cent growth it was bound to end in tears. The share price dropped like an old pair of trousers from 580 to 504p, putting the stock on 13 times forward earnings.

The market's reaction seems unfair. If M&S had similar growth, the shareholders would be hanging banners in the street. The full-year figures, showing pre-tax profit up from £167m to £195m on the back of sales up from £1.24 billion to £1.43 billion, were respectable enough.

But what was more exciting was Next's plan to grow its online shopping service, with forecasts of £12m of sales through the Internet next year. The company is leveraging off the successful Next Directory, which already has a distribution and warehousing network, and the e-commerce venture cost just £120,000 to set up.

The only real difficulty with Next is that it is operating in an unloved sector. Even the advent of Next.co.uk is unlikely to push the shares up further in the short term, although the share buyback plan, announced yesterday, may have a positive effect.

Source: *Daily Telegraph*, 24 March 2000.

Chairman's statement

The year to January 2000 was another period of good growth for Next, with record profits and earnings per share. The trading profit before tax of £195.6m was 20 per cent higher than the previous year. Shareholders' funds increased by £63m to £606m and we continued to earn a post-tax return of 24 per cent on the enlarged capital. This strong performance enables the Board to recommend a final dividend of 14p, making a total of 21p for the year, which is an increase of 10 per cent. Over the last five years, dividends have increased by 133 per cent compared with a 91 per cent increase in trading profits.

Our strategy is to continue to build our market share in the UK and Eire by expanding our store space and by moving into new related product areas. We believe this presents the best opportunity for profitable growth.

During the year, we completed the £100m warehouse development programme, which will provide sufficient capacity to service our anticipated growth.

At the end of January we had net cash balances of £123m, an increase of £62m for the year. Your Board believes that Next will continue to generate a strong cash flow and that shareholder value can be enhanced by returning surplus capital to shareholders.

Source: Next plc, 2000.

Q Questions

1 What costs might be involved in developing and launching the online ordering service?

2 How might a retailer like Next fund the expansion into online ordering?

3 What changes have there been to the profitability of Next from 1999 to 2000?

4 What are the advantages and disadvantages of increasing the earnings per share?

5 What changes have occurred to the assets of Next from 1999 to 2000? How has Next financed these changes? (*Hint*: Use the information from the balance sheet.)

6 What might happen to the profit and share price of Next over the next few years? Explain your answer.

E Extension

Use the Internet or write to a similar retail outlet to Next (e.g. Marks & Spencer, Debenhams, Bhs) and obtain information on its accounts, including the balance sheet, profit and loss account and share price. Compare the two companies' performance and asset structure.

Cash flow and working capital

This unit is about the role of cash flow and working capital in business.

At the end of the unit, students should be able to:

- explain the importance of cash to a business

- understand how cash flow operates in a business

- understand how businesses may encounter cash flow problems and how the business investigates ways to improve cash flow

- explain the term working capital

- understand the importance of working capital in larger companies

- investigate ways in which companies can adjust their working capital to suit their needs

- apply their knowledge of cash flow and working capital to the accounts of a business.

What is cash?

In Unit 23 we defined cash as the asset that the business holds, which allows it to buy supplies and pay wages. We also explained the difference between cash and profit. In this unit we will look in more detail at the importance of cash to a business.

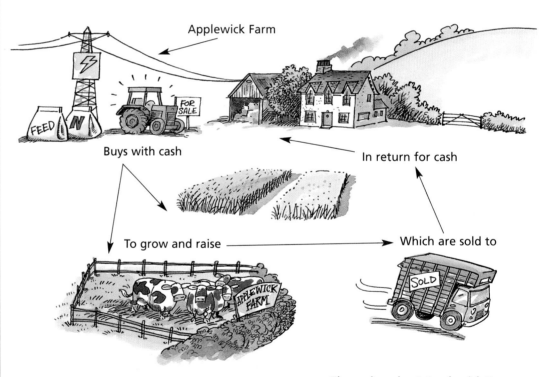

Applewick Farm

Buys with cash

In return for cash

To grow and raise

Which are sold to

The cash cycle at Applewick Farm

All businesses need cash to survive. Cash includes money that is held in the business, e.g. in a cash till or safe for meeting everyday transactions and money held in a bank or building society account to which there is immediate access. For small businesses the availability of cash to keep the business operating is vital. Take the example of Applewick Farm shown in the diagram, which produces a mixture of arable crops and beef cattle.

Applewick needs cash to pay a mortgage on the farm buildings, rates for the farm, to buy seeds, animal feed and fertiliser from suppliers, to pay wages to the workforce, and to pay interest on a loan for the machinery.

Applewick gets its cash from selling its wheat and barley to milling companies, and its beef cattle at the local market.

Unfortunately the times when the farm receives cash from its sales do not match the times when it has to pay out cash to its employees and its creditors.

Cash in:

Sales of beef cattle between April and December

Sales of wheat and barley between August and October

Cash out:

Payment of wages on monthly basis

Payment of electricity/heating every 3 months

Payment to suppliers on monthly account

Payment of rates annually in April

Payment of interest to the bank monthly

Payment of mortgage monthly

Therefore there will be several months of the year (January to March) when Applewick will be paying bills, but will be receiving no income. There will be other months, like April, when payments will be larger than revenue. For a business like Applewick Farm, it will be important that there is enough cash available during these months to meet the payments that have to be made. Otherwise the farm may not be supplied with seed, or animal feed or fertiliser; the bank may take possession of the machinery and the mortgage may be closed.

The flow of cash is the life blood of a business and needs to be carefully managed.

Cash flow

A **cash flow** shows when money is expected to come into or go out of a business over a period of time, and where it is coming from or going to. It was shown above that any business will need to keep a careful record of its cash flow. The cash flow for Applewick Farm for 2000 is shown in the spreadsheet:

Actual cash flow of Applewick Farm in 2000 (£000s)

Month:	Jan	Feb	Mar	Apr	May	Jun	Jul	Aug	Sep	Oct	Nov	Dec
Receipts:												
1 Sales of crops	–	–	–	–	–	–	–	8	15	12	–	–
2 Sales of beef cattle	–	–	–	3	5	7	6	5	4	8	9	10
3 **Total cash in:** (1 + 2)	–	–	–	3	5	7	6	13	19	20	9	10
Payments:												
4 Supplies	1.5	1.5	1.5	1.5	1.5	1.5	1.5	1.5	1.5	1.5	1.5	1.5
5 Wages	2	2	2	2	2	2	2	2	2	2	2	2
6 Owner withdrawals	1.2	1.2	1.2	1.2	1.2	1.2	1.2	1.2	1.2	1.2	1.2	1.2
7 Electricity	–	–	1	–	–	1	–	–	1	–	–	1
8 Heating	–	–	1.3	–	–	1.3	–	–	1.3	–	–	1.3
9 Rates	–	–	–	8	–	–	–	–	–	–	–	–
10 Mortgage payment	0.5	0.5	0.5	0.5	0.5	0.5	0.5	0.5	0.5	0.5	0.5	0.5
11 Interest on loan	0.2	0.2	0.2	0.2	0.2	0.2	0.2	0.2	0.2	0.2	0.2	0.2
12 **Total cash out:** (4 + 5 + 6 … + 11)	5.4	5.4	7.7	13.4	5.4	7.7	5.4	5.4	7.7	5.4	5.4	7.7
13 **Net cash flow** (3 – 12)	-5.4	-5.4	-7.7	-10.4	-0.4	-0.7	0.6	7.6	11.3	14.6	3.6	2.3
14 **Opening bank balance**	35	29.6	24.2	16.5	6.1	5.7	5.0	5.6	13.2	24.5	39.1	42.7
15 **Closing bank balance** (14 + 13)	29.6	24.2	16.5	6.1	5.7	5.0	5.6	13.2	24.5	39.1	42.7	45.0

Applewick's cash flow statement shows that it had £35,000 at the start of the year in its bank account. This was enough to cover the January to March period when it had no income coming into the business and the months of April, May and June when its costs were still higher than its revenue.

The owners of Applewick may also try to predict the next year's cash flow by drawing up a **cash flow forecast**. This would have the same structure as the spreadsheet above, but the figures would be estimates rather than actual figures.

TASK 1

The owners of Applewick Farm have decided to draw up a cash flow forecast for the coming year (2001). They have estimated that their revenue from sales will be as follows:

	Sales of crops (£000s)	Sales of cattle (£000s)
Jan	–	–
Feb	–	–
Mar	–	–
Apr	–	3
May	–	5
Jun	–	8
Jul	–	7
Aug	9	14
Sep	16	20
Oct	13	21
Nov	–	10
Dec	–	11

They have also worked out what they might be paying in costs, and are worried about some increases. Their figures for likely payments are as follows:

- wages to rise to £4,000 per month
- payment to suppliers to rise to £3,000 per month
- electricity to rise to £6,000 per year
- heating to rise to £8,000 per year
- rates to rise to £12,000.

It looked as though only their mortgage and interest payments would stay the same. They did not feel that they could take any more themselves for their own expenses than the £1,200 a month at present.

a From the information above draw up a cash flow forecast for the next 12 months for Applewick Farm. If possible, use a spreadsheet to do this.

b What problems, if any, do you see the business facing?

c How might Applewick Farm overcome some of the problems you have identified?

You could produce a report using desktop publishing software on the cash flow of Applewick Farm that includes the spreadsheet, the problems and the solutions.

Managing the cash flow

A business will often find that the inflows and outflows of cash do not balance and that problems occur. This may be particularly true for small firms which may find that their cash flow is very erratic. The causes of cash flow problems can include:

- A fall in sales will reduce receipts, e.g. if the business loses an important customer.
- A sudden increase in orders, though eventually leading to higher sales, will require an increase in expenditure on materials and supplies.
- An increase in the price of an important material will increase expenditure.
- A new competitor may suddenly take away a number of customers and reduce sales.
- The interest rates paid on loans or a mortgage may go up, which would increase the level of payments.
- Customers may be slow in paying for a service or goods received; receipts might therefore be delayed.

Where the lack of cash becomes severe, organisations may find themselves unable to pay bills, suppliers and wages. If this continues in the long run, the result may mean the closure of the firm (see Unit 26).

Companies therefore need to be able to find ways of managing the cash flow and reducing any problems that they may face. Possible solutions include:

- Encourage prompt payment from customers; ask for cash with sales.
- Try to arrange trade credit with suppliers, so that payment is delayed until the goods being produced with the supplies are sold.
- Reduce prices to increase sales and compete better against other businesses.
- Attempt to reduce expenditure through finding cheaper suppliers or reducing the use of electricity, heating etc. Reduce the level of stocks being held.
- The owners might draw less from the business during a period when the cash flow is unfavourable.
- Alternatively the owners might put more capital into the business to overcome any cash shortage.
- Through careful forecasting, it is possible to identify a future problem, and arrange an overdraft in advance.

TASK 2

A newly appointed manager at McBurgers has been asked to draw up a cash flow forecast for the restaurant. The first six months' cash flow forecast is outlined below.

	Jan	Feb	March	April	May	June
Opening balance	0	-3105.5	-2481	-894	-2072	-1917
Receipts						
Revenue from sales	1592.5	4062.5	5435	3770	4045	4317
Total income (A)	1592.5	4062.5	5435	3770	4045	4317
Outgoings						
Purchases to make burgers	490	1250	1660	1160	1360	1445
Heat and light	0	0	300	0	0	300
Advertising	250	30	30	30	30	30
Telephone	130	130	130	130	130	130
Promotions	300	200	200	100	100	100
Tax and insurance	58	58	58	58	0	0
Stationery	10	10	10	10	10	10
Rent and rates	500	500	500	500	500	500
Property insurance	0	300	0	0	0	0
Wages	960	960	960	960	960	960
Leasing	0	0	0	0	800	0
Franchise fee	2000	0	0	2000	0	0
Total outgoings (B)	4698	3438	3848	4948	3890	3475
A – B	-3105.5	624.5	1587	-1178	155	842
Closing balance	-3105.5	-2481	-894	-2072	-1917	-1075

a How might drawing up the cash flow forecast (CFF) help the manager with the restaurant?

b What problems are you able to identify from the CFF?

c What solutions might there be? Why might your suggestions not always work?

Working capital

We have already seen the importance of cash in a business. In larger businesses, cash remains an important asset, but there will be other sources of short-term funds which may help the business to survive from day to day.

Working capital is the difference between a firm's **current assets** (cash, debtors, cash, etc.) and its **current liabilities** (overdraft, creditors, etc.), and is calculated as:

Working capital = Current assets − Current liabilities

This can be shown in a working capital cycle. In the diagram you can see the following stages:

1 Parry Games Ltd has the choice of buying its raw materials either using cash or on credit, with 30 days to pay. By using credit it will need less cash.

2 These raw materials are added to those the company already holds in stock.

3 The stocks are used to manufacture the games it makes.

4 When made the games are held as finished stock. But the company does not want to keep them as stock too long.

5 It will hope that the stocks are soon sold to customers – large toy and games retailers – who will buy them either using cash or on credit, that is the customers will have a certain time to pay.

6 The company will eventually collect its cash from its debtors, and with the other cash be able to purchase or pay for more raw materials.

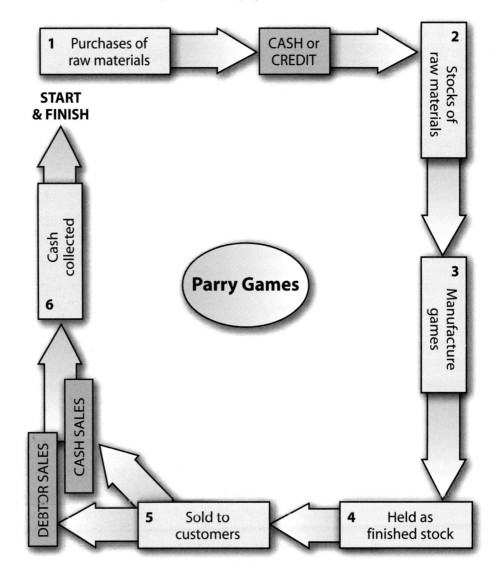

Working capital cycle for Parry Games

TASK 3

Dartington Glass

Dartington is one of Britain's leading manufacturers of glass, exporting to more than 50 countries. It has a workforce of 300 and retail sales of £20 million per year. The photographs show Dartington glass being made.

Six glassmaking teams at work. Every piece is produced by a team of glass blowers, led by the Master Blower

Molten glass is rolled on a smooth plate called a marver, after which the first bubble is blown

Molten glass from the furnace is sheared on to create a foot for the glass

a From the pictures, identify any elements that would form part of the working capital of Dartington Glass.

b Draw a working capital cycle for Dartington Glass, including any other elements that do not appear in the pictures.

c Why is working capital important for a company like Dartington Glass?

Controlling working capital in a company

Larger firms will seek to manage their working capital in a similar way to that in which smaller firms try to manage their cash flow in order to ensure that:

- it does not run out of working capital, because then it would have to stop production

- it does not hold too much working capital, because the money might be better used for other purposes, e.g. buying new machinery to expand the business.

If a company is short of working capital, there are a number of solutions. It could:

- take out an overdraft at the bank – or increase an existing one

- sell off some of its stocks to increase sales revenue, perhaps by offering lower prices (a sale)

- buy more of its raw materials on credit – or take longer to pay

- ask its customers to pay using only cash – or reduce the time given to debtors to pay up

- sell off a fixed asset, e.g. an item of machinery, to raise some cash.

TASK 4

Kwik-Fit Holdings plc

Consolidated Balance Sheets at 28 February 1999 and 28 February 1998

	1999 £m	1998 £m
Fixed assets		
Intangible assets – goodwill	74.6	–
Tangible assets	300.5	212.1
Investments	–	2.0
	375.1	214.1
Current assets		
Stocks	72.9	53.0
Debtors	54.5	41.0
Cash and short term deposits	34.6	26.4
	162.0	120.4
Creditors: amounts falling due within one year	(200.3)	(148.8)
Net current (liabilities)	(38.3)	(28.4)
Total assets less current liabilities	336.8	185.7
Creditors: amounts falling due after more than one year	(120.9)	(9.4)
Provisions for liabilities and charges	(16.6)	(12.0)
Net assets	199.3	164.3
Capital and reserves		
Called-up share capital	17.9	17.8
Share premium account	53.7	52.2
Profit and loss account	127.7	93.9
Equity shareholders' funds	199.3	163.9
Minority equity interests	–	0.4
Total capital employed	199.3	164.3

Source: Kwik-Fit Holdings plc, 2000.

a Why would Kwik-Fit hold stock?

b Calculate the working capital for 1998 and 1999. What has happened to working capital and why?

c What strategies might Kwik-Fit use in future years to ensure that it is not short of working capital?

Joe has decided to set up a sandwich shop to sell sandwiches and snacks to local offices. He has already done some market research and established that he can sell sufficient numbers of sandwiches to make a profit. His bank manager is happy with the progress he has made so far but would like him now to draw up a cash flow forecast to see how the cash can be managed.

Joe has estimated the following information to help with the cash flow forecast:

- At the start of the business (January), Joe will have £200 cash available in his bank account.

- Most of Joe's customers are individuals and pay in cash on the day. He expects to earn £400 per week from sales and that this will rise by £40 each month.

- One customer, a company, has agreed a contract with Joe where it will be invoiced for the month. Joe gives it the invoice on the 25th of the month and the company pays him on the 5th of the following month. He anticipates the monthly bill to be £550.

- His rental for the shop and kitchen is £450 per month; rates are a further £50 per month.

- He has estimated his fuel, heating and lighting bill at £80 per month.

- The wage bill for himself and a part-time worker comes to £600 per month.

- Joe will have to pay suppliers in cash as he is a new business with no credit rating. He has estimated that this will cost him £300 in the first month, rising by £30 per month as sales increase.

- Joe has decided not to buy a van, but to use his own car to make deliveries. His suppliers deliver his stock to the shop. The repayments on the car are £70 per month and he has calculated other running costs including depreciation and road tax at a further £15 per month.

- Administration costs, advertising and other expenses average £40 per month.

Q Questions

1 Use the information above to work out the first six months' cash flow forecast (CFF). (You may want to refer to the cash flow forecast earlier in the unit to help you with the layout.) It is best to set this up on a spreadsheet.

2 What reaction might Joe and the bank manager have to the CFF?

3 The bank manager thinks that Joe has underestimated some of his expenses. What might the bank manager ask Joe to re-estimate and why?

4 Joe's suppliers decide to raise their prices by 5 per cent. Calculate the effect that this will have on the cash flow.

5 Joe has considered raising the price of his sandwiches to cover the increased cost of supplies. Would you advise Joe to do this?

6 Draw up a table of the current assets and current liabilities for Joe.

E Extension

Small businesses complain that they have suffered with cash flow problems because of late payment by larger companies that they subcontract to. To try to help this, the government brought in legislation called the Late Payment of Commercial Debts (Interest) Act (1998). Find what the legislation did to help small businesses and investigate any cases where the legislation has been used.

Analysing the accounts

This unit is about how businesses keep accounts to measure their performance.

At the end of the unit, students will be able to:

- interpret a company balance sheet and profit and loss account

- understand the different methods used to measure the success of a company

- calculate ratios on profitability, liquidity and investment and interpret their findings.

Looking at the accounts of a business

In Unit 23, we identified that a range of stakeholders would want to know how well a company was doing. The list included the shareholders, who might want to know what dividend they are going to receive, and workers, who may use profitability as an indicator of their job security.

While most companies will identify a range of factors to determine how well they are doing, including market share, turnover and the value of their assets, the most frequently used measures will be made from the accounts of the company. The profit and loss account and the balance sheet allow companies not only to judge their own performance over time, but also to judge themselves against competitors.

When a company chooses to measure its success by looking at profit levels over time, it may find the picture misleading. Look at the information below:

Company ABC	1999	2000
Sales	£870,000	£900,000
Net profit	£35,000	£36,000

At first glance, the company is doing well. Sales have increased by £30,000 and profit by £1,000. While the comment that the company is doing well is not incorrect, the situation may require a little more attention. If we calculate the percentage change in the figures, the picture should become clearer.

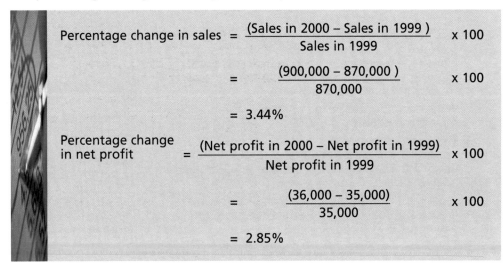

$$\text{Percentage change in sales} = \frac{(\text{Sales in 2000} - \text{Sales in 1999})}{\text{Sales in 1999}} \times 100$$

$$= \frac{(900,000 - 870,000)}{870,000} \times 100$$

$$= 3.44\%$$

$$\text{Percentage change in net profit} = \frac{(\text{Net profit in 2000} - \text{Net profit in 1999})}{\text{Net profit in 1999}} \times 100$$

$$= \frac{(36,000 - 35,000)}{35,000} \times 100$$

$$= 2.85\%$$

This shows that although the level of sales and net profit were both rising, they were not rising at the same rate. Sales were in fact increasing at a faster rate than net profit and the firm may, as a result, want to look at ways of reducing costs to keep net profit margins higher.

TASK 1

Look at the five-year financial history of Next plc.

Five-year history, Next plc

Year ending January	2000 £m	1999 £m	1998 £m	1997 £m	1996 £m
Turnover	1,425.4	1,239.1	1,176.8	946.8	773.8
Profit before interest	186.8	157.9	173.2	145.6	129.1
Net interest income	7.9	9.0	10.8	13.2	12.8
Profit before taxation	194.7	166.9	184.0	158.8	141.9
Taxation	(54.5)	(43.0)	(47.4)	(40.6)	(36.4)
Profit after taxation	140.2	123.9	136.6	118.2	105.5
Dividends	(76.4)	(69.1)	(66.6)	(55.6)	(44.0)
Profit transferred to reserves	63.8	54.8	70.0	62.6	61.5
Shareholders' funds	606.7	542.8	489.6	420.6	359.0
Dividend per share	21.0p	19.1p	18.0p	15.0p	11.75p
Earnings per share	38.4p	33.9p	36.9p	32.0p	28.6p

Source: Next plc, 2000.

Using the raw data, plus your own calculation, write a financial section for the annual report, outlining how well Next is doing. (*Hint*: You may want to use a spreadsheet to make calculation easier, and some of your results on trends might be presented as graphs.)

Ratios

To help companies compare their performance more effectively, accountants will use **ratio analysis** – a mathematical way of comparing one figure with another. The company can then use these ratios to:

- compare their own performance over time
- compare their performance to that of other companies (usually of a similar size and in the same sector).

There are three areas that ratios are used to judge:

- Profitability – ratios in this area measure how well a company is doing by comparing profit to other factors such as sales and capital invested.
- **Liquidity** – ratios in this area seek to establish whether or not the company can pay its debts.
- Return on investment – this area is usually important to existing and potential investors who might want to know what returns are likely on their investment.

Throughout this unit, we will be referring to the profit and loss account and balance sheet for Windsor Gifts Ltd that first appeared in Unit 23.

Profit and loss account of Windsor Gifts Ltd for the year ending 31.12.2000

		£	£
	Sales revenue		830,000
less	Cost of sales		417,000
	Gross profit		413,000
less	Expenses		305,000
	Profit before tax		108,000
less	Corporation tax		32,000
	Profit after tax		76,000
	Dividends paid		46,000
	Retained profit		30,000

Windsor Gifts Ltd Balance Sheet as at 31 December 2000

		£000	£000	£000
	Fixed assets			
	Premises		350	
	Fixtures and fittings		80	
	Vehicles		75	
			505	
	Current assets			
	Stock	168		
	Debtors	120		
	Cash at bank	45		
		333		
less	*Current liabilities*			
	Trade creditors	140		
	Taxation owed	32		
	Dividends owed	46		
		218		
	Working capital		115	
	Net assets employed		620	
	Financed by:			
	Shareholders' funds			
	Ordinary share capital			
	(300,000 shares at £1)	300		
	Reserves	100		
	Retained profit	30		430
	Long-term liabilities			
	Bank loan			190
	Capital employed			620

Profitability ratios
There are three useful ratios that help to measure profitability:
- return on net assets employed
- gross profit margin
- net profit margin.

Return on net assets employed

This ratio measures the profitability of a company by assessing the profit made from the capital invested in it. The higher the return, the better the company is performing and the happier the owners and managers.

Return on net assets employed is calculated by using the ratio:

$$\frac{\text{Net profit before tax}}{\text{Net assets employed}} \times 100$$

For Windsor Gifts Ltd, in 2000 the net profit before tax was £108,000 (from the profit and loss account) and the value of net assets employed was £620,000 (from the balance sheet). Therefore its ratio for 2000 would be:

$$\text{Return on net assets} = \frac{£108,000}{£620,000} \times 100 = 17.4\%$$

This figure means that for every £1 invested in the company, 17.4p is earned in net profit before tax. It shows how well the management of the business has used the assets employed in the business to generate profits. It could be used to compare with previous year's results or with other firms in the industry in order to assess how well the company is performing.

Gross profit margin

This ratio measures the profitability of a company by assessing the gross profit made from the level of sales. Again, the higher the figure, the better.

Gross profit margin is calculated by using the ratio:

$$\frac{\text{Gross profit}}{\text{Sales revenue}} \times 100$$

For Windsor Gifts Ltd in 2000, the gross profit was £413,000 and the sales revenue was £830,000. Therefore its ratio for 2000 would be:

$$\text{Gross profit margin} = \frac{£413,000}{£830,000} \times 100 = 49.75\%$$

This figure shows that for every £1 of sales, the company was making just under 50p of gross profit.

Net profit margin

This ratio measures the profitability of a company by assessing the net profit made from the level of sales. Again, the higher the figure, the better.

Net profit margin is calculated by using the ratio:

$$\frac{\text{Net profit before tax}}{\text{Sales revenue}} \times 100$$

For Windsor Gifts Ltd in 2000, the net profit before tax was £108,000 and the sales revenue was £830,000. Therefore, its ratio for 2000 would be:

$$\text{Net profit margin} = \frac{£108,000}{£830,000} \times 100 = 13.0\%$$

This figure shows that for every £1 of sales, the company was making 13p net profit.

The difference between gross and net profit before tax is expenses. Comparing the two ratios over time allows the company to compare the effect of expenses on profit. For example, look at the results for Windsor Gifts Ltd for 1999 and 2000 shown in the table below.

	1999	2000
Gross profit margin	49%	49.75%
Net profit margin	16%	13%

While the gross profit margin had improved slightly, the net profit margin had fallen. This is accounted for by an increase in expenses, an area that the company may wish to investigate more fully.

TASK 2

Look at the profit and loss account for Company ABC Ltd. Using your knowledge of profitability ratios, write a report to the managers of the company, explaining how well the company is doing.

Profit and loss account for Company ABC Ltd
for the years ended 31 March 1999 and 31 March 2000

	1999 (£000s)	2000 (£000s)
Turnover	414	400
− Cost of sales	305	280
Gross profit	109	120
− Administration fee	83	80
Operating (net) profit	26	40
− Tax on profit	6	10
Profit after tax	20	30
+ Balance brought forward	20	4
	40	34

Liquidity ratios

Liquidity is the term used to define assets that can quickly be turned into cash. Assets such as stock are considered more liquid than the premises, for example, because it is easier to sell stock than dispose of the premises. Cash/cash flow is vital to a company's ability to pay debts, and therefore a ratio that measures how easily cash can be raised to pay immediate bills is important. There are two useful ratios that help to decide whether or not the company can pay its debts:

- current ratio (working capital ratio)
- acid test ratio.

Current Ratio

This ratio shows how well a business is able to meet its short-term debts from its current assets.

Current ratio is calculated by using the ratio:

$$\frac{\text{Current assets}}{\text{Current liabilities}}$$

Windsor Gifts' ratio for 2000 is:

$$\text{Current ratio} = \frac{£333,000}{£218,000} = 1.5$$

For Windsor Gifts, the figure 1.5 means that for every £1 of debt, the company has £1.50 of current assets. Ideally, the figure for the current ratio should be between 1.5 and 1.8. If the figure gets below this, there may be insufficient assets to cover the debt. A figure much higher than 1.8 does not indicate cash shortages, but it suggests that the assets are not being put to a sufficiently profitable use. It is pointless to hold too much cash and stock.

Companies, as with all ratios, may also use the current and acid test ratios to compare their performance over time and against rivals.

Acid test ratio

This ratio is a much tighter way of looking at whether or not a company can pay its debts. Stock is removed from the calculation of current assets because the company may not be able to sell it quickly or at the right price.

Acid test ratio is calculated by using the ratio:

$$\frac{\text{Current assets} - \text{Stock}}{\text{Current liabilities}}$$

For Windsor Gifts, the ratio would be:

$$\text{Acid test ratio} = \frac{£165,000}{£218,000} = 0.76$$

For Windsor Gifts, the figure 0.76 means that for every £1 of debt, the company has £0.76 of current assets minus stock (mainly cash and debtors). Ideally, the figure for the acid test ratio should be between 0.5 and 1. If the figure gets below this, there may be insufficient cash to cover the debt, a worrying sign for the company.

TASK 3

ABC Company Ltd balance sheet as at 31.12.2000
(Figures for 1999 are in brackets)

	£m	£m
Fixed assets		33 (35)
Current assets		
Stocks	14 (12)	
Debtors	9 (7)	
Cash	3 (4)	
	26 (26)	
Current liabilities		
Trade creditors	12 (8)	
Overdraft	6 (4)	
	18 (12)	
Working capital		8 (11)
Net assets employed		41 (46)
Financed by		
Shareholders' funds		
Issued share capital		18 (18)
Reserves and retained profit	18 (23)	
Long-term liabilities		
Mortgage loan		5 (5)

a Calculate the current ratio of ABC Company Ltd for 1999 and 2000.

b Calculate the acid test ratio for 1999 and 2000.

c Using your results, write a short report on the liquidity of the company.

Return on investment ratios

Current and potential investors will want to be able to measure how good their investment is or could be. They may be considering a variety of potential investments including the bank, and want to know which option will give them the best return on their investment. The two ratios which might be helpful here are:

- return on capital employed (ROCE)
- gearing.

Return on capital employed

This ratio shows how successfully the management of the business has used the money invested by shareholders.

Return on capital employed is calculated by using the ratio:

$$\frac{\text{Profit after tax}}{\text{Shareholders' fund}} \times 100$$

For Windsor Gifts the ratio for 2000 is:

$$\text{ROCE} = \frac{£76,000}{£430,000} \times 100 = 17.7\%$$

This figure shows that for every £1 of shareholders' money invested, the company has made 17.7p. The higher the figure, the better. It should be remembered that there are external factors that may affect company profit levels including economic recession, legislation and trade policies.

Gearing

This ratio shows how much the business is using outside loans to expand its operations. As loans are thought to be more risky than share capital because they have to be paid back, a low gearing is considered favourable.

Gearing is calculated by using the ratio:

$$\frac{\text{Loan capital}}{\text{Total capital}} \times 100$$

For Windsor Gifts, the loan capital is £190,000 and the total capital is £620,000 (both figures from the balance sheet).

The ratio for 2000 is:

$$\text{Gearing} = \frac{£190,000}{£620,000} \times 100 = 30.6\%$$

This figure shows that 30.6% of all the capital invested in the company came from loans. This helps to expand the business faster but it is risky because the loans eventually have to be paid back. The higher the gearing, the faster the business can grow but the more risk if there is a sudden problem because the company has to be able to pay the higher levels of interest on the loans. Shareholders might feel safer with a gearing of less than 30 per cent.

These ratios therefore can help some of the users mentioned earlier to analyse a company's accounts. Other sources of information, such as company reports, articles in newspapers and annual shareholders' meetings will also provide useful non-numerate information about the business.

TASK 4

Look at the balance sheet for ABC Company Ltd in Task 3.

a Calculate the return on capital employed ratio for 1999 and 2000.

b Calculate the gearing ratio for 1999 and 2000.

c Using your results, write a short report on how good an investment ABC Company Ltd is.

Liquidity – the ability to convert an asset into cash.

Ratio analysis – a way of comparing one figure with another, used to look at the accounts of a business.

Asda plc Balance sheet at 27 April, 1996

	1996 £m	1995 £m
Fixed assets		
Tangible assets	2,502.6	1,927.7
Investments	1.0	75.7
Colleague share ownership plan	33.0	16.7
	2,536.6	2,020.1
Current assets		
Stocks	307.4	275.2
Debtors	96.2	103.0
Investments	315.2	428.6
Cash at bank and in hand	22.4	14.7
	741.2	821.5
Creditors: amounts falling due within one year		
Borrowings	(93.1)	(110.7)
Other creditors	(880.9)	(757.5)
	(974.0)	(868.4)
Net current (liabilities)/assets	(232.8)	(46.9)
Total assets less current liabilities	2,303.8	1,973.2
Creditors: amounts falling due after more than one year		
Borrowings (including convertible capital bonds)	(515.1)	(328.4)
Other creditors	(0.1)	(0.3)
Provisions for liabilities and charges	(130.9)	(151.3)
	1,657.7	1,493.2
Capital and reserves		
Called up share capital	731.8	726.2
Share premium account	306.8	302.6
Revaluation reserve	98.8	83.9
Profit and loss account	520.3	380.5
Equity shareholders' funds	1,657.7	1,493.2

Source: Asda plc, 2000.

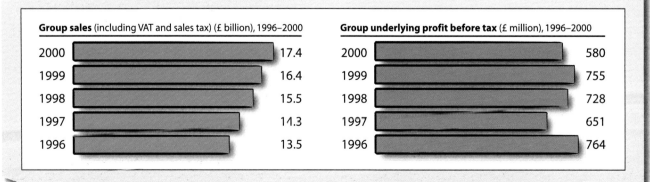

Group sales (including VAT and sales tax) (£ billion), 1996–2000

2000	17.4
1999	16.4
1998	15.5
1997	14.3
1996	13.5

Group underlying profit before tax (£ million), 1996–2000

2000	580
1999	755
1998	728
1997	651
1996	764

Source: J Sainsbury plc, Annual Report and Accounts 2000.

Asda plc five-year statistics

	1996 £m	1995 £m	1994 £m	1993 £m	1992 £m
Turnover, excluding value added tax	6,042.3	5,285.3	4,822.2	4,613.8	4,529.1
Results before exceptional items:					
Operating profit	316.7	251.1	196.7	190.0	180.0
Share of profits of associates	3.1	2.7	1.3	1.2	2.1
Net interest	(15.2)	(7.6)	(15.0)	(50.8)	(95.3)
Profit before tax	304.6	246.2	183.0	140.4	86.8
Earnings per share (pence)	7.71	5.90	4.36	3.97	1.20
Number of stores	206	203	202	201	206
Total sales area (000 square feet)	8,436	8,210	8,134	8,099	8,241
Average sales area per store (000 square feet)	41.0	40.4	40.3	40.3	40.0

Source: Asda plc, 2000.

Asda plc Group Profit and Loss Account 52 weeks ended 27 April 1996

	1996 £m	1995 £m
Sales	6,531.1	5,682.6
Value added tax	488.8	397.3
Turnover	6,042.3	5,285.3
Operating costs	5,725.6	5,034.2
Operating profit	316.7	251.1
Share of profits of associated undertakings	3.1	2.7
Release of provision for reorganisation of group businesses	–	11.0
Profit on ordinary activities before interest	319.8	264.8
Net interest payable	(8.3)	(7.6)
Profit on ordinary activities before taxation	311.5	257.2
Taxation	(83.2)	(78.6)
Profit for the financial year	228.3	178.6
Dividends	(75.5)	(63.9)
Retained profit for the financial year	152.8	114.7
Earnings per ordinary share	Pence	Pence
Basic	7.96	6.16
Before exceptional items	7.71	5.90
Dividend per ordinary share	2.65	2.20
Total recognised gains and losses relating to the year	243.2	178.6

Source: Asda plc, 2000.

Q Questions

1 Calculate the profit to sales ratio for Asda for 1995 and 1996 (use either operating profit or profit before tax).

2 Calculate the annual percentage change in sales from 1992 until 1996.

3 Do you think that Asda is doing well?
(*Hint*: Use the evidence from Questions 1 and 2.)

4 Has Asda got a liquidity problem?
Explain your answer.

5 What other indicators could you use to measure how well Asda is doing?

6 Compare the profitability of Asda to its rival, Sainsbury's. Using evidence, decide which company you would prefer to be a shareholder in.

(Alternative: Students could collect their own annual reports and produce group presentations analysing how well the company has done compared to previous years and rivals.)

E Extension

Obtain a copy of the balance sheet and profit and loss account for J. Sainsbury plc. Answer question 6 by using detailed, comparative ratio analysis.

Success and failure in business

This unit is about how businesses measure success and failure.

At the end of the unit, students should be able to:

- explain how success can be measured in a company

- understand factors that may influence the success and failure of a company

- explain how a company is wound up

- comment on strategies to improve profitability.

Success

Many of the leading companies like Microsoft, Virgin and Marks & Spencer grew out of successful, small companies. An indicator of their success was the profit that they made and this profit allowed them to put more money into the business to help it expand, and attracted other people to invest in the company. In 1991, a survey of small businesses by Coopers & Lybrand asked a group of entrepreneurs how they measured the success of their business. The rankings they gave to the measures are shown in the graph.

Ranking of how small business proprietors measure success

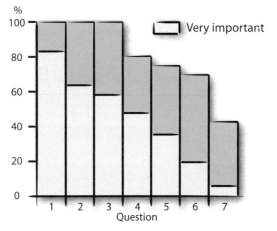

How do you measure success?

1 Quality of product/service
2 Financial performance
3 Development of an effective management team
4 Ability to sleep at night
5 Standing in industry
6 Balance of work/leisure
7 Standing in business community

Source: 1991 Coopers & Lybrand survey

The survey showed that financial success alone is not sufficient for these entrepreneurs. They saw quality and customer service as the most important factor, with financial success as the second most important factor. Being able to develop a good team to run a business was seen as another important factor.

There is a number of reasons why making most profit might not be seen as a major success factor for a small business:

- If the owners have to work too hard to achieve maximum profit, they might prefer to gain less profit, but be able to sleep at night.

- Getting the quality of a product or service right might mean that costs are higher, and short-term profits lower, than if corners are cut.

- Too much financial success would lead to higher tax to pay and may make the business an attractive one to be taken over by a larger company.

- The owners might have different objectives for the business (see Unit 3).

- The owners may be looking towards long-term survival rather than short-term profit.

TASK 1

Hewlett-Packard's profits soar

Computer company Hewlett-Packard has announced higher-than-expected profits, giving rise to hopes the results will spark a fresh rally in technology stocks.

The sharp growth was largely due to the company's cost cutting and surging sales of printers and home computers.

Hewlett Packard earned $1 billion, or 99 cents per share, in the third quarter, compared with $696 million, or 66 cents per share, in the same period last year.

Analysts had forecast the company would make 85 cents a share in the quarter.

In after-hours trading in the US, Hewlett-Packard's shares roared ahead to trade at more than $120 after closing at $111.5.

'We posted what I would characterise as superb results,' Hewlett-Packard chief executive Carly Fiorina said.

'We had a great quarter, we made truly remarkable strides.'

The company's revenues came to $10.7 billion, up from $9.53 billion, boosted by a 62 per cent surge in home computer revenues and a 93 per cent rise in notebook revenues.

Ms Fiorina also said the company planned to concentrate on new Internet businesses and sell off assets, such as its specialised software business.

'We're on target with our vision of a world where literally everything is connected,' she said. 'That all is supported by an Internet infrastructure that is always on.'

Source: BBC News Online, 17 August 2000.

a What reasons are there for the higher than expected profits?

b Why would people want to buy shares in Hewlett Packard as a result of the announcement?

c Why do companies use analysts to forecast sales and profit levels for them?

d What factors may affect the profit of Hewlett Packard? Is the company able to control all these factors?

TASK 2

Research a company that you believe to be successful.

a What measures do you think indicate the success of the company? Give evidence to support your answer.

b In groups, look at the range of success indicators that you have chosen and produce a composite list of how success can be measured in a company.

c Have you found anything in your research that you think detracts from the success of the company? What was it and how did it affect the success of the company?

In a larger company, there are more stakeholders and more views on how success can be measured. Different people may use different ways to look at a simple measure like profit. These could include:

- Shareholders – they will be interested in the profits of the company, the size of the dividends paid and the earnings per share (profit after tax per share issued).

- Outside investors – they will also be interested in profits, dividends and earnings per share as they will be comparing them with other companies on the Stock Exchange.

- Managers – for them profit will be important as a low profit may lead to a takeover which could cost them their jobs. But they will also measure success by sales levels and market share. These will be important to give them status with other managers.

- Employees – if there is an incentive scheme, then they will want good profits or sales to increase their bonus. But they might also measure success by the number employed or the percentage wage increase they might get.

It is possible for these different measures to conflict with each other. A business might cut jobs, close factories and reduce pay in order to reduce costs and increase profits and dividends. In the eyes of the shareholders the business is a success. But in the eyes of redundant workers it is a failure.

A business might reduce prices to increase sales and increase market share – but profits and dividends are cut. The managers might be happy if the business is bigger in the market, but the shareholders will be unhappy as their earnings are reduced.

With larger businesses therefore it is more difficult to say what is a successful business.

Failure

If profit is generally seen as the measure of success, then loss is the measure of failure. Loss occurs when the costs of the company exceed the revenue. While companies may suffer loss at particular points in their history, continuous losses will eventually lead to the closure of the company.

Failure in a small business

When an unlimited liability company like a small business fails, the result can be far more serious for the owners than if a limited liability company fails. This is because the owners might lose not just what they put into the business, but other possessions until all the debts are covered. The result might be that the owner becomes **bankrupt**. This is the process where the creditors of the business (e.g. a bank which has loaned the owner money, or a supplier who has provided goods but not been paid for them) asks a court to declare the owner bankrupt. The assets of the business – and possibly the owner – are then sold off and the proceeds divided between the creditors.

Why do small businesses fail? There are a number of possible reasons:

- Lack of business expertise – the entrepreneur might lack some of the all round skills needed to run a business alone.

- The market was just not there or had fallen due to recession – the number of customers that a business attracts may be too low to sustain it.

- Shortage of finance – either the amount of capital might be too low, or the business might run out of cash as sales are lower than expected. This might well occur if the business tries to expand too quickly.

- Too much is withdrawn from the business – there is a temptation for sole traders to take money out of the business for their own income, rather than using it to meet future bills.

It was a feature of the recession in the UK in the early 1990s that many small businesses went out of existence. While some may have gone bankrupt, there are other reasons why small businesses cease to exist:

- They might become limited companies, or change their name.

- They might be taken over by another business.

- The owner might decide that he or she could earn more money in another business.

- The owner may retire or die.

Failure in a large company

Unlike a sole trader, a private limited company or a plc is set up by law. Therefore the process of winding up a company is more complicated.

These are the stages leading to a company being wound up:

- The company makes a loss or there is a sudden fall in sales.

- The creditors of the company – banks, suppliers, the government – are worried that they will not be paid back or the shareholders are worried that they will lose all their investment.

- Creditors or shareholders ask a court to appoint an **Official Receiver** who will take over and run the company.

- The Official Receiver may see if he or she can find a buyer for the company as a going concern.

- If not, the Receiver will sell off the assets of the firm, and pay off the creditors. Any money remaining will be divided between the shareholders.

- This final stage is known as **liquidation**; the company ceases to exist.

Many companies which face losses do not end up being wound up. The management and shareholders might find another company willing to take over the business before a Receiver is appointed. It might be a competitor which wants to increase its market share. The takeover of a loss-making Habitat (part of the Storehouse Group) by the Swedish furniture retailer IKEA is a good example. In recent years a number of companies have been bought by their management in order to keep them going (a **management buy-out**).

TASK 3

Character shares fall 17%

Shares in Character Group, the struggling UK toys distributor, dropped 17 per cent on Friday after it warned that full-year results would fall short of market expectations.

Character, which distributes products for the *Star Wars*, *Chicken Run* and *Toy Story* films, blamed poor summer weather for the sales decline.

It said the usual upturn in August business had not materialised this year as retailers deferred their Christmas orders due to difficult trading conditions in the toy market.

'The losses experienced in the second half are unlikely to be significantly less than those experienced in the first half, Character said.

Earlier this year, the company blamed large quantities of unsold *Star Wars* goods for a significant first-half loss.

In addition to film-related toys, Character also commands a large share of the UK water gun market where sales suffered as the British summer remained elusive.

Richard King, chairman, said 'A water gun is not exactly a necessity when it's pouring down with rain.'

He said a time consuming and expensive reorganisation also contributed to the ailing balance sheet.

Mr King predicted that the company would return to profit by expanding its range to encompass products that also appeal to teenagers and adults.

In the coming year, the group will focus on its international business, including Japan, where Character's new digital camera has taken a 10 per cent market share after four weeks on sale.

Source: FT.com, *Financial Times*, 18 August 2000.

a What factors led to the Character Group making a loss?

b Will the loss mean that the company will have to be wound up? Explain your answer.

c What might be the problems of expanding the range of products to return the company to profit?

d What other methods could the company use to restore profits other than by expanding its range?

Ways of improving profit/ minimising loss

Businesses that find themselves making a loss or experiencing falling profit levels will seek to rectify the problem as soon as possible. Profit is the difference between revenue and costs and therefore there are three options for the business:

• Reduce costs.

• Increase revenue.

• A combination of both.

Reduce costs

For many loss-making companies, the first possible way to improve profitability is to cut costs. This will be an option only if the company has been run with some degree of inefficiency, or has costs that can be cut without affecting output. As with revenue, each option will bring with it drawbacks as well as benefits and cost cutting methods have to be carefully planned. The most common cost cutting options include:

• cutting labour costs, e.g. redundancies, reducing bonuses and restructuring the organisation

• reducing the size of the plant to reduce rent and rates

• renegotiating deals with suppliers or changing suppliers to buy cheaper raw materials

• reducing promotions and sponsorships

• cutting investment in equipment, e.g. not replacing machines as early as had been planned, stopping new projects

• reducing bills and administration costs, e.g. raising awareness of the need to keep fuel usage to a minimum, sending post second class.

Increase revenue

Revenue is calculated as:

Revenue = Average selling price x Output

For a business to increase revenue there is the option of altering price, volume of sales or both. This is not as simple as it may seem, as altering one variable often affects the other, e.g. a decision to alter price may affect the level of sales.

- Alter the price. Businesses can seek either to raise or lower the price. The decision rests on a number of factors. These include the following:
  - The price charged by competitors – will customers simply go somewhere else if it is cheaper?
  - Availability of competitors – if you raise your price but there is no other choice locally, customers may be forced to continue buying your product.
  - Loyalty of customers – customers may be prepared to pay a higher price because they are loyal to the business, perhaps because it offers a good after-sales service or it is a branded item.

M&S banks on drastic new makeover

More than 4,000 jobs axed and 38 European stores closed in attempt to reverse slide

The ailing Marks & Spencer store group yesterday embarked on a radical retrenchment in an attempt to restore its faded fortunes, slashing 4,390 jobs and closing its 38-strong chain of European stores.

The store chain – which has been battered by a sea change in shopping habits as consumers have deserted the middle market in favour of discounters and designer brands – is also axing its loss-making mail-order business and has put its two US businesses up for sale.

At the same time the huge new flagship M&S store in central Manchester – built after the city centre was devastated by an IRA bomb – is to be sliced in half, with the unwanted half being sold to rival Selfridges.

Chairman Luc Vandevelde said he intended to concentrate on improving the UK stores and winning back previously loyal customers. The priority, he said, would be to concentrate on 'classically stylish' fashions with the quality and fit M&S was once famous for. Prices will also be cut.

The pressure on Mr Vandevelde to turn the business round is growing almost daily. When the Belgian supermarket boss was headhunted to join M&S a year ago, he said it would take two years to rebuild M&S. Halfway to that self-imposed deadline, there is still no sign of any improvements, and yesterday he admitted that M&S was in far worse shape than he thought when he took the job. 'If I had known then what I know now, I would have acted earlier.'

The 38 European stores, including 18 in France, will close by the end of the year at the cost of 3,350 jobs.

A further 690 jobs will be lost in the mail-order business and

350 in the group's Baker Street head office. Mr Vandevelde said he was sorry 'to disappoint the large number of staff who have been doing an excellent job'. It will cost £300m to close the European and mail-order operations – and save £50m a year.

Mr Vandevelde described his new plan as 'a dramatic, urgent, thorough correction' to halt the decline of the group, which until 1998 was viewed as the gold standard for the retailing business. At that point, the chain's sales fell off a cliff and it has been unable to halt the slide ever since. Its profits have slumped from more than £1bn to £557m, and City analysts are expecting M&S to bring in £100m less than that this year.

M&S has made several vain attempts to win back business - from special offers to its 'I'm normal' advertising campaign last year featuring a naked size 16 model running across fields. It has changed its trademark carrier bags, started buying more clothes from abroad to cut

costs and launched an expensive range of upmarket designer clothes under the Autograph label. Every member of the board has been replaced and at one point the chain had more than 30 firms of outside consultants working on improving the store.

So far, however, its efforts have had little effect. Its advertising campaign was panned and the Autograph range has fallen short of sales targets.

The chain's new answer is to concentrate on shoppers aged over 35 – who account for 70% of the clothing market. Mr Holmes said M&S will now focus on items ranging from skirts and blazers to classic white shirts, sweaters and jeans. Meanwhile, Autograph will continue to provide higher priced fashion from designers like Hussein Chalayan and milliner Philip Treacy. Two thirds of the stores are to be given low-cost revamps. Out will go beige walls, wood and worn carpets. In their place will be bright white walls and more

Source: *The Guardian,* 30 March 2001

Marks & Spencers is trying to combine reduced costs with increased revenue to boost profits

Businesses will need to know how sensitive their customers are to price changes before altering the price. In markets where there is plenty of competition and little loyalty, even a small change in price can see revenue falling dramatically.

- Increase the volume of sales. Businesses may consider methods that will increase their sales. These could include the following:
  - Altering the price of the product or service. Normally, lowering price will increase sales, but for luxury goods, the opposite may be true – the more expensive the good, the more exclusive it seems and the more people will buy it.
  - Promoting the item. Increased advertising, repackaging the good and offering special deals such as 'buy one get one free', can increase sales, although often at a cost.
  - Market research. Finding out what the customer wants (and doesn't want) may help the company to improve sales, but again there is an initial cost before any improvement in sales will appear.

There is no guarantee that any of these methods will work and the company may find that it has to remove products from the market or spend a lot of money redesigning and relaunching the product before it sells.

TASK 4

Sainsbury profits slump 30%

J Sainsbury, the UK-based supermarket chain, on Wednesday announced annual pre-tax profits down 30 per cent, slightly below expectations, as the company announced it was to focus its efforts on its 'core supermarket business'.

The company had been expected to report falling profits affected by strong price competition from rivals Asda and Tesco, the UK's largest supermarket chain, accompanied by rising labour and rent costs.

Operating profit was down from £857 million to £640 million including exceptional items of £112 million.

The figures are the first since Sir Peter Davis, chief executive, took the helm at the supermarket chain, whose brands include Shaw's supermarkets in the US, the Homebase DIY chain and Sainsbury's Supermarkets.

Sir Peter said as the results were announced: 'Recovery will take time. As I said when I rejoined the company, I am determined to make Sainsbury's somewhere special to shop again.'

Source: FT.com, *Financial Times*, 31 May 2000.

In groups, act as business consultants to Sainsbury's. Create a presentation, explaining what strategies Sainsbury's could adopt to improve its profits and why some of your suggestions might not work. You should aim to conclude your presentation with a recommended strategy.

About Gap

Gap Inc. was founded in 1969 in San Francisco, California with a single store and a handful of employees. Today, Gap Inc. is a global company with three distinct brands – Gap, Banana Republic and Old Navy – and revenues topping $9 billion. The company has world headquarters in the San Francisco Bay Area, product development offices in New York City and offices coordinating sourcing activities around the globe. Currently, it employs over 110,000 people worldwide and operates more than 2,900 stores in the United States, Canada, France, Germany, Japan and the United Kingdom.

Stores in operation as of January, 2000	
Gap, GapKids and babyGap	
United States	1,700
Canada	134
France	40
Germany	16
Japan	51
United Kingdom	133
	2,074

Company milestones:

1999 Old Navy brings its sense of fun to the Internet at www.oldnavy.com
Banana Republic goes online at www.bananarepublic.com
Gap Inc. opens more than 400 new stores this year.

Gap's key financial statistics

Net sales (US$ billions)

89	90	91	92	93	94	95	96	97	98
1.6	1.9	2.5	3.0	3.3	3.7	4.4	5.3	6.5	9.1

Net earnings (US$ millions)

89	90	91	92	93	94	95	96	97	98
98	145	230	211	258	320	354	453	534	825

Earnings per share (US$)

89	90	91	92	93	94	95	96	97	98
.15	.23	.36	.33	.40	.49	.55	.71	.87	1.37

Return on average shareholders' equity (%)

89	90	91	92	93	94	95	96	97	98
32	36	40	27	26	26	23	27	33	52

Dividends paid per share (US$)

89	90	91	92	93	94	95	96	97	98
.04	.05	.07	.07	.09	.10	.11	.13	.13	.13

Sales per average gross square foot

89	90	91	92	93	94	95	96	97	98
389	438	481	489	453	444	425	441	453	532

Source: Gap Inc., 2000.

Worse to come for clothing retailers

The tough trading environment for middle-market retailers is due to get progressively worse over the next five years as competition from grocers and discounters intensifies, a study forecasts today.

Verdict, the retail consultancy, says moves by Asda, Tesco and Sainsbury's to develop their non-food offering will see the value of clothing sales out of grocers jump from £1.4 billion in 1999 to £2.6 billion by 2005. At the same time, discounters such as Matalan and Primark will continue to advance, with sales forecast to rise from £1.9 billion to £3.5 billion in the period.

Much of the increase in sales will come from retailers with strong brands, such as Gap and Hennes & Mauritz, occupying space vacated by C&A, which is pulling out of UK retailing. Verdict estimates that these retailers will contribute an additional £350 million annually to spending on clothing.

'People have plenty of money but prefer to spend it on home-related products,' the report says. 'There will be more casualties among those who lack brand differentiation. Anyone anticipating brighter horizons over the next five years will be greatly disappointed, as it will be the most difficult trading climate for decades.'

Verdict estimates that by 2005, sales growth among specialist retailers will have fallen to just 2 per cent, from 5 per cent during the mid 1990s.

The study estimates that discount retailers' share of the clothing and footwear market will grow from 6 to 10.3 per cent, with grocers taking 7.5 per cent by 2005, against 4.4 per cent this year. Middle-market retailers, such as Marks & Spencer, Bhs, Littlewoods and Arcadia, are cutting prices by 10 to 20 per cent this year.

Source: *The Independent*, 21 August 2000.

Mind the Gap

In the enthusiastic advertisements for Gap Inc, the slender, trendy-looking models sing in cowboy boots, dance on ice skates or just go plain khaki-happy. But Gap executives have little to smile about these days, and shareholders don't find the company's recent results entertaining at all. Last week the company that sold America blue button-down skirts and khaki pants for years, reported a 6 per cent decline in second-quarter profit and warned for the fourth time in three months that future earnings won't meet analysts' expectations.

This is the first time since 1996 that the retailer – parent of the Gap, Banana Republic, a preppy, casual line for twenty- and thirty-somethings, and lower-priced Old Navy chains – hasn't beaten its previous performance. Profits fell to $183.9 million in the second quarter, or 21 cents a share, from $195.8 million, or 22 cents per share a year ago. Sales in the quarter ended July 29 rose 20 per cent to $2.95 billion from $2.45 billion.

Shares of the retailer, based in San Francisco, hit a new 52-week low after the earnings shortfall was announced, and are down 41 per cent this year, losing more than $23 billion in market value, after returning gains of 23 per cent, 18 per cent and 78 per cent in the previous three years.

Gap executives have also warned that if retail market conditions continue, its third-quarter earnings might fall to or below last year's level of 35 cents a share. Fourth-quarter results might also be at risk, says Heidi Kunz, the company's executive vice-president and chief financial officer. 'We are in an uncertain retail environment,' she says. 'We do see risks.' So what's exactly the problem? Like a bad mid-life crisis in full throttle, Gap went after the young. 'When we get tricky, when we get young, when we get gimmicky at the Gap, we kind of lose it,' says the Gap chief executive Millard S Drexler, known to the retail world as 'Micky'.

Kurt Barnard, president of Barnard's Retail Trend report in Montclair, New Jersey, says: 'Every time Gap has tried to liberate itself from what made it famous – the blue jeans, blue shirt and things that went with it – it has failed.' This year's roster of deviations included red leather pants at Gap Kids, shirts with asymmetric hems at Banana Republic and Hawaiian print T-shirts at Old Navy.

Industry watchers note that the handwriting on the wall began appearing late last year. Two years ago the popularity of khaki pants boosted Gap to 17 per cent growth in same-store sales. But analysts began to report that Gap Inc was cannibalising itself as Old Navy stole customers from the core Gap stores with lower prices for similar merchandise. This year the problems are across the company. From February through June, same-store sales for the core Gap stores and both its offshoots fell about 2 per cent from a year earlier.

But most industry watchers say the biggest culprit in this spate of problems is Old Navy. The company took a strategic risk, focusing on notoriously fickle teens at its Old Navy stores. Parents came in to shop for their children, but found nothing for themselves.

'We knew that appealing to teens at Old Navy would have its positives and negatives,' says Mr Dexter. 'Now we're feeling the negative. After five years of extraordinary growth, we're experiencing growing pains at Old Navy.'

The company has also looked at expansion plans overseas. That could mean more Gap stores popping up on British high streets. 'The popularity of Gap among UK consumers has been a major driver of our international growth,' says Jack Dougherty, a spokesman for Gap. Executives told analysts there's plenty of room for expansion since several communities still have no Gap, Banana Republic or Old Navy. That kind of aggressive expansion helped boost profits by 37 per cent in the most recent fiscal year, to $1.1 billion on overall sales of $11.6 billion, a gain of 28 per cent.

Does Mr Drexler have the magic touch to turn Gap around again? The company's greatest competition may be its own stellar record. Between 1997 and 1998, sales grew 57 per cent. Between 1998 and 1999, they were up 38 per cent. This year, sales are projected to increase only 19 per cent.

That poses a formidable challenge for Mr Drexler, who needs to return Gap to its previous glory and, for a change, give investors something to sing and dance about.

Source: Adapted from *The Independent*, 16 August 2000.

Q Questions

1 Using the evidence, give reasons why Gap could be thought of as a successful company.

2 Why might the managers and shareholders of Gap be concerned about its future?

3 Write a report, suggesting the actions that Gap might take to ensure that falling profits do not become loss. Evaluate these suggestions.

4 Gap has proposed concentrating on its UK stores in the near future. What conflict may that cause for all the stakeholders?

5 Old Navy, a brand in the Gap company, appears to be struggling to maintain sales. Why might another business wish to buy this part of Gap?

E Extension

Stag Furniture is a recent example of a company being wound up. Using this, or any other example, describe the financial and social costs and benefits caused by the closure of a company.

THEME 5

People in organisations

The internal organisation of business

This unit is about how the people who work in a business are organised so that they can work effectively to deliver a business's aims.

At the end of the unit, students should be able to:

- draw up an organisation chart for a known business

- identify and explain hierarchy, span of control and delegation by referring to an organisation chart

- compare the different ways that companies might be organised

- explain the advantages and disadvantages of centralisation/ decentralisation

- assess the impact of informal organisation on a business.

Formal organisation

When any group of people joins together to work towards a common goal, there needs to be organisation. A rowing team working towards competing at the Olympics needs trainers and coaches, team doctors, a manager and other support workers. A school fête needs an organising committee, people to set up stalls, people to run the stalls and people to collect and count the money. In a small business like a café, the owners will do most of the work, but may also employ other people to help them buy and prepare the food, serve the customers or keep the café clean. In a large business there will be many activities that need to be completed and people will work in specialised teams, known as departments, to deliver each activity.

The way in which any business is structured internally is known as its **formal organisation**. The easiest way to show how a business is organised internally is to use a simple **organisation chart**. In any business the way the different departments are organised may look like this:

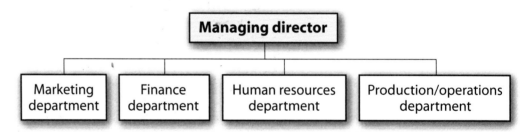

Managing director

| Marketing department | Finance department | Human resources department | Production/operations department |

TASK 1

a Find out how your school is organised. You may use the school prospectus to help you or you could look on the school's web site if it has one. Alternatively, you could ask the Headteacher or one of the teaching staff to explain the organisation to you.

b Draw an organisation chart of the teaching staff in your school. Illustrate it with the names of the various posts in the school.

c What other organisations exist within the school? Try to add these to your organisation chart, or draw separate charts.

d Is your school's organisation similar to or different to that of a business? Explain your answer.

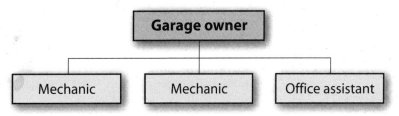

Organisational structure in a sole trader, a privately owned garage.
This is a structure with only two levels of hierarchy

Hierarchy and span of control

Most businesses have some sort of **hierarchy,** that is, levels of responsibility and accountability, in order to aid decision making.
In a sole trader, the organisational structure is likely to be broad with only a few levels to the hierarchy. The owner/manager will be at the apex (top) of the pyramid.

In a partnership, the organisational structure might look different, particularly where each partner has a slightly different area of responsibility. For example, the organisation chart of an independent firm of estate agents could look like the one below. There are three levels of hierarchy in this structure.

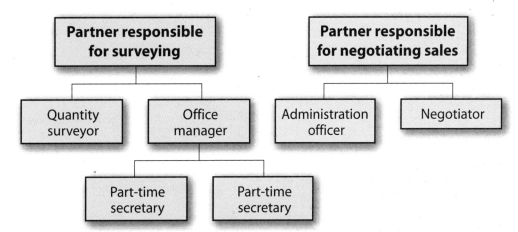

Organisational structure in a partnership: a firm of estate agents. One partner is responsible for surveying and the other partner is responsible for negotiating sales.

The **span of control** is the number of employees for whom the person in the tier above has direct responsibility. In the first example of the garage, the garage owner has a span of control of three. In the second example of the estate agency, each partner has a span of control of two people. The office manager also has a span of control of two people. The organisation is more tightly structured than that of the sole trader because there are two separate parts to the business.

Such an organisational structure will work only because in a small firm all employees know each other and organisation is very informal.
Although employees may have clearly defined responsibilities, the organisation is small enough for everyone to be able to communicate directly with all other employees.

In large firms, organisation charts tend to take the form of a tall pyramid with a narrow base. Larger businesses are usually more hierarchical.
This type of organisation has the manager at the top with many levels in the hierarchy below. The span of control varies from a narrow one, that is, each person is responsible for two or three others, to a much wider one. The organisation chart represented by the pyramid would look like the one shown below.

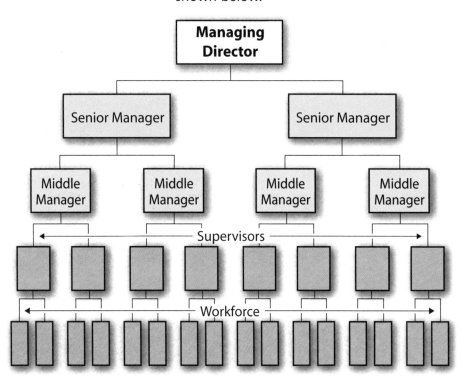

This organisation chart has five levels in its hierarchy with each manager or supervisor in the top four levels having a span of control of two, that is, he or she is responsible for two other workers.

The more levels of hierarchy that an organisation has, the longer it will take for decisions to pass from the top to the bottom and ideas from the bottom to the top. The managers in charge are also a long way from the customers and they might lose touch with them.

Hierarchical organisation chart

TASK 2

Look again at your school's organisation chart that you drew in Task 1.

a How many levels of hierarchy are there in your school?

b What is the span of control of the following people in your school:

   i the headteacher

   ii a deputy headteacher

   iii a head of department or head of faculty

   iv the school secretary

   v a head of year?

c Do you think your school organisation is effective? What changes would you suggest to the present organisation?

Types of organisation

Many companies group workers within a hierarchy according to their function, that is the job which they do. This is known as a **functional organisation.** Workers are grouped according to the department in which they work. For example, a human resources department's organisation structure is shown on the right. This would be one part of the business's whole organisation chart.

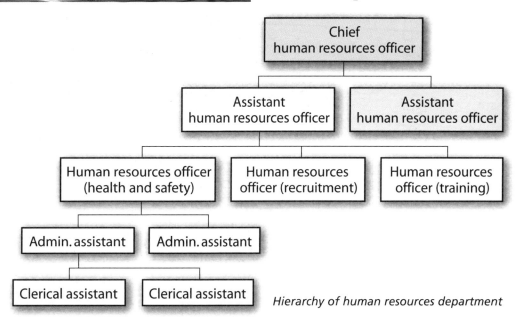

Hierarchy of human resources department

The human resources department shows five levels of hierarchy within the department. The head of human resources has a span of control of two, whereas the assistant human resource officers have spans of control of three.

The advantage with this type of structure is that each function is carried out by specialists who can concentrate on their particular activity. However, a functional organisation can lead to competition between different departments. There may also be poor communication and liaison between the departments.

For this reason a company may use a different type of organisation to help solve complex problems or to work on a strategy that cuts across department boundaries. A **matrix organisation structure** has people working across traditional boundaries. For example, a company may draw workers from all departments to solve the problem of opening a new manufacturing plant. In the diagram below the conventional structure is shown by the top line whereas the use of the workers to solve the problem of opening the new plant is shown by the diagonal lines.

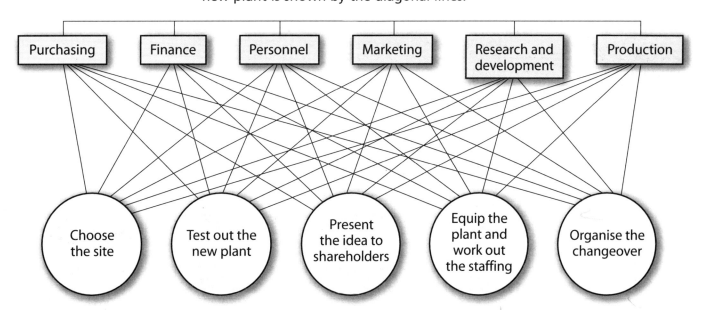

For example, teams drawn from a number of departments will be involved in choosing the site, testing out the model of the new plant, presenting the idea to shareholders and so on. Some companies might have staff permanently organised in a matrix pattern.

TASK 3

Below is the organisation chart of Walton's Lawnmowers, a medium-sized family firm which makes petrol driven lawn mowers for large gardens, parks and sports grounds.

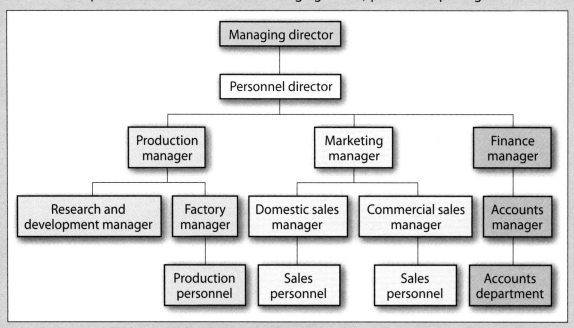

a What type of organisation does Walton currently have?

b How many levels of hierarchy are shown on the chart?

c What do you think is wrong with the present way in which Walton's is organised?

d Draw up a new chart which you think is a better way of organising Walton's. Explain your reasons for making any changes.

Centralisation versus decentralisation

Organisations may have centralised or decentralised decision making. **Centralised decision making** is when control is held by those at the centre of the organisation. The managing director and the senior managers in charge of the major departments often take all the decisions and those below them are responsible for carrying out the decisions.

Decentralised decision making is when the responsibility for making all decisions is passed down to lower levels. For example, in a local council there might be no central human resources department. Each of the separate parts of the council – education, social services, housing, etc. – would include its own human resources officers and they would make their own personnel decisions.

There are advantages and disadvantages to both approaches to decision making, as shown in the table.

Advantages	Disadvantages
Centralised decision making allows someone to have a complete picture of what is going on in the company.	Centralised decision making can demotivate the workforce who have no real responsibility for what is going on.
Centralised decision making can be rapid and may be helpful in times of crisis.	Centralised decision making can be slow as all decisions are taken centrally.
Decentralised decision making allows decisions to be made by those who know most about that particular aspect of the business.	Decentralised decision making can lead to problems as conflicting decisions might be made by different departments.

The process of **delegation** means giving the responsibility for tasks to a subordinate although ultimate responsibility remains with the superior. This can act as a powerful motivator for the subordinate and prepare him or her for positions of greater responsibility in the future. However, delegation will work only if the leader has trust in his/her subordinates and can leave them to carry out the task themselves. One way of maintaining control over the subordinate in order to ensure that nothing goes wrong is to have regular meetings which keep the leader informed of the progress made.

TASK 4

Waterstone's is the largest specialist bookseller in the UK and Ireland. It has more than 200 branches and employs 4,200 people. The shops are familiar sights in high streets, in airports, and on university campuses. Recent developments include an Internet bookstore where books can be ordered electronically and a book superstore in London's Piccadilly.

A typical company will have an organisation structure like the one shown below. Communication is one way from top to bottom.
The organisation chart in Waterstone's is turned upside down.

Waterstone's superstore in Piccadilly, London

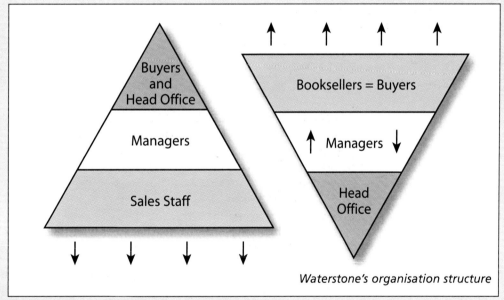
Waterstone's organisation structure

Within Waterstone's individual branches have the freedom to make their own decisions about how to serve their customers and manage their part of the business. For example, the variety of books on offer in any one shop will depend upon the size of the branch and customer needs in each catchment area.

Source: www.mbapublishing.co.uk/cd/casestudies

a Explain what the two diagrams in the above case show.
b Is this an example of decentralisation or centralisation? Give your reasons.
c What are the benefits for   i   customers
                   ii the business from this type of organisation?
d Which decisions might the manager of the large bookstore in London be able to take?

Informal organisation

The organisation chart shows the formal roles and responsibilities of the people employed in an organisation. But in every business there are many everyday contacts between people, often cutting across the formal organisation. This is known as the **informal organisation**. In most small businesses the owners and workers will know each other and work closely together whatever the formal organisation. In larger businesses there will also be important informal links.

Some examples of informal groups within a business might be:

- families and relations who work in different departments
- those who meet outside work in the social club, at the local church, at the football club or at the pub
- workers and managers who have trained together or who have worked on projects together
- employees who have been promoted or moved between departments may well keep loyalties and friendships in their old department.

These informal links are important for employees as they help to promote job satisfaction, they help to keep people informed about what is happening and they encourage co-operation across departments. However, they can cause problems for a business. Rumours can spread quickly through the business even if not based on fact. Informal groups may go against the aims of the business and may undermine what official groups are trying to do. Some people may have more power because of their informal links than their position in the business would give them.

TASK 5

a Make a list of all the formal and informal groups that you are in at school.

b What is the difference between these two types of group at school?

c Which are the most important groups that you are in? Explain your answer.

Reorganisation at the BBC

Greg Dyke, the new director general of the BBC, chose pink as his backdrop when he addressed the BBC's 23,000 staff at Television Centre in Shepherd's Bush, London. He said that a change of culture was essential: 'Our aim is to create one BBC where people enjoy their job and are inspired and united behind the common purpose of making great programmes.'

He told them of his plans to make the BBC a happier and more inclusive organisation. He indicated to his staff that the days of hierarchical departments were over. He presented his new management structure shaped like a huge daisy-like flower. Each petal represented different aspects of programme making in contrast to the previous regime when administrators and strategists were at the top. There is now one director of television and one director of radio, each of whom is one of Mr Dyke's top 17 executives. There is a new creative director who is responsible for BBC Drama and Films as well as children's programmes. There is also a new head of factual programmes and a single sports department.

Mr Dyke said: 'We have taken out a complete level of management in the new structure. It is flatter, inclusive and will result in … less internal competition.' He has scrapped the previous broadcast and production departments as well as the corporate centre and policy and planning unit. He has also pledged to reduce the number of business units in the BBC from the present 190 to a more manageable 50.

His overall aim is to cut duplication at many levels. Hundreds of jobs will be lost. The shake-up should give back to the programme makers a certain amount of guaranteed output which will help them to cover their overheads. The new system should help reduce the worst aspects of the internal market that operated at the BBC.

Source: Adapted from *The Observer*, 30 January 2000.

Q Questions

1 a What type of business organisation is the BBC?
  b Who do you think are the BBC's major competitors?

2 What problems did the above article suggest the BBC faced under its old management structure?

3 How would you describe Mr Dyke's new organisation structure? What clues are there in the article?

4 Why has Greg Dyke brought in these changes at the BBC?

5 Why do you think that Greg Dyke created one sports department across the BBC in his reorganisation?

E Extension

1 Explain why Greg Dyke might want to move away from the 'internal market' that was operating at the BBC.

2 By using the BBC web site – www.bbc.co.uk – try to find out all the new departments that Greg Dyke has set up and draw the 'daisy' diagram that he presented to staff.

Communication in business

What is communication?

Communication is the process of conveying information from one person to another in such a way that an accurate message is received and can be acted upon. A simple model of communication could be an archer firing an arrow.

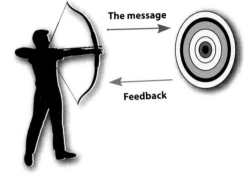

The message

Feedback

The archer represents the person sending the message. The arrow is the message itself. The target is the person to whom the message is being sent. The archer will not know if the arrow has hit the target until he or she receives feedback, that is knowing the result of the communication. Has the person heard the message? Has he or she done something as a result?

In business, the archer might be a company producing sports magazines. The message might be an advertisement on television telling customers about a new athletics magazine. The target will be the segment of the market that the business is aiming at, e.g. 18–40-year-olds interested in athletics. The feedback will be the level of sales when the magazine first goes on sale.

TASK 1

This is a class activity. Your teacher will draw on a piece of paper two irregular four-sided objects that are joined together. A member of the class should take the piece of paper and stand behind a screen so that he or she cannot see the class and the class cannot see the drawing. The student should now describe the figure and each class member should try to draw the figure as described. There should be no other communication between the group and the person behind the screen. When everyone has made an attempt at drawing the figure, check the accuracy against the original.

a How long did this communication take?

b How accurate was the communication? Explain the reasons.

c What is lacking in this form of communication when compared with the archer/target model above?

Now repeat the activity with a new drawing of a different four-sided figure. This time the volunteer can describe the figure and answer any questions from the group. But he or she must not show anyone the drawing. When everyone has finished, again check the accuracy against the original.

d Compare the results with the first experiment. Was the communication quicker? Was it more accurate? Explain the reasons for your results.

e What does this whole exercise say about what makes good communication?

How communication takes place

Within a business, communication can take place in various directions. The main directions are:

- upwards
- downwards
- horizontal
- diagonal.

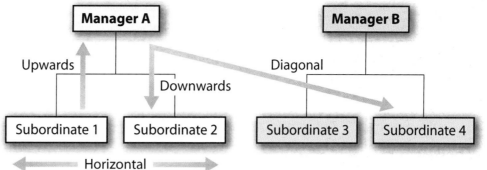

Directions of communication within a business

Upwards communication

This takes place from subordinates to managers, e.g. from the workers to the managers. Workers can provide detailed practical information about products, processes and customers. **Upward communication** is likely to be an important positive feature of a small business but more difficult in larger businesses. Larger companies now use methods such as suggestion schemes and quality circles (see Unit 19) to enable employees to give their own ideas to management.

Downwards communication

This takes place from managers to subordinates. It will consist of instructions, decisions and policies being passed down to the workforce. It is important that major decisions and policies are discussed with the workforce before they are put into practice. **Downward communication** allows the workforce to have its say and perhaps influence the final decision or policy. Companies often have staff or workforce consultative committees, containing representatives of the employees, whom they talk to before making major decisions. They might also consult trade union representatives (see Unit 32).

Horizontal communication

This takes place between employees at the same level in the hierarchy. **Horizontal communication** is likely to occur frequently as people exchange information about procedures, difficulties and successes as a normal part of their work. Sometimes communication between departments is more difficult as employees might not have specialist knowledge about another department's work.

Diagonal communication

This takes place across the hierarchy between people at different levels. For example, in the organisation chart of the estate agency shown in Unit 27 (page 209), **diagonal communication** could take place between the partner responsible for negotiating sales and the office manager. He or she may want to introduce a different procedure into the office which is specific to his area of responsibility.

TASK 2

For each of the following examples say in which of the above directions is communication taking place and why you have made that choice:

a The management of Ford consulting with the Transport and General Union about the proposed ending of car production at Dagenham in Essex.

b Headteachers in England and Wales writing to the Secretary of State for Education to complain about the amount of bureaucracy that they have to tackle every day in school.

c The manager of the marketing department at Marks & Spencer headquarters sending an e-mail to all the branch managers about the launch of the new spring collection.

d A member of the IT department making a presentation to the department managers of an NHS hospital trust on the benefits of a new information management system that is being installed.

e The management team of a large theme park meeting every morning at 8 am before it opens to review the previous day's business and identify any changes needed for the coming day.

Methods of communication

Methods of internal communication are those which are used within the business for communication between workers or between workers and owner. The small number of employees in a small firm means that much of the communication is informal.

In a larger business, communication will be more formal as individual workers will come into personal contact with few others outside their own area of work.

The most usual methods of internal communication which a business would use are:

- **oral**
- **written**
- **electronic.**

Oral communication

Face-to-face communication involves holding a conversation in person. For example, in a small office employees will be able to communicate face to face rather than by phone. The advantages and disadvantages of this method of communication are shown in the table.

Advantages	Disadvantages
The message can be clearly communicated.	Non-verbal communication, that is, gestures and facial expressions, may act as a barrier to effective communication.
Feedback is immediate.	

The **telephone** is an important method of internal communication in all businesses as well as a major method of external communication. Employees may work in separate buildings and a telephone will make communication easier. The table shows the advantages and disadvantages of communicating by telephone.

Advantages	Disadvantages
It enables long-distance communication to take place.	It is possible for the message to get distorted if the line is unclear or the person receiving the message works in a noisy environment.
It saves time.	
It enables immediate communication to take place when necessary.	There is no non-verbal communication to give the listener any clues.
Feedback is immediate.	

The **tannoy** is a way of broadcasting a short message to all the workers at once in, for example, a large warehouse or factory. It might be used to warn people that the fire alarm is to be tested. A tannoy is often used in large shops to request a member of staff to go to a certain part of the store. This is quicker than finding the worker in person. The advantages and disadvantages of tannoy communication are shown below.

Advantages	Disadvantages
A message can be passed quickly to a large number of people.	Noise in the workplace may make the message difficult to hear.
The message can be repeated until the communication gets through.	It is difficult to give detailed messages over a tannoy.

TASK 3

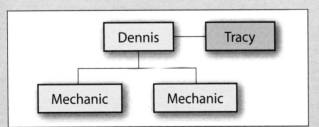

Wreckers is a small business that sells spare car parts and repairs vehicles involved in accidents. It is run by Dennis in partnership with his friend Tracy. The organisation chart is shown here.

Suggest in what direction communication would take place and what would be an appropriate oral method of communication in each of the following situations:

a Dennis needs to reprimand a mechanic for his poor time keeping.

b Tracy needs to tell one of the mechanics that she has an urgent phone call.

c The mechanics need to sort out among themselves who tackles which vehicles.

d Dennis is delivering a lorry load of parts to a friend's garage when he is asked whether he has any more mini seats in stock.

e One of the mechanics wants Tracy to sort out his pay. He reckons his hours have been wrongly worked out for the third week running.

Written communication

Notices, **bulletins** and **newsletters** are methods used to keep the workforce up to date with what is going on. Notices may relate to vacant posts, holiday arrangements, union matters or social events and are likely to be displayed on a noticeboard. Sometimes important notices are included with wage or salary slips. Bulletins and newsletters are regular publications which are intended to keep workers informed and also make them feel a part of a large company. The advantages and disadvantages of notices, bulletins and newsletters are shown below.

Advantages	Disadvantages
They can contain detailed information and the information can be presented in a variety of ways using graphics and pictures.	They are impersonal methods of communication, that is, the same communication is sent to all the workers.
Newsletters can draw people together by creating a strong company identity.	Although they are sent to everyone, not everyone will read newsletters.
	Notices lose their impact if they are not changed frequently.

Letters are mainly used for external communication but can be used as a formal internal communication tool. Letters will often be used by the personnel department to inform workers of wage rises, promotions or redundancy and disciplinary procedures. They have both advantages and disadvantages, as shown below.

Advantages	Disadvantages
Letters are confidential and can be targeted exactly at the right person.	The sender will only know the impact of the message when he or she receives a reply.
They provide a record of what has been discussed or agreed and the message should be clear to the receiver.	Letters are formal methods of communication and feedback may be slow.

Even where it is easy in a business for people to communicate face to face a **memorandum,** or **memo,** is used because it is a way of committing questions, answers and general information to paper so that a record is kept. A memo sets out the date, sender, recipient, topic for discussion and contains a short note of the content. A memo can be self-carbonated so that the sender can keep a copy. Look at the example of a memo.

MEMORANDUM

FROM: Office Manager
TO: All partners
DATE: 1 March 2001

Office routines
The meeting on Monday to discuss updating office routines will start at 2.15 pm prompt.

Advantages	Disadvantages
A written record of the message is kept.	Pieces of paper can get lost or ignored so there is no guarantee that the message is received.
The message is communicated in written format and therefore should be unambiguous.	If too many memos are sent receivers may not be able to identify the important messages.

A **report** is a more formal written method of communication than a memo. It usually communicates important information and is used in business to record the position at a particular point in time. For example, the office manager referred to in the memo might be asked to submit a report on office routines and why they need updating as a basis for a meeting with all the partners. A report is usually typed or word processed. It should include recommendations for action, and normally uses the following format:

- Report to...
- Report by...
- Subject
- Date
- Introduction
- Main findings
- Conclusions
- Recommendations
- Action by...

The advantages and disadvantages of reports are given in the table.

Advantages	Disadvantages
A report can contain detailed information including data.	A report is a formal method of communication and is therefore time consuming to prepare.
It provides a written record of the business at a particular moment in time.	Because of the length of reports, they may not be read in detail.
By including recommendations a report can give the receivers useful advice to help future decisions.	People may need help in understanding difficult information.

TASK 4

Supermart is one of a large chain of supermarkets in the west of Wales.

Which method of written communication would be appropriate in the following situations and why?

a The store manager in Wales needs to send the latest sales figures to the head office in Birmingham.

b To advertise a vacancy for a section supervisor to be filled internally.

c To inform staff of the closure of a branch and offer them work at other local branches.

d To keep the workforce up to date with the company's developments in TQM (Total Quality Management).

e To organise coverage of the information desk throughout the coming week.

f The store manager in Wales is asked to provide head office with the results of a recent promotion of the store on Channel 4.

Electronic communication

Fax is a way of sending documents through the telephone system. In a large company it is often essential for documents and important reports to be seen immediately by a number of employees. Fax is an instantaneous method of sending written information both between two offices in the same building and between two offices in different parts of the world.

E-mail (electronic mail) enables one computer to talk to another via a modem which accesses the telephone lines. Many companies send messages, memos and reports by electronic mail. Employees have to check their e-mail post box in the same way as they would check an intray or pigeon hole for letters. E-mail has the potential to replace most forms of written communication provided all people involved have access to their own e-mail address.

Many business people are now equipped with a **mobile phone** so that they can communicate with customers (external communication) and with their base office (internal communication) while on the move. Some mobile phones can be connected to pocket book computers to receive and send faxes and some mobile phones can receive and store messages and e-mail. Mobile phones can now be used to access the Internet as well.

Staff who work in large buildings and who may be in any part of the building at any one time are often equipped with **pagers**. For example, doctors on call in hospitals are contacted through pagers if they are needed urgently. Very simple pagers just alert their owner to a need to contact a base office, while more sophisticated ones are capable of storing longer messages. The advantages and disadvantages of electronic communication are shown in the table.

Advantages	Disadvantages
Messages can be sent quickly and responses received quickly.	There may be no permanent record of the messages being sent.
A large number of people can be contacted electronically via e-mail, with a worldwide range.	It is possible to intercept electronic messages so it is not a good way of sending confidential messages.
Documents can be transferred instantly by e-mail and the receivers can make their own amendments to reports, etc.	The cost of communication via mobile phones at peak times is higher than using land lines.
Employees can quickly access important information when they are travelling or working away from base.	Not all receivers have access to fax or e-mail.

TASK 5

You may get an opportunity to visit a local business as part of your Business Studies course or through your work experience placement. While you are there, find out about the methods of electronic communication used inside and outside the business.

Write up your research as a short report concentrating on the advantages to the business of communicating in the ways it uses. Also identify in your report any possible improvements that could be made in the way the business communicates.

Barriers to communication

At the start of the unit, it was shown that for communication to be successful the message has to be received and acted upon. However, there are many things that can get in the way of good communication. These are known as **communication barriers**. They can occur at all stages of communication in business:

- The sender – he or she might not be a good communicator, or might not have enough influence over the person being communicated with. For example, employees on the shop floor often find it difficult to get management to listen to their ideas.

- The message – this may be too complicated, may be too long, may contain too much 'jargon', or may just be sent at the wrong time. For example, a specialist accountant may find it difficult to explain to the production department why cuts in finance are necessary due to increased interest rates.

- The medium – the sender may choose the wrong way to send a message. For example, sending out letters to the workforce announcing possible staffing cuts rather than face-to-face communication may lead to unnecessary worry for workers.

- The receiver – he or she might not be listening to the message, or may not want to hear the message because it involves doing something that he or she is against. For example, a sales person may not read a memo about cutting down on travelling expenses because the individual regards the expenses as part of his or her salary.

- The feedback – the sender may not provide an opportunity for feedback to take place, or may not listen to the feedback received. For example, a council might announce the closure of a local library without giving people a chance to say whether they agreed with the decision.

TASK 6

In the following situations, who and what has been the cause of the breakdown in communication?

a You have just returned home from a club at 1 am. Your mum or dad is angry with you as they told you to be in by midnight. You would have phoned, but you had run out of top-ups for your mobile phone.

b The staff of a fast-food outlet have just received training from a human resources manager from head office about a new system for assessing their performance and deciding their pay. But nobody on the staff could understand the new system and they were worried that their pay would fall.

c An announcement that an Internet company is to close at the end of the week because of losses had been sent to staff by e-mail on Monday morning. The staff could not believe it and promptly walked out, refusing to continue working.

Electronic communication in Tameside Council

Tameside Local Education Authority is a metropolitan authority in the north west of England, to the east of Manchester. It controls some 100 primary and secondary schools.

It has recently produced the following policy for improving electronic communications between the council and the schools in the authority.

1. All schools should by July 2000 be able to set up e-mail addresses for all their staff, both administrative and teaching.

2. All schools will have their own 'domain' name, i.e. @schoolname.tameside.sch.uk.

3. From September 2000 day-to-day correspondence between council officers and schools will be sent by e-mail.

4. Sensitive or confidential letters will be sent by post.

5. Lengthy documents or policies will be sent by post, but also such literature will be available on the council's web site.

6. The Tameside web site will be developed to include news, recent documents and links to other sites

7. There will be guidelines produced for all staff on how to use e-mail.

8. Training will be run by the council for school and council staff on using e-mails.

9. E-mails should be checked on a regular basis (at least twice a day).

10. There is an expectation that both schools and council staff will read and respond to e-mails much quicker than a letter.

"PLANNING TOGETHER... WORKING TOGETHER..."

A Strategy to improve communications and consultation in Tameside's education service

Tameside
Metropolitan Borough

Education and Cultural Services

Source: Tameside LEA Communication Strategy, September 2000.

Q Questions

1 Identify and explain three methods of communication mentioned in the above extract.

2 Why would Tameside Council want to use e-mail to communicate with:

 a headteachers

 b teachers

 c administrators in Tameside schools?

3 Compare the use of e-mail with the use of the post for organisations like schools and councils.

4 What are the benefits of web sites for:

 a public sector organisations like councils

 b private sector organisations like retailers?

5 What barriers to communication might still exist between the schools and Tameside Council even after this policy has been introduced?

E Extension

1 a Why might it not be possible for all the communication between the council and schools to take place electronically?

 b Give examples of other types of communication that might be needed, and explain why.

2 Evaluate the web site of your school or your local council. What is communicated well on the web site? What could be improved?

Recruitment, training and redundancy

This unit is about how businesses expand and train their workforce and how a reduction in the size of the workforce is managed.

At the end of the unit, students should be able to:

- identify why recruitment is needed

- draw up a job description and person specification for a given post

- assess the different ways in which recruitment can take place

- select the right candidate for a job

- compare the different ways staff are trained

- understand what happens when staff are made redundant.

Why are new staff needed?

A sole trader who can operate on his or her own does not need to recruit staff. For example, a self-employed computer programmer who works from home for a number of companies will be able to organise himself or herself and keep his or her own financial records and will not need another employee. But as soon as the work of the business starts to increase so does the work of running the business. The computer programmer might have to recruit someone part time to keep his or her books.

There are a number of choices that a sole trader could make faced by a growing workload:

- Turn down the extra work, but this will result in a loss in possible income.

- Find someone to subcontract the work to, that is pay someone else to do the work for you (see Unit 16). This allows the business to keep the customers, but it reduces the amount of profit that the sole trader will receive.

- Employ part-time workers or seasonal workers, that is, people to help out at certain times of the week or the year. Part-time work is now becoming very common because it is easier to reduce or increase the hours of part-time workers than full-time ones. Seasonal workers are common in agriculture and in the tourism industry where they might be taken on for the holiday period.

- Employ full-time employees either to help carry out the main work of the business, or to do some of the administrative work and therefore to free the owner to deal with more customers.

In any large organisation there will be a regular need to take on new staff. Businesses will need to recruit new employees for a number of reasons:

- to meet an increased workload due to increased demand for products or services

- to replace staff who are leaving on a permanent basis

- to replace staff who have been promoted within the organisation

- to replace staff who are leaving for a temporary period.

Large organisations will draw up a **human resource plan** to help them decide how many staff they need in the future.

Who should be recruited?

If a business decides that it does need to recruit a new employee, then two important tasks need to be carried out:

- drawing up a **job description** – what is the nature of the job that has to be done?
- drawing up a **person specification** – who would be the ideal candidate for the job?

Job description

This should include a description of the following:

- job title
- purpose of the job
- place in the organisation
- specific duties
- other responsibilities
- location of work
- hours of work and working conditions.

A large packaging manufacturer which operates in the UK and Germany needs to recruit a manager for its market research department. The managing director of the company has drawn up the following job description:

Job title	Manager, Marketing Research
Purpose of the job	To manage the company's market research programmes
Place in the organisation	Within the Marketing Department, responsible to the Marketing Manager
Specific duties	To identify needs and opportunities in the market for packaging through research into: • product awareness • brand image with manufacturers • advertising • customer satisfaction
Other responsibilities	To administer the market research department To manage and appraise market research assistants and other department employees To contribute to the wider activities of the marketing department.
Location of work	At the company head office in Manchester.
Hours and conditions of work	Hours as required by the Marketing Manager Salary by negotiation 30 days' holiday plus statutory holidays Private health insurance Company car

The job description needs to be a useful and up-to-date document. It will form the basis for the job advertisement and for any information sent by the company to applicants for the job.

Person specification
This could include the following:

- educational attainments
- previous experience
- general intelligence
- specialised skills
- interests
- personality
- physical make-up.

The packaging company drew up the following person specification.

Post	Manager: Market Research	
Educational attainments	Degree level qualification	Essential
	Professional qualification in market research	Essential
Previous experience	Senior market research role in manufacturing company	Essential
General intelligence	Understanding of paper/packaging industry	Desirable
	Knowledge of European Union rules	Desirable
Specialised skills	Ability to speak and write in German	Essential
	Skilled in use of PCs and electronic communication	Essential
Personality	Good interpersonal skills	Essential
	Self-motivated	Essential
	Enquiring mind	Essential

Such a person specification would be used by the company when the application forms are being looked at and when the interviews take place. It is common for businesses to identify those features that are essential, and those that are desirable.

TASK 1

a Draw up a possible person specification for the job of new product development manager described in the advertisement, adding any other information you feel is needed.

b Which items from the advertisement are likely to appear in a job description for a new product development manager?

Product Development Manager
Huntress Systems, Croydon

This demanding role will call upon your many years of experience in product development, buying and distribution. As an accomplished manager, you will enjoy autonomy, relish challenge and perform at your best in a pressurised but fun environment. Commitment and a dedicated work ethic will be rewarded with an excellent salary plus performance related bonus and company car.

For details email office.croydon@huntress.co.uk or visit our website at www.huntress.co.uk.

Recruiting staff

There are a number of methods that businesses can use to recruit their staff.

TASK 2

Nina Moya owns a sandwich bar which serves the office workers at lunchtime in the centre of Nottingham. She has two part-time assistants who work from 10 am to 2 pm but now she wants to stay open until 5 pm to catch the afternoon shoppers. Neither of her present team wants to work full-time, so she has decided to recruit a full time employee to work from 9 am to 5 pm. She is looking for a willing worker and is not worried that the recruit may not have any previous experience.

1 Recommend a suitable method of recruitment for the sandwich bar.

2 Explain why you chose that method rather than other possibilities.

3 What alternatives to recruiting an extra worker might there be for this business?

Personal contact

This is likely to be the most common way for a small business. The owner will make personal contact with individuals he or she knows would be interested in working for the business. They might be one of the family or a friend, or it might be someone the owner has come across during his or her day-to-day business. This will save the cost of advertising a job and make it more likely that he or she will actually take on the person after an interview.

Internal advertisements

These will appear on noticeboards or in company newspapers or bulletins. They will attract candidates looking for promotion within the business. There might also be people who are looking for redeployment if their jobs are under threat in one part of the organisation. However, a small business will probably be unable to recruit from within its existing staff. It also may not have full-time employees to help it with recruitment.

External advertisements

These will appear in newspapers, both local and national, on radio, and through the Internet. Large companies will tend to look for specialist workers through national and regional advertisements, and general employees through local advertising. Small businesses will use local newspapers and even card advertisements in order to recruit. The advantages of this are that the candidates for the job know the local area and markets, and are willing to accept local rates of pay. Also the rates for advertising are lower. However, the right candidates with the right skills may not be available locally.

Recruitment agencies

Private agencies like Alfred Marks and Manpower are used to find certain types of employee. **Recruitment agencies** often specialise in certain categories of workers, such as office workers, construction workers, professional workers. They will therefore have a database of suitable candidates from which the business can choose. This will reduce the time it takes to find suitable employees. However, the business will have to pay a fee to the agency for finding the employee, and the employees from the agency might only be looking for temporary work. There are also selection consultants and 'headhunters'. These companies would charge a substantial fee or commission for finding or selecting candidates.

Job centres

These are run by the government through the Department for Education and Skills and are designed to bring people looking for jobs in contact with people in the local area with jobs to offer. They are therefore a low-cost way of recruiting staff, but the Job Centre might not have the right candidate for a specialised job.

Careers services

These are now run by a variety of private and public sector organisations, directly funded by the government. Careers officers have regular contact with school leavers and may be able to find new employees for an organisation. They also keep in touch with employers to find out about vacancies. A new service, Connexions, is being set up in 2001 which brings together the Careers Service with Youth Services. It aims to increase the support for school leavers who find it difficult to get a job with training.

Learning and Skills Councils (LSCs)

These run a similar placement service for adults looking for or returning to work. They are also responsible for funding and promoting Youth Training schemes. These provide training up to National Vocational Qualification (NVQ) Level 2 for young people but do not guarantee a job at the end of the training. They would thus be a good source of trained employees for a small business. They also promote Modern Apprenticeships, where larger organisations take on trainees full time and train them up to NVQ Level 2 or 3.

Selecting the right candidate

For a company the most important aim in selection is to get the right candidate for the job. But it will also want the cost of the process to be reasonable, and to keep a good image as an employer with both the successful and unsuccessful candidates.

A business might go through three stages in the selection process.

Application forms and curriculum vitae

An application form acts as the first means of selection. It will be used to find out a range of information about the candidate: age, qualifications, training, previous employment and interests.

As an alternative to an application form, the candidate might have a **curriculum vitae**, that is, a short account of his or her qualifications and experience so far.

A letter of application will be important in helping to select a shortlist of preferred candidates.

Interviews

Interviews are commonly used in selection. They will help to provide the employer with additional information about the candidate, and to see if he or she will fit into the organisation. These are some of the general questions that might be asked:

- Why do you want to work for this business?
- What have you done previously that makes you a suitable candidate?
- What are your personal strengths and weaknesses?
- What skills have you got that you could use in the job?
- How will your qualifications help you in this job?

The answers to questions like these, the way the candidate reacts, and the general appearance of the candidate, will help the employer decide if he or she wants to offer them the job. However, interviews can be quite subjective if the interviewers are not well trained, and they need to make sure that each candidate is asked the same questions and is treated fairly. Because of problems with interviews, many companies also use other selection techniques, such as aptitude tests, or personality tests.

Offering the job

If the interview is successful and a choice of candidate has been made, the business will ask for references from people who know or have employed the candidate. These help to check that candidates have done what they have said they have done, and that they are honest and reliable.

TASK 3

The following four candidates were shortlisted and interviewed for the post of marketing research manager at the packaging company described on page 225.

Candidate A: Gautam Sharma, age 32	**Candidate B: Jane Dellamere, age 39**	**Candidate C: Josie Martinez, age 27**	**Candidate D: Peter Brotherton, age 40**
Degree in Chemistry	Masters degree in Management Science; degree in Business Administration	Degree in Marketing; no higher qualifications	Degree in Engineering; no higher qualifications
Member of the Institute of Marketing	14 years' experience in market research working for various research agencies. At present manager in a small market research company.	4 years' experience in market research department of large supermarket chain – joined as a graduate recruit. Limited knowledge of IT systems. Placement in Germany as part of degree – fluent in language.	18 years' experience in paper industry – 12 years as engineer and for last 6 years in product development at a rival packaging company. Responsible for small department at present.
10 years' experience in marketing department of large chemical company carrying out variety of marketing functions. Confident with IT. Worked extensively in European Union member countries, and fluent in German and French.	Extensive IT experience. No previous work in EU. German to A level.	Interview: showed potential and motivation, but uncertain about management role. Excellent communicator.	Confident with IT. Good knowledge of European market. No language qualifications or expertise.
Interview: showed confidence and motivation; would fit into the team well; has not had any senior management responsibilities in his existing job.	Interview: strong personality; confident and well motivated; likes to lead from the front; no real knowledge of packaging, but a real understanding of market research.		Interview: a reserved candidate, showing extensive understanding of packaging industry; not very assertive, but good team member.

a Using the job and person specifications shown on pages 225 and 226, draw up a list of the advantages and disadvantages of each candidate.

b Which candidate do you think the company will appoint? Give your reasons.

Induction and training

Induction is a programme to introduce a new employee to a job. The aims of induction are to:

- familiarise the employee with the job
- make the employee as efficient as possible
- encourage new entrants to be committed to the organisation.

TASK 4

An older member of your family wants to set up a small retail sportswear business. But she feels that she needs some training in setting up on her own first.

a Make a list of all organisations in your area that might provide such training. You might get some names from your local Careers Office, Job Shop or Business Link centre.

b Contact these organisations and find out about the courses that they offer: their duration, content, method of study, cost and whether they lead to a qualification.

c Choose the most appropriate course for your relative to go on.

A possible induction programme might involve a tour of the company, an introduction to the company's organisation, details about payment, holiday entitlement and company policies, an introduction to training programmes on offer, and the chance to meet other new entrants and to ask questions.

Some organisations run a mentor scheme where new employees are linked to an experienced worker for the first few months to help them settle into the job.

Training involves providing new or existing employees with new skills and experience in order to make them more efficient.

On-the-job training involves workers being trained as they do the job. Apprenticeships, where workers learned their skills alongside an experienced worker, were once common in industries like manufacturing but until recently have been in decline. A Modern Apprenticeship initiative was launched by the Government in 1993 to help employers train their employees. Available to young people aged 16 and above, Modern Apprenticeships provide training lasting typically around three years and leading to a qualification at NVQ Level 3 or higher.

Many professional workers – solicitors, accountants, architects, teachers – do an important part of their training on the job. The advantages of on-the-job training are that employees gain direct experience, that they are able to apply the skills they are learning, and that they are doing a job of work as well as being trained. However, much can depend on the quality of the training and the availability of **off-the-job training** to learn the theory.

Off-the-job training involves the worker being trained away from the workplace, either in the company's own training office or in a college or training workshop outside the company. A company may run a one-off course for its employees on a new computer system that is being installed, or a new product development, or it may offer a longer induction or management training course. Many large organisations are now providing courses which lead to a qualification. As an alternative a company may allow its employees to have day-release to study at a college towards an NVQ, a vocational A Level or GCSE, or a professional qualification. People working for small organisations may go on courses giving training on how to run your own business. Such courses may be run by local colleges or by the Learning and Skills Council.

The advantage of off-the-job training is that a wider range of job-related skills and knowledge can be covered by expert trainers and that for the employee a qualification can be a useful basis for career development. The disadvantages are the training costs and the lost production while the employee is off site. In addition, the employee might leave and join another company shortly after training.

In practice, most companies will use a combination of on-the-job and off-the-job training for individual employees.

In recent years, large UK companies have shown more commitment to training. The Confederation of British Industry has promoted the idea of training targets for all companies, and recent governments have backed the idea of National Learning Targets.

National Learning Targets for 2002	
Targets for 16-year-olds	50% of 16-year-olds getting 5 higher grade GCSEs
	95% getting at least 1 GCSE
Targets for young people	85% of 19-year-olds with a Level 2 qualification (5 A*–C GCSE or GNVQ Intermediate or NVQ Level 2)
	60% of 21-year-olds with a Level 3 qualification (2 A Levels or vocational A Level or NVQ Level 3)
Targets for adults	50% of adults with a Level 3 qualification
	28% with a Level 4 qualification (a degree or NVQ Level 4)

Labour turnover, dismissal and redundancy

There will be a variety of reasons why employees will leave an organisation:

- They might have found a better job elsewhere.
- They might be leaving the area.
- They might be bored with their job.
- They might be retiring at the end of their working life.

The number of employees leaving a company over a period of time is known as **labour turnover**. If the level of turnover is high, then a business will need to reduce this as it leads to costs in recruiting, selecting and training new staff.

There will also be reasons why a company might want to reduce the number of people it employs:

- Demand for its products might have fallen.
- To reduce labour costs in order to reduce total costs – known as downsizing (see Unit 19).
- The introduction of new technology might have reduced the number of workers the company needs to employ.

There are various ways that a company can reduce the size of the workforce:

- offer early retirement to those nearing 60 years of age
- invite employees to apply for voluntary **redundancy**, that, is to leave their post voluntarily in return for a cash payment
- not filling posts when they become vacant – natural wastage
- making posts part time rather than full time
- imposing compulsory redundancies, that is, identifying certain workers who will be asked to leave because their job is being cut.

All these choices would involve costs for the business. The government requires businesses to make minimum redundancy payments based upon the number of years' service, and many companies will have their own scheme which has been negotiated with the trade unions. Any programme of redundancies would have to be carefully discussed between management and employee representatives, especially if it involves compulsory redundancy.

A business might also want to dismiss an individual worker as a result of misconduct, or if he or she is not capable or qualified to do a job, e.g. a bus driver might be dismissed if he loses his driving licence due to speeding.

The Employment Protection Act of 1978, plus more recent amendments, gives most employees protection against **unfair dismissal**. Some examples of unfair dismissal would be:

- selecting someone for redundancy just because he or she was a member of a trade union or active in a trade union
- sacking a woman because she is pregnant
- sacking a worker for incompetence when no training has been given
- dismissing someone solely because of their gender or race.

In all these cases the employee would be able to appeal against the unfair dismissal to an **industrial tribunal**. This is a panel of experts which can consider each case. If the dismissal is found to be unfair, then the worker might be reinstated, or given compensation.

KEY TERMS

Curriculum vitae – a brief account of the qualifications and experience so far that a person has, often used in job applications.

Induction – a programme to introduce a new employee to a job.

Industrial tribunal – a panel of experts which considers appeals in cases of unfair dismissal.

Job description – a document that describes the nature of a job that someone is doing.

Labour turnover – the number of people leaving a company over a period of time.

Off-the-job training – training which takes place away from an employee's workplace, e.g. at a college or training centre.

On-the-job training – training which takes place at an employee's workplace while doing their work.

Person specification – a document that describes the type of person that would best be suited to a particular job.

Recruitment agencies – organisations that help companies find full-time or part-time staff in return for a fee.

Redundancy – when employees leave an organisation because their job no longer exists.

Training – providing employees with new skills, knowledge and experiences so that they can better carry out their job.

Unfair dismissal – where an organisation ends an employee's contract without good reason.

Training in Autoglass

Autoglass, the car windscreen repairers, was formed in 1974 and by 1983 it had over 40 branches and 100 mobile fitting units. When it merged in 1984 with a rival company it continued to grow and today has 180 branches and 900 mobile fitting units.

On average, a motorist will need to replace a windscreen every 10 years. A new windscreen is a grudge purchase – most motorists wish they didn't have to buy one. Therefore Autoglass sees its core purpose as overcoming the customer's natural unhappiness by providing good customer service. And it also links customer satisfaction with employee satisfaction. The company wants a highly motivated, enthusiastic, well-trained workforce.

The company has identified a number of core skills that help employees to improve customer service and the training they offer focuses on those skills. There are a number of levels of training:

- 'Startline', a course for new employees that contains both technical training for their particular job and elements to ensure that everyone understands how the business works.

The trainees spend time in each of the departments of the business.

- Fitters have 18 months' training leading up to NVQ standards – 80 per cent of all NVQs in Automotive Glazing have been gained by Autoglass employees.
- Call-centre operators are monitored when receiving calls and this enables their team leader to identify areas where the operator can improve and to be given some direct training.
- Senior managers receive training in management skills, some taking a Business Management degree course at Loughborough University.

Autoglass feels that its emphasis on training has brought benefits. Labour turnover has fallen and there have been more internal appointments to senior jobs within the company. Also the company gets more innovative ideas from its employees as they know the company so well.

Source: Adapted from www.mbapublishing.co.uk/cd/casestudies/

Q Questions

1 Why are windscreens 'grudge' purchases by consumers?
2 Explain the type of training involved in each of the following, showing which ones are on-the-job or off-the-job training:
   a 'Startline'
   b Business Management degree at Loughborough University
   c Training provided for the call-centre operators
   d The NVQ in Automotive Glazing.
3 How does employee satisfaction lead to good customer satisfaction?
4 Identify some of the core skills that you think are needed at Autoglass to improve customer service.
5 Why do you think Autoglass feels that the training is a worthwhile business cost?

E Extension

1 Why in the 'Startline' training would new employees spend time in each of the business's departments?
2 How would Autoglass find out whether the training it offers is effective? What measures could it use?

Financial motivation at work

This unit is about how financial rewards are used to motivate people who work.

At the end of the unit, students should be able to:

- understand why people go to work
- explain Maslow's hierarchy of needs
- identify what motivates workers
- identify what makes workers dissatisfied with their work
- understand how wages and salaries are used to reward the workforce
- calculate total pay and net pay
- compare different payment systems
- understand bonus pay.

Why do people work?

Everybody is different. The differences we are born with, and the differences we get from how and where we live, help to make us different. We are different in intelligence, in personality, in physical appearance and in our physical skills. We therefore have very different needs and wants which drive us on. One person may want to be prime minister. Another may want to see England win the World Cup. Another may want to help famine relief in Somalia. Another to own their own business.

If the question is asked, 'Why do people work?', there will be as many different answers as there are workers. But although everyone's needs are different, these needs can be put together under a number of headings. This was first done by Abraham Maslow in 1954 and has become known as Maslow's **hierarchy of needs**.

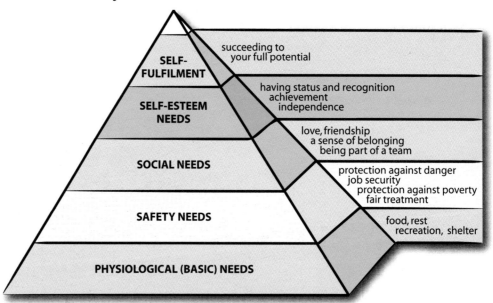

Maslow's hierarchy of needs

A hierarchy means that those things at the top are more important than those at the bottom. At whatever age people start work, they will be motivated by physiological or basic needs. They will want to earn enough money for food and recreation and perhaps for shelter if they have left home. They will also hope that the job is secure and the working environment safe and pleasant (safety needs). As they move through their working lives these aspects may become less motivating. They will want to feel a part of the organisation they work for and to develop friendships (social needs). They will want to gain promotion and be given additional responsibilities and more pay (self-esteem needs). They will finally want to feel that they have achieved something and become a success (self-fulfilment needs).

TASK 1

This task would be best carried out individually at first, and then in groups so that you can compare what you have written with someone else.

a Imagine that you have just taken a part-time job as a check-out operator at your local supermarket.

　i What needs do you think such a job would satisfy in your present position?

　ii What needs do you think it would not satisfy?

　Explain your answers.

b Imagine that you have just moved on to an A Level, vocational A Level or NVQ course in your school or in a college.

　i What needs would you hope that the school or college would meet during your course?

　ii Compare your answer with the needs you identified for the part-time job. What are the differences? Why do you think the two lists are different?

There are three conclusions from Maslow's hierarchy which are important for business:

- As soon as one need is satisfied it no longer motivates. For example, if a group of workers feels that they are paid enough to meet their basic needs, then paying them more will not motivate them to work harder. They will need other forms of encouragement, like being able to make some of their own decisions.

- If a need is not satisfied, then it can lead to frustration. For example, if a manager feels that he or she has been ignored for promotion, the individual might well not put much effort into his or her job and look for alternative employment.

- If a lower need is suddenly not being met, then higher needs are ignored. For example, if a group of workers is threatened with redundancy, any incentive scheme run by the management will soon run into problems.

Working in large organisations

Working in large organisations often means working on production lines similar to the one shown in the picture.

Production lines were introduced in the early part of the twentieth century to allow the mass production of consumer goods like cars to take place. Every job on a production line was simple and repetitive, and required little training for the worker. Few skills were involved and the work was boring. On such production lines, only the basic needs of workers from their job would be met – pay, a job, a safe working environment. But the threat of losing a job was also there. Each worker could easily be replaced by another worker, and at times when demand for goods was low, production lines could be shut down.

Despite the lack of motivation from working on production lines, employees and management accepted them for over 80 years and today many goods are still made on production lines throughout the world. But for a workforce to be productive, more is needed than simply regular pay and safe working conditions. New ways of organising work have been developed in Europe, the USA and Japan in order to make the job itself more rewarding for the worker.

There are a number of advantages and disadvantages of working in a large organisation as shown in the table.

Advantages	Disadvantages
More opportunities for promotion and career development.	Many workers will have low skilled and poorly paid jobs.
More opportunities to take responsibility and make decisions when higher up the organisation.	Less job security if the company is unsuccessful.
	Close supervision over what workers are doing.
Higher wages and bonuses for some workers if the company is successful.	Production line jobs are boring and repetitive.
More people to meet and make friends with.	Poor communication and relations between workforce and management.
Company pension schemes and better health and safety schemes.	

Frederick Herzberg carried out some research during the 1960s to find out people's opinions about their jobs. He took a sample of people at different levels in different jobs and asked them two questions:

1 *What is it about your job that you dislike?*

In the answers the following were identified:

- salary and job security
- working conditions
- supervision by the boss
- company rules and policy
- relationships with subordinates.

Herzberg gave these the name *hygiene factors*. If these factors are satisfied, they do not make employees any happier, they just remove unhappiness.

2 *What is it about your job that you like?*

In the answers the following were identified:

- the job itself
- being given responsibility
- achieving success and being recognised by management
- gaining promotion
- personal development.

He gave these the name *motivators*. It is these factors which really motivate the workforce. Notice that they are similar to the top two levels of Maslow's hierarchy of needs (see above).

TASK 2

Jason Leigh works in the postroom of a large food manufacturer. His responsibilities involve the sorting of mail coming into the organisation and its delivery to departments; the collecting, sorting and delivery of internal mail within the organisation; and the collection and stamping of mail being sent out of the company. He left school at 16 with two GCSEs to join the company and has been with it for three years. He earns £8,500 per annum for a 40-hour week. He works with seven others under a supervisor.

Elaine Morgan works in the product development department of the same organisation. She is responsible for the research and development of new food products, including testing and trialling with consumers. She has responsibility for a team of five home economists, and reports to the product development manager. She joined the company three years ago on completing a degree in Food Technology and earns £22,250 per annum but has no stipulated hours in her contract.

1 What areas for dissatisfaction might exist in
   i Jason's job
   ii Elaine's job?
2 What opportunities for motivation might exist in
   i Jason's job
   ii Elaine's job?
3 Why are your answers about Jason's work different from answers about Elaine's?

Rewarding the workforce

In any type of business, the basic reward for working for the business will be by the payment of a **wage** or **salary**.

A wage is a sum of money that is usually paid on an hourly or weekly rate in return for the labour provided by the employee. For example, general labourers might be paid £5.00 an hour working on a building site; if they work for 45 hours in one week they will earn £225 that week. A school secretary might be paid £200 per week for working during school term time. If there are 42 weeks of school a year, she will earn £8,400 per year. There is now a national minimum wage of £4.10 per hour for adults and £3.50 for 18–21-year-olds (as from October 2001) that the government has set. No business should be paying its workers less than this amount.

A salary is a sum of money that is agreed on an annual basis as a reward for working, but will be paid monthly. An engineer working for a partnership of builders may have an annual salary of £30,600 but would be paid monthly as £2,550 per month.

A third method of payment is payment by results. This might be based upon the number of products an employee produces – known as piece rate. Pea pickers on a farm in East Anglia might be paid £3.00 for every 5kg of peas they pick. If they can pick 100kg in a day, they will earn £60 for the day's work. Or it might be based on the number of products someone sells. A door-to-door seller of cosmetics might be paid 10 per cent of every £1 worth of goods that he or she sells. If he or she sells £1,800 of cosmetics in a week, the sales person will receive £180 as earnings in the form of sales commission.

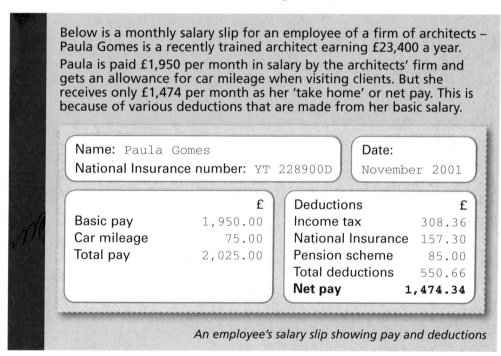

Below is a monthly salary slip for an employee of a firm of architects – Paula Gomes is a recently trained architect earning £23,400 a year.

Paula is paid £1,950 per month in salary by the architects' firm and gets an allowance for car mileage when visiting clients. But she receives only £1,474 per month as her 'take home' or net pay. This is because of various deductions that are made from her basic salary.

Name: Paula Gomes
National Insurance number: YT 228900D
Date: November 2001

	£	Deductions	£
Basic pay	1,950.00	Income tax	308.36
Car mileage	75.00	National Insurance	157.30
Total pay	2,025.00	Pension scheme	85.00
		Total deductions	550.66
		Net pay	**1,474.34**

An employee's salary slip showing pay and deductions

Everyone who works has to pay income tax, that is, a percentage of their income as a tax to the government. For most employees this is taken out of their pay before they receive it and is known as Pay As You Earn (PAYE). People who are self-employed, e.g. a sole trader, also have to pay income tax.

Each employee makes a contribution towards the cost of retirement pensions, the National Health Service, etc. through paying National Insurance. Employers have to make a contribution for each employee; the self-employed also make contributions.

There may be other deductions to a person's salary. In the case of Paula above, she makes an additional payment to a private pension scheme which will top up her state pension when she retires. There might be other deductions for savings schemes, charitable donations or union dues.

As well as basic wages and salaries, there are other sources of income for employees, including **overtime** and **bonus pay**.

Overtime is where someone is paid for working more hours in a week than is stated in his or her **contract of employment**. Overtime is not available in all jobs, but where it is, it is usually paid at a higher rate than the basic pay for the job. For example, the general labourer who is paid £5.00 per hour for a 45-hour week may be paid time and a half, that is £7.50 per hour, for every hour worked over 45 hours. If he or she works 50 hours in a week, his weekly pay would be:

45 hours at £5.00 per hour	=	£225.00 +
5 hours at £7.50 per hour	=	£37.50
Total pay	=	£262.50

This figure would be before any deductions were made.

Bonus pay is where extra money is paid if the employee or the organisation achieves a certain target. It might be tied to the employee's output – known as a productivity bonus. It might be tied to the employee's sales – known as a sales bonus. Alternatively, it might be linked to the output, sales or profitability of the whole organisation. Such bonus schemes are more common in large organisations than in small ones. They are explained in more detail later in this unit.

TASK 3

The following jobs were recently advertised in a local newspaper of a large city.

HEAVY GOODS VEHICLE DRIVERS
required for work driving refrigerated lorries
Days £5.00 per hour
Nights £6.00 per hour

SWITCHBOARD OPERATOR
wanted for new hotel:
£4.55 per hour
for 37-hour week

SALES REPRESENTATIVE
required for furniture company
£22,000
plus commission

Expert Gents Hairstylist
required for City Centre Salon
£10,400 plus bonuses per annum

EXPERT FISHMONGER
required to work in local branch of a chain of fish shops
£240 per week plus bonus

TRAINEE RECRUITMENT OFFICER
wanted by an engineering recruitment company
Starting at £15,000 pa

a In which of the above jobs are employees earning a wage and in which a salary? Explain your answers.

b Why is the HGV driver paid more for night time work than daytime?

c What type of bonuses might the fishmonger and the hairstylist earn?

d What is meant by 'plus commission' in the advertisement for the sales representative?

e Another switchboard job is on offer at a solicitor's office paying £175 per week. Is this a better job to apply for than the one in the hotel? Explain your answer.

Payment systems

In large organisations complicated payment systems have been developed to provide incentives for the workforce. Businesses have also developed non-financial ways of motivating the workforce. These will be looked at in the next unit.

In large businesses there will be many employees doing a wide range of jobs. For example, in a large department store there will be shop assistants, department managers, clerical assistants, maintenance people, warehouse and stock control staff, office managers, security staff and many more jobs. In a large manufacturing company there will be many levels of production worker from unskilled to skilled to supervisory, and many staff levels from technicians and clerks to managers. Such organisations have developed payment systems to reward their workers. An example of the payment systems for a large department store is shown below.

Payment Systems at Ashton Department Store Ltd

Employees move up a point for every year served with the company.

Shop floor assistant and clerical assistant	Grade 1	New entrants		Department manager	Grade 1	Departments employing 5–10 staff
	Point 1	£10,000			Point 1	£19,000
	2	£10,250			2	£20,000
	3	£10,500			3	£21,000
					4	£22,000
Shop floor assistant and clerical assistant	Grade 2	Experienced assistants			5	£23,000
	Point 1	£10,750				
	2	£11,250		Department manager	Grade 2	Departments employing over 10 staff
	3	£11,750				
	4	£12,500			Point 1	£24,500
	5	£13,250			2	£25,500
					3	£26,500
Section supervisor	Point 1	£14,250			4	£27,500
	2	£15,250			5	£28,500
	3	£16,250				
	4	£17,250		Senior management – salaries by negotiation in the range £31,500 – £36,500		
	5	£18,250				

Such a payment system would be the result of negotiation between management and employee representatives. It would have to take into account:

- what each job involves
- the need to reward experienced or skilled workers at a higher rate than inexperienced or unskilled workers
- any national or local pay agreements in the industry
- the overall levels of pay in similar companies
- the profitability of the company.

TASK 4

Use the information on payment systems at Ashton Department Store to answer the following questions:

a What would be the pay of the following individuals working for Ashton's:

i the accounts manager, responsible for 14 employees in her department, who has been a manager for eight years

ii an accounts clerk who has just completed his first year in the office

iii a supervisor in the jewellery department who gained promotion three years previously

iv the manager of the jewellery department who joined the company this year and who is responsible for eight employees

v the managing director?

b What evidence is there from the pay scales that Ashton Ltd is trying to motivate its workforce through the payments system it uses?

Bonus systems

In addition to the basic payment system, businesses might also have a bonus system which is tied to the actual performance of the employee.

There are several types of bonus payments:

- Productivity bonuses – for those directly involved in producing a good or service. An individual or group would receive extra pay if an output target is reached.
- Sales bonuses – for employees directly involved in selling a product or service. A bonus would be paid based on the value of sales over a period.
- Performance related pay – for staff not directly involved in the production or selling of goods and services. An additional payment tied to carrying out certain duties or achieving certain targets.
- Annual bonuses – workers have traditionally been paid an annual bonus, often at Christmas, as a reward for loyalty and hard work during the year.

In most of these cases a piece rate element has been added to the basic time rate. This is in order to motivate the workforce to achieve higher output, sales or profit. For many employees such bonuses now form an important part of their total pay. There are, however, disadvantages to bonus systems:

- There is uncertainty as to how much will actually be paid each month.
- If machinery breaks down or equipment fails, a bonus might be lost through no fault of the employee.
- If groups of workers are paid a bonus, some of the group might not deserve the bonus.
- Competition between individuals or groups might lead to a poorer quality product.
- For some groups of workers, e.g. nurses, teachers, police, etc., it is difficult to measure the contribution that an individual has made to the overall performance of the organisation.

TASK 5

A vacancy has arisen for a highly motivated
SALES PERSON
required to sell a full range of Mercedes Benz commercial vehicles products at our very busy dealership. The right applicant must be smart and presentable and able to use their own initiative. A competitive salary and a company vehicle will be provided to the right candidate,
Please apply to Brian Tuxford,
Used Vehicle Sales Manager
0161 230 6808

Ashton Foods Limited

Maintenance Technicians

Ashton Foods is a leading manufacturer of pre-packed bacon and cooked meat products, supplying major British Retailers.

To support our business we are currently seeking to strengthen our Engineering Team by appointing additional Maintenance Technicians.

Ideally, we are looking for multi-skilled Engineers preferably with electrical bias and 16th edition regulation certificate with "hands-on" experience of high speed Food Production Machinery.

The successful candidates will be highly motivated, team players who can work a rotating shift pattern in a highly pressurised environment.

Opportunities exist for further development to Supervisory/Team Leader positions for the right candidate.

All interested candidates should send a full CV and letter of application to
Gill Warburton-Hall (Personnel Manager),
Ashton Foods Limited, Mackeson Road, Off Queens Road, Ashton-under-Lyne, Lancashire, OL6 8HZ.

HARRY RAMSDEN's
Require Full & Part Time
*Waiting On Staff
*Bar/Hosting
*Kitchen Assistants
*School Leavers Needed
Flexible hours to suit students
Company benefits package available
Please call DUTY MANAGER on
0161 832 9144
To arrange interview

EDUCATION

ICT TEACHER
Maternity Cover
Required for Autumn Term 2001
Salary MPS. Hours 0.4
Required for Autumn Term 2001. An enthusiastic and IT literate member of staff to join ICT department of this oversubscribed Beacon School and work in KS3 two days per week. We have an excellent scheme of work developed in-house. ICT is a rapidly expanding area at Blue Coat School and the department is growing
Informal Enquiries to Mr G McGuffie
(Deputy Headteacher)
Tel 0161 624 1484
Application forms from and returnable to:
Mr K W Pleasant BA, Headteacher
The Blue Coat School
Egerton Street
Oldham
OL1 3SQ
Please mark the envelope ICT post
Email:secretary@blue-coat.oldham.co.uk
Closing date 12th July 2001

a For each of these jobs, identify and explain a possible bonus system which might be used to motivate the post holder.

b Choose one of the jobs. Identify any problems that might exist in using this method of bonus payment from the point of view of: **i** the employee **ii** the employer.

KEY TERMS

Bonus pay – extra money paid if the employee or organisation achieves a target.

Income tax – a percentage of a person's income paid as a tax to the government.

Hierarchy of needs – a way of presenting the needs of people at work with basic needs at the bottom and higher needs at the top.

Overtime – payment made for work outside the stated hours in a worker's contract; often paid at a higher rate.

Salary – basic form of payment based on a reward for a year's work, but usually paid in monthly instalments.

Wage – basic form of payment based on the number of hours or weeks that a person works.

Average Hourly Earnings, 2000	
Industry	**Earnings per hour (£)**
Agriculture	6.24
Education	11.78
Finance	14.29
Health and Social Services	9.67
Hotels/Catering	6.65
Manufacturing	9.72
Public Administration	10.55
Retailing/Wholesaling	8.82

Source: *Monthly Digest of Statistics*, March 2001

How salaries compare

Public sector professionals, long said by their unions to be underpaid, are placed high in a pay league compiled by the Office for National Statistics. For example, secondary school teachers, paid on average £16.04 per hour, get better pay than accountants, architects and civil engineers. Financial managers however top the list with hourly wages of £26.38. Doctors, solicitors and management consultants have all shown annual salary increases of more than 10 per cent in 1999/2000.

Teachers argue that this figure is misleading because their working week is officially very short which is why the hourly rate appears high.

The average hourly rate is above £10 but this is increased by a number of people with very large salaries who can throw out the averages. Almost 3,000 people are earning in excess of £1million which is a five times increase over 1994.

These figures do not take into account overtime which can boost hourly wages considerably. They also do not reflect other incentives that employees get.

Source: Adapted from *Metro News,* 24 July 2000.

Q Questions

1 Explain from the table how the average earnings have been calculated.
2 Why are the average earnings in the finance industry the highest in the list?
3 Why might the article provide misleading evidence about the average pay of secondary school teachers?
4 Why do you think public sector professionals have seen their income increasing in recent years?
5 a From the table, which are the two lowest paid industries?
  b What policy has the Government introduced in the last three years to improve pay in low-paid industries?

E Extension

1 Explain why the average hourly wage of £10 may be distorted by a number of people with very high wages.
2 How might **a** employers, and **b** unions use the information above to support their particular viewpoints?

Non-financial motivation

This unit is about how the people who work are motivated by non-financial rewards.

At the end of the unit, students should be able to:

- understand different methods used by business to motivate workers

- explain the advantages and disadvantages of each method

- compare motivation in the private and public sectors

- understand how contracts protect the rights of the workforce

- analyse methods of discrimination against workers

- apply own understanding of discrimination to case studies.

What motivates?

In the 1970s and 1980s in industries where workers were well paid, such as printing and motor manufacture, there was still considerable worker dissatisfaction. This led to, for example, resistance to new technology or changes in working practices. Considerable numbers of working days were lost due to industrial action as a result of this resistance.

By the 1990s business managers had realised that money should not be used as the only method of motivation. The work of people like Maslow and Herzberg (see Unit 30) showed them that workers are motivated by being given new challenges and opportunities, by being involved in their work and by being give training to improve their skills. British managers were also able to learn from methods of motivation developed in other countries.

Since the 1980s several large overseas companies have bought or set up companies in the UK. For example, Nissan and Honda from Japan set up car manufacturing factories in Sunderland and Swindon respectively. New methods of motivation began to be used in such factories. There are also examples of UK companies – such as British Airways and the John Lewis Partnership – which have employed non-financial methods of motivation for several years.

The methods employed attempt to meet the higher needs of the workforce that Maslow and Herzberg identified. They have involved giving employees more say in decision making and more responsibility for their work.

TASK 1

Use the Biz/ed web site to find out how different companies motivate their workforce. Go to www.bized.ac.uk and click on Company Facts. Choose three of the companies listed and look at the frequently asked questions. Click on 'Can you tell me how employees are motivated?' Print off each of the answers from the three companies.

a Identify:

   i methods of financial motivation that are being used by the companies

   ii methods of non-financial motivation that are being used by the companies.

b Which company in your opinion would be best to work for? Explain why.

Methods of non-financial motivation

There are a number of methods that different companies have used:

- **Job enrichment** involves making a job more interesting by giving workers more control over what they are doing. This might involve, for example, training machine operators to carry out their own quality control or allowing them to order their own materials. It does not mean making the job larger but it does allow workers more of their own control over how a job is done.

- **Team working** involves allowing a group of workers to produce the whole product and to decide for themselves how they organise their own work. This was pioneered by Volvo in Sweden and has been copied by many companies since. It means that teams can share their ideas and make use of everyone's skills and knowledge to the best effect. However, teams do not always work well together if there is not the right combination of skill and experience in the team.

- **Quality circles** are groups of workers who meet regularly to talk about and introduce improvements in the way particular tasks are carried out and in the quality of the product. They are more commonly found in foreign-owned companies than in British companies. To work, managers must be willing to listen to and act upon the ideas that come out of the quality circles. Otherwise the workforce will feel that they are not a good use of their time.

- **Consultative committees** involve management seeking the views and advice of employees on a regular basis through meetings and discussions with employee representatives. In some organisations they are known as Works Councils. In these committees the management puts up ideas in order to see what the response of the workforce might be. They might discuss proposed changes in working conditions, production, training or even pay. These groups, however, do not make the final decisions – the managers may or may not follow the feedback they get from the workforce. Under recent European Union (EU) legislation, all companies with over 1,000 employees and which exist in two or more EU countries must set up a European Works Council to give information and consult with employees on important company decisions.

- In a **single status company** there are no distinctions between management and workforce, e.g. everyone is paid monthly, there is no clocking on, everyone wears the same company clothing, everyone eats in the same cafeteria. The working conditions (but not the pay) of the management are the same as the working conditions of the workforce.

- **Profit sharing** is where the workforce become owners of the company through receiving shares as a bonus or by receiving a share of the profits of the company. The department store group John Lewis Partnership has run such a scheme since the company was set up. It is now becoming more common in other businesses where the workforce is rewarded with shares which have the potential to increase in value in the future. However, the value of shares may also fall if the business becomes unsuccessful.

- **Investors in people** is a kitemark awarded to companies that encourage training and development and good communication with their employees. It is therefore not a method itself, but by achieving the award this shows that the company follows good practices with its workforce.

INVESTORS IN PEOPLE

TASK 2

Turning Japanese

Nissan's day shift begins at 8 am, but Kevin Jones, a 26-year-old supervisor in the press shop, gets there early. The 20 men under him are divided into two teams, each with a team leader. Jones has control of three 2,700-ton presses. His main responsibility is to meet the day's target for production.

Next to the press shop is the meeting room, where supervisors, engineers and managers all have their desks, and where the manufacturing staff can have their breaks. There are no partitions or separate rooms.

At 8 am the teams leave the meeting room and go on to the shop floor. They meet by the presses and Jones tells them about the day's target. Yesterday there was a problem; a number of faulty pressings were passed on and the mistakes only showed up in the paint shop. 'We have to support the inspection in the paint shop,' says Jones, 'one of us must go through the stacks of parts awaiting painting and catch the faulty ones. Lee – you've drawn the short straw!' Lee briefly pulls a face, then sprints off to the paint shop. The rest of the men move to the presses and begin work on the thousands of bits of motor car they will make today.

Source: Adapted from *The Independent Magazine*, 12 September 1992.

a What examples are there in the extract which show that Nissan is using non-financial methods of motivation?

b Do you think that Kevin Jones' higher needs are being satisfied by working at Nissan? Explain your answer.

Problems with non-financial motivation

While such methods have helped many companies to motivate their workforce, some problems with their use have been experienced:

- Many of these schemes involve time and cost to set up throughout a business. For example, considerable staff training is needed before team working or job enrichment can take place. The results from any changes also may take a long time to show in increased output, sales or profit.

- People have to change their usual working practices. There is always some resistance to change in any organisation and this might make new methods of working difficult to put into practice.

- Many jobs within organisations do not have enough scope to be 'enriched'. It is difficult to make certain unskilled jobs, e.g. stacking in a warehouse or cleaning in a hospital, more varied and interesting. It tends to be those workers in more highly skilled work who get the benefit of job enrichment.

- Managers are accused of giving employees more to do rather than helping to motivate them. If there is no increase in pay, but an increase in the range of work that someone is expected to do, then the workforce may well resist new practices. New schemes to motivate the workforce may have to be introduced alongside new bonus payment schemes.

- Redundancies in a company might make such schemes less motivating as workers worry about job security. If a lower need on Maslow's hierarchy is not being satisfied, then it becomes the one that most affects the workforce. For example, recent job losses in the UK's banks have seriously affected relations between management and bank employees.

TASK 3

We're not happy, you're for it

Many new web companies need to learn an important lesson from the past – if you don't give an employee job satisfaction, then they will find their own, perhaps with disastrous effects. In industries like the docks and the car industry job satisfaction was kept high by warfare with the employers over wage rates.

If wage demands were not met, the workforce took strike action collectively and this gave them considerable power. They worked in teams but against the interests of the managers.

Workers in the web companies are unlikely to go out on strike, but they will have other ways of showing dissatisfaction with the company. They might change or remove important data, they might hack into the company's computer or they might work in teams against the interests of the company, e.g. by setting up a rival operation.

E-commerce managers will need to show that they value their employees, that they can be trusted, that they communicate well and that they are willing to listen to employees. As yet most e-commerce managers are too young to learn from the experience of the past.

Source: Adapted from *The Observer*, 24 September 2000 (based upon information from www.ftknowledge.com).

a Why might working in teams not always be in the best interest of a company?

b List three ways in which workers in an e-commerce company might work against the company.

c How could managers promote job satisfaction in the new web companies?

Motivation in the public sector

The public sector is among the largest employers in the country. About two million people are employed by central government. This includes, for example, all central government departments such as the Inland Revenue, the Department for Education and Employment, the Home Office, and the National Health Service. The UK's National Health Service is, in fact, one of the largest employers in Europe. About another two million people are employed by local government. These workers include teachers, police, librarians, refuse collectors and those employed in the local council's offices. Also included in the public sector are those employed in public corporations like the Royal Mail and the BBC and members of the armed services. The size of the public sector changes over time. Its size depends on the government's views of the need for services and its ability to finance them. It also depends on political policy.

Because public sector organisations and departments are generally large there are advantages and disadvantages to working in them. These are similar to the advantages and disadvantages of working in any large business, shown in Unit 30 (page 234).

Research (by Livingstone and Wilke) has been carried out into the levels of morale and motivation among workers in the public sector and into ways in which these levels can be maintained or improved. The research shows that satisfaction is usually increased when:

- work is seen as a challenge
- workers' achievements are recognised
- there is a pleasant physical environment
- there is some freedom to carry out the job.

However, dissatisfaction is likely where there is:

- a lack of a challenge
- the feeling that workers are no more than a 'cog' in a large machine
- a lack of freedom
- a lack of promotion prospects
- poor training
- low salary
- a lack of appreciation from clients, that is, the public.

Public sector workers largely provide a service rather than make or sell products. It is therefore difficult to introduce bonus payment systems for such workers. However, a number of non-financial strategies have been employed by public sector managers to help promote high levels of motivation and satisfaction. These include:

- the introduction of targets, e.g. schools and teachers are set targets of increasing the number of pupils achieving 5 or more GCSE A*–C grades; hospitals and doctors are set targets of reducing waiting times
- improved communication between managers and other workers, e.g. through the use of newsletters, consultative committees or focus groups
- use of quality circles to improve the quality of a service being offered
- the introduction of mission statements and corporate aims to create an identity for an organisation just as in the private sector
- reporting achievements to the public through annual reports, meetings, news releases and other public relations methods.

TASK 4

Interview your headteacher or a member of the school's senior management team. Try to find out:

a the targets that have been set for your school by either the local education authority (LEA) or the school's governors – there may be targets for Key Stage 3, Key Stage 4 and the sixth form.

b what the school and teachers are doing to help them meet these targets

c whether the pay of any of the staff is linked to these targets

d the opinion of the head or senior managers about the use of targets and whether they motivate staff.

Write a short report which summarises your findings. Do you feel that target setting acts as a motivation for the teaching staff at the school?

Protecting the workforce

An employee of any business has certain rights which are protected by law. One of the most important is the right to have a written **contract of employment**. Provided they work for more than 16 hours a week for someone, all employees should have a contract.

Every contract must contain certain information. This includes:

- the job title
- the date when employment begins
- the rate of pay or the way the pay will be calculated
- the hours of work
- the amount of holidays that the employee is entitled to
- any provision for sickness pay
- the length of notice needed to end the contract by either side, or the date when a fixed-term contract ends
- any disciplinary code which applies to the job
- the identity of a person to whom the employee could apply if dissatisfied with his or her job.

The importance of having a contract is that if the employer or employee breaks any part of it, then the other side is protected by the law. This should allow either side to get things put right, or at least get some form of compensation. For example, if a garage mechanic is paid less per week by the garage owner than is stated in the contract, he or she should be able to get back pay to make up the difference; or if an employee leaves a job without giving any notice, the employer would not have to pay any wages from the day the employee left the job.

There are other areas where employees now have legal protection in their work. Again, these apply to all types of business organisation, and to both full- and part-time workers:

- **Equal pay** – female employees should be paid the same wage as male employees for work rated as of equal value in terms of effort, skills and decision making. The work does not have to be the same for it to be of equal value. For example, a cook in a small building business might expect to receive equal pay to painters and plasterers employed by the business.

- **Sex discrimination** – female or male employees should not be at a disadvantage in their employment just because of their sex. For example, a woman should not be overlooked for promotion just because she is married and might start a family. This protection also applies to the recruitment process for jobs and other aspects of employment such as hours of working and dismissal.

- **Racial discrimination** – employees should not be disadvantaged at work because of their ethnic origin. This should be applied to recruitment, pay, other conditions of employment, promotion and also dismissal.

- **Disability discrimination** – it is illegal for an employer to treat an employee who is disabled less favourably than anyone else. Employers must make 'reasonable adjustments' to buildings, equipment, facilities, training, etc. if the disabled person is at a substantial disadvantage compared to able-bodied employees. This also applies to job applicants.

- **Health and safety** – all employers are required to have rules and policies that ensure that the working environment is safe and healthy for the workforce. All employees are expected to follow any safety rules that exist but it is the duty of the employer to make sure that the workforce knows the rules and follows them.

- **Unfair dismissal** – employees have the right to complain if they feel that they have been dismissed for an unfair reason. This would be when they feel that the employer has broken his or her side of the contract. They can go to an industrial tribunal (see Unit 29) to put their case for being given their job back, or for receiving compensation.

The trouble with laws, however, is that they can be expensive for a small business to apply. There are many examples where employees in small organisations are not provided with all the legal rights they should have. It can also take an employee a long time to get a matter put right. In small businesses especially, both sides rely largely on each other behaving properly within the law. In larger organisations which have personnel departments and trade union representatives, it is easier to ensure that workers' rights are protected (see Unit 32).

TASK 5

This task could be carried out in pairs or in groups of four.

For each of the cases:

a make a list of the arguments that the employer might use.

b make a list of the arguments that the employee might use.

c come to a decision in your pair or group as to which of the two sides is acting correctly.

Case A

When Ray Leyland took on Jason Knight to work for his parcel delivery business, Jason signed a contract of employment saying that he would carry out deliveries anywhere in the UK. However, at the time of signing the contract Ray and Jason made a verbal agreement that he would not be sent to Scotland on deliveries. Jason did not want to be away from his family for too long. But when two years later Jason refused to make a delivery in Scotland, Ray dismissed him for breaking his written contract.

Case B

When Sonia Joseph applied for a part-time post at a local law firm she thought she would stand a good chance of getting the job. Before having her three children she had worked for eight years as a legal secretary. She also had excellent references. But despite being invited for interview, the job went to another candidate who was new to legal work. When she asked the head of the law firm why she didn't get the job, she was told that the firm thought she would be unreliable because of the demands of her children.

Case C

Leila Shanks was a part-time machinist in a small textiles business which employed eight full-time and 18 part-time workers, all female. She had not been employed long by the business when she realised that the part-time workers received less than half the pay of the full-time workers, even though they worked half the hours. When she asked her boss about this, she was told that the lower rate was paid because the part-time workers' machines were lying idle for longer and therefore unit costs were higher. Also, the part-timers had more chances to earn overtime than the full-time workers.

Case D

Nick Kirker, a chemist working for British Sugar, was chosen for redundancy on the basis of a selection test in which he scored no points for performance, competence and potential. However, he was suffering from glaucoma and was therefore partially sighted. He maintained that the real reason he was being made redundant was because of his disability.

Hundreds of women share £12m bias payout

The National Health Service is to pay 351 speech therapists £12 million to settle one of the longest running sex discrimination cases in legal history.

Payments of up to £70,000 each will be made in back pay to female speech therapists who have fought for 15 years for equal pay with professionals working in clinical psychology and pharmacy who tend to be male.

Speech therapists train for up to four years and work with people with a range of speech and communication problems.

Senior National Health Service managers think that the pay of therapists will now have to be raised to match those of other health professionals. The agreement could also open the way for similar deals for physiotherapists and midwives who are also claiming equal pay with colleagues in male-dominated fields.

Liz Panton, a speech therapist with Newcastle City Health Trust, argued that patients would benefit because therapists would now be able to command more resources from the NHS managers.

Roger Lyons, general secretary of the Manufacturing Science Finance Union, which represents the therapists, said that the agreement was a great victory, not only for the women concerned, but also for women working in other professions.

'This is a David and Goliath story. A small group of female professionals overcame the might of an antagonistic Tory government.' he said, adding that the settlement was a testament to the present government's commitment to equal pay.

Source: *The Independent,* 8 May 2000

Q Questions

1 Why did the speech therapists accuse the NHS of sex discrimination?

2 What arguments would the representatives of the therapists have put forward in support of the case?

3 What arguments would representatives of the NHS put against the therapists?

4 Explain how the outcome from this case might affect the salaries paid to other workers in the health service.

5 What types of non-financial motivation might workers like speech therapists benefit from in their jobs?

E Extension

1 How might this case affect the salaries of workers outside the National Health Service?

2 Use the Internet to find out other examples of recent 'discrimination at work' cases. What arguments were used for and against each case? What were the outcomes for the employers and employees?

Negotiation and bargaining

This unit is about how employers and employees come to agreements over pay and working conditions and what happens when negotiations break down.

At the end of the unit, students should be able to:

- explain what is meant by collective bargaining

- understand the roles of the two sides in collective bargaining

- identify the benefits of trade union membership

- analyse why industrial relations might break down

- compare the different types of industrial action.

Collective bargaining

> # No longer a job to bank on
>
> ## Unions threaten action over cuts in Sunday pay
>
> # Today's rail strike
>
> ## Rail union to ballot on peace plan
>
> ## Car workers fear drift of work to Eastern Europe

The type of participation at work talked about in Unit 31 has been added to a more traditional way in which workers have taken part in decisions. For many years workers and managers have met on a regular basis to negotiate over pay and working conditions. This is known as **collective bargaining**. By being part of a large organisation, workers have realised that they have a certain power if they put their views together rather than individually. Therefore they choose representatives to put their case about pay or conditions. At the same time management would prefer to talk to a representative rather than meet with each worker individually. Collective bargaining has been an important part of the industrial relations between employers and workers.

Who is involved in collective bargaining will vary between one large organisation and another. Most of the representatives of the workforce will be full time employees of the company, but companies are required by law to give them time off for union business. The table shows who would be involved in the negotiations on each side.

The management side	The workers' side
An *employers' federation* – in some industries like building, engineering, printing, there are national groups which negotiate pay and conditions on behalf of all the companies in an industry.	A *trade union negotiator* – workers might be represented by a trade union which negotiates with employers on a national basis. There may be several trade unions represented in a large organisation and each will want to be involved in any negotiation.
The *personnel* (or *human resource*) *manager* – a specialist manager in a company who will have responsibility for negotiating with the workforce.	A *shop steward* – unions with a large number of members in a business may have shop stewards representing groups of workers in different parts of the business.
Other *managers* and *supervisors* – who will be involved in day-to-day discussions on the shop floor with workers' representatives.	A *convenor* (the leader of the shop stewards) might also exist, e.g. in large car making factories.
	An *employee representative* – often in white-collar jobs or where workers are organised in local staff associations there will be employee representatives who negotiate with management.

TASK 1

At the engineering depot of a telecommunications company a dispute has arisen between the installation engineers, represented by the Union of Communication Workers (UCW), and the company's managers. For the last two years the engineers have been required to complete a maximum of four jobs during each working day. But, because management wanted to increase the engineers' productivity, this had now been increased to five. The engineers were angry because they had not been consulted on this change. Although it meant the possibility of more overtime, some of the engineers were unwilling to work longer than their 7½-hour day on a regular basis.

The engineers have called in their local UCW representative to negotiate with the management either to restore the four jobs per day limit, or else to pay extra basic pay for the increased work. Management has said that the increased number of visits (jobs) would help the company provide a better service to its customers.

a What is the dispute at the company about?

b Explain the role of the trade union negotiator in the dispute.

c Suggest a reasonable solution to the dispute on which both sides might agree. Explain your solution.

The front page of a leaflet encouraging workers to join the Manufacturing, Science and Finance Union

The role of trade unions

Trade unions exist to represent the interests of employees when they are negotiating with their employers. Between 1980 and 1998 membership of trade unions declined from 13 million to 6.7 million. This was due to the decline of industries such as coalmining, shipbuilding and manufacturing, where membership had been strong, and the reduction in public sector employment due to privatisation and government cutbacks. However, since 1999 membership of trade unions has started to rise again. The Employment Relations Act (1999) means that if 50 per cent plus one of the workforce want to be represented by a union, then that union must be recognised by management. Employers are now more positive in wanting to work with unions.

The majority of trade unions are members of the **Trades Union Congress (TUC)** which represents trade unions in national discussions with the government and employers' organisations like the Confederation of British Industry (CBI).

Each individual trade union represents certain groups of workers. These groups might be in one industry or profession, e.g. the NUT (National Union of Teachers), or the RCN (Royal College of Nursing). There are other unions which represent workers in several industries, for example the TGWU (Transport and General Workers Union) and the AEEU (Amalgamated Engineering and Electrical Union). During the 1980s and 1990s, when the decline in membership of trade unions took place, several unions merged in order to make it easier to negotiate with large companies and employers. For example, the Agriculture Workers and the Seamen joined with the TGWU; two print unions – SOGAT (Society of Graphical and Allied Trades) and the NGA (National Graphical Association) formed one union, the GPMU (Graphical, Paper and Media Union). The largest union is Unison, representing local government employees, with 1.4 million workers. The smallest is the Engineering and Fastner Trade Union with 240 members.

For the employee, trade unions provide a number of benefits:

- the power of being part of a large group when negotiating with employers
- protection against unfair dismissal or victimisation at work
- help on health and safety matters in the workplace
- legal assistance if the employee is looking for compensation from the employer
- in larger unions, strike pay if the employee takes industrial action (see later in this unit)
- insurance schemes where the employee can get lower rates.

For companies there are also benefits from negotiating with trade unions:

- It is easier to negotiate with one group representing a number of workers than individual workers.
- Once a deal is agreed, a union will help to see that it is applied to all its workers.
- A union may take a more realistic and long-term view than would individual workers.
- Unions have built up many years of expertise about an industry or company.

John Monks, the General Secretary of the TUC, addresses the annual conference

A problem for companies has been that in any one business there might be several unions represented. Therefore each issue would have to be negotiated with several groups. In some companies there is now a **single union agreement** so that only one union represents all the workforce, e.g. the AEEU and News International, publishers of *The Times* and *The Sun*, have such an agreement.

TASK 2

In a recent survey of 3000 union members, the following ratings were given to the question 'What do you want unions to do for you?'

Job security – 77 per cent
Preserving pay and pensions – 62 per cent
Increasing pay – 52 per cent
Better pensions – 50 per cent
Union influence with management – 42 per cent
Health and safety – 37 per cent
Shorter working hours – 27 per cent

Unison's television advertisements about the power of the little ants when they stand together against the big bears has struck a deep chord. According to the TUC there were 75 recognition deals between employers and unions in the first 10 months of 1999. In the same survey, the TUC estimated that there might be 5 million people who would like to be members of a trade union. The large number of company mergers and the transfer of workers from public to private sector has created fertile ground for unions.

Source: Adapted from *The Observer*, 9 April 2000.

a Explain the results of the survey given above.

b What do you think 'the power of the little ants when they stand together against the big bears' means in terms of being in a union?

c Why might many more people now want to be part of a trade union?

Negotiations

Some of the following issues may be the basis for collective bargaining:

- Basic pay – how much is earned weekly or monthly?
- Overtime pay – what extra is earned if longer hours are worked?
- Bonus schemes – what extra is earned if production increases?
- Conditions of employment – are there to be changes to the hours of work or length of holiday?
- Redundancies and dismissals – will there be voluntary or compulsory redundancies? What redundancy pay might be offered?
- Organisation of jobs – will individuals be expected to take on more duties?
- Training – how many days' training will be offered to each employee?
- Rules and discipline – are new rules being introduced by management?
- Equal opportunities – is there an equal opportunities policy? Are all groups being treated fairly?
- Health and safety – what safety training is being provided for the introduction of new machinery; what increased protection is being offered?

Although collective bargaining will be different in each company, most negotiations will follow a similar pattern, almost like a television serial:

Episode 1: Both sides meet separately to decide on their specific demands and on their negotiating strategy.

Episode 2: Both sides meet together and state their initial demands or conditions. These are often unrealistic and neither side would expect the other to agree to them. The first meeting is usually short and breaks up without agreement.

Episode 3: Separate meetings, with each side deciding what they might accept from the other to move the two sides closer.

Episode 4: Both sides meet again, and make concessions to each other. New information might be introduced to make the situation clearer. Both sides will move closer towards an agreement. This might be a long meeting, or several meetings.

Episode 5: When both sides feel that they have achieved some of their targets, and that to go further would cause damage, then they will come to an agreement. A written summary will be produced to which both sides can agree.

Once an agreement is reached, it is important that it is communicated to those that it affects, that is the workforce. It has to gain their acceptance before being implemented. Collective bargaining agreements are not legal contracts and they are often broken by both sides. There has been a trend in recent years for some companies to move away from taking part in collective bargaining and to impose decisions on the workforce. But this might well affect the motivation of the workforce.

There has also been a trend for local bargaining to replace national bargaining. This may help some areas where there is low unemployment and shortages of workers and where pay rates tend to be high. In less well-off areas local bargaining may not help to raise the pay of the workforce in comparison to other areas.

Most collective bargaining is between the management of a company and the unions. In the public sector, however, the government is the direct employer or provides the funding. Pay in occupations such as teaching, nursing or the police is determined by committees which include representation from national or local government, from public sector unions and often independent experts.

Another role for unions representing workers in the public services has been to attempt to influence the changes taking place in the structure and organisation of the public sector. There is an increasing trend towards the 'commercialisation' of public sector services; that is the transfer of private sector practices into the public sector or the 'out sourcing' of public sector activities to private organisations. For example, Islington Local Education Authority has been taken over by Nord Anglia, a private sector education organisation, which is now running Islington schools.

TASK 3

Pike Paper Ltd makes paper decorations, selling the majority of its products to wholesalers in October in time for Christmas. It employs 150 workers on the shop floor (120 women and 30 men) as well as 25 office staff. Shop floor workers are paid £220 for a 40-hour week but can earn overtime during busy periods at time and a half. In the office there are two groups: general clerical workers paid £180 per week and designers paid £300 per week. All the workforce is represented by the TGWU. It is April and time for the annual wage negotiation. Management and shop stewards are preparing their policies for the negotiations. Information that both sides are looking at includes the following:

- Pike's profits have fallen over the last year from £250,000 to £25,000 as sales have fallen due to overseas competition.
- A similar business to Pike's, only five miles away, closed down in March.
- Last year's pay rise was only 3 per cent, and 10 production workers accepted voluntary redundancy and were not replaced.
- The present rate of inflation is 2.7 per cent but expected to fall; average pay rises for similar workers have been 4 per cent this year.
- The company has recently won a large order from Asda for next Christmas which could keep the present workforce employed for the next two years.
- There are rumours that the company is considering compulsory redundancies to keep its wage costs down.

a Decide what pay claim the union might make for the coming year and explain your decision

b Decide what offer management might make for the coming year and explain your decision.

c What strategy might the union adopt if the initial pay claim is rejected?

d What strategy might the management adopt if its initial offer is rejected?

e What might be the final outcomes for the negotiations? Explain your reasons for choosing these outcomes.

Industrial action

For both sides the aim of collective bargaining will be to reach an agreement. If such an agreement is not possible, then in large organisations a range of alternatives might be followed:

- Conciliation – the two sides might decide to call in a conciliator, that is someone who is independent and will try to bring the two sides together.

- Arbitration – they might call in an arbitrator, that is someone who is independent and who will actually decide what should be the outcome. **ACAS**, the **Arbitration and Conciliation Advisory Service** might provide such independent people.

- Industrial action – a final alternative for the workers may be to take some form of action at the workplace.

There are a number of different types of industrial action, including the following:

- A strike – a withdrawal of labour for a period of time, e.g. the 2001 London Underground strike. This may be official, that is, recognised by a union, or unofficial, that is, not recognised by a union.

- An overtime ban – where workers work only their contracted hours.

- A work to rule – carrying out work strictly to the rule book and therefore creating a 'go-slow' as corners are no longer cut.

- A boycott – refusing to carry out a duty or refusing to use a particular machine or equipment, e.g. the teaching unions' boycott of National Curriculum testing in 1993.

- A lock out – in this case management keeps groups of workers out of the premises until they sign a new agreement e.g. the dispute at the Timex watch factory in 1993.

The right to take industrial action is a basic freedom for all workers, but in the 1980s the government introduced a series of laws which have affected this right:

- Unions are required to hold a **secret ballot** before they can call for industrial action, and the majority of workers must be in favour.

- A strike can be called only 'in furtherance of a trade dispute in a single organisation or company'. Any unofficial action, or a sympathy strike in support of a group of workers in another company, is not covered by this. Employers therefore could sue the workforce or union for such action to compensate for loss of production.

- Picketing – standing outside a factory to persuade non-strikers to join a strike – can be organised only by the people directly involved and must occur only at the factory where the strike is taking place. This makes 'flying pickets' illegal.

- If employees are dismissed for taking part in an unofficial strike they cannot claim that it is an unfair dismissal to an industrial tribunal (see Unit 29).

Through these laws the government has tried to reduce the number of strikes taking place, in particular unofficial and sympathy strikes. The effect is illustrated in the graph below.

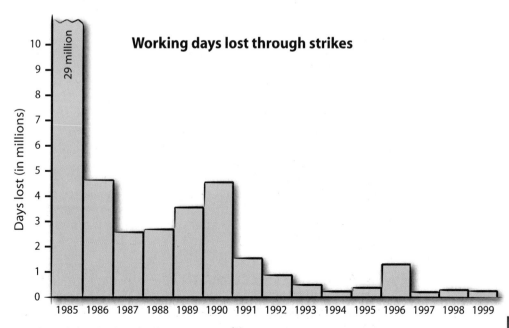

Working days lost through strikes

Source: Annual Abstract of Statistics 2001

TASK 4

Ford faces strike at Dagenham

Ford is heading for a clash with its workforce after union leaders failed to persuade the group to drop plans to halt car production at its Dagenham plant in Essex.

Union officials have called for a meeting of the plant's 7,000 employees and will send out strike ballot papers. The union fears that if the company closes the assembly unit at Dagenham other Ford factories in Britain could face the same fate.

When the strike ballot result is known, the unions will seek a meeting with Ford and the government to discuss job levels at the other factories. The unions claimed that Ford management had promised that the new Fiesta would be built at Dagenham, but that Ford then announced that it would be made in Germany.

Ford said that it would halt car production at Dagenham in 2002 but it would expand the diesel engine plant on the site. Only 1,300 planned redundancies would be made and Dagenham would continue as the largest industrial site in London.

a What is the dispute at Dagenham about?

b What are the arguments that both sides are putting forward in this dispute?

c Why is it necessary for the union to hold a strike ballot before meeting with management at Ford?

d Who do you think is right in this dispute? Explain your reasons.

ASLEF – the train drivers' union

Connex, the French-owned owners of several south-eastern rail services, have just granted their drivers a shorter working week after a one-day strike by their drivers, who are members of ASLEF, the train drivers' union. Connex lost about £1 million in ticket revenue due to the one-day strike and could not afford to let the industrial action go on any longer.

ASLEF is a very centralised and strong union. The rail operating companies are operating on very narrow profit margins and cannot afford to lose passengers. They are also approaching the time when their franchises for the areas they control are coming up for renegotiation.

A driver's basic pay of £26,000 per annum is above that of nurses and teachers.

Job	Gross weekly earnings, including overtime and bonuses (£)
Bar staff	184
Sales assistant	219
Car factory worker	357
Nurse	385
Secondary school teacher	496
Train driver	506
Management consultant	769
Air traffic controller	940
Doctor (GP)	952

With overtime, drivers can earn up to £35,000. The table above shows some comparative earnings.

There is a shortage of drivers at present as a number of older drivers took redundancy deals when the railways were privatised. This means that many drivers have to work on their rest days or work 11-hour shifts. It is a very stressful job, working long hours and with up to 800 people travelling behind the drivers.

As well as the Connex settlement, ASLEF has already done a deal with South West Trains and Virgin train drivers have put in a claim for a rise in basic pay to £35,000 per year. An ASLEF spokesman said: 'We do not aim to use industrial action as our negotiating tool: it is the final resort. But if the train operating companies are resisting meaningful negotiations we have to use the strike wherever and whenever it is necessary.'

Source: Adapted from *The Observer,* 30 January 2000.

Q Questions

1 What type of industrial action is described in this article?
2 From the article, was ASLEF or Connex in a stronger position during the industrial action? Explain your answer.
3 What does the table tell you about the pay of train drivers in comparison with other workers?
4 Can you explain why train drivers earn more than teachers or nurses?
5 If you were the management of Virgin trains, what arguments would you make against the train drivers' claim for basic pay of £35,000?

E Extension

1 How might the safety problems that occurred on the railways at the end of 2000 have affected the bargaining position of ASLEF and the railway companies?
2 Explain why the split up of the railway industry into separate companies might have increased the power of unions like ASLEF.

The changing nature of work

This unit is about the way in which changes in the economic structure, in technology and in society have been having a major impact on the way people work.

At the end of the unit, students should be able to:

- identify key changes in the structure of employment in the UK

- explain the reasons for the decline in employment in manufacturing

- analyse the changes taking place to the number of women at work

- assess the advantages and disadvantages of different types of flexible working

- carry out individual research into the advantages and disadvantages of self-employment

- evaluate different viewpoints about working at home and teleworking.

The changing industrial structure

For the past 40 years the developed countries in the western world such as the USA, Canada, Germany, France, Italy, Spain and the UK have seen a gradual change in their industrial structure. The number of businesses involved in primary production and manufacturing have gradually declined while the number of businesses involved in providing services have gradually increased. As a result of this, the number of jobs in manufacturing has steadily fallen and the number of jobs in services has steadily risen. In some countries this has led to periods of high unemployment as manufacturing workers have found it difficult to retrain for service jobs. But over time the service jobs in western economies have tended to replace the lost manufacturing jobs.

In the UK the trend has been quite dramatic. In 1978, 7 million people were employed in manufacturing. By 2000, this had fallen to 4.2 million, a decrease of 39 per cent. At the same time the number of people employed in the service sector has risen by 36 per cent from 15.6 million to 21.2 million. By 2009 the UK government expects a further 670,000 manufacturing jobs to be lost. Yet more people are now employed in the UK (27 million in 2000) than ever before. The pie charts show how the balance of employment has continued to change since 1971 and will continue to change in the next decade.

Employment by sector

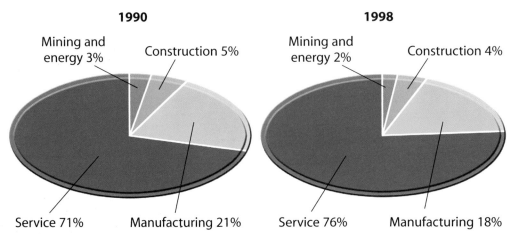

1990
Mining and energy 3% Construction 5%
Service 71% Manufacturing 21%

1998
Mining and energy 2% Construction 4%
Service 76% Manufacturing 18%

In the UK the major decline in jobs in manufacturing has been in engineering, steel-making, car manufacture, clothing and textiles. The largest expansion in services has been in business services such as advertising and customer services. More people in the UK are now employed in call centres responding to customer enquiries and complaints than in steel-making and car manufacture combined.

There are a number of reasons for the decline in manufacturing employment:

- Competition from global producers, especially in countries which pay lower wages, has meant that western manufacturers have lost sales and market share. Textile producers in the UK have found it difficult to compete with producers in Asia, for example.

- Manufacturing companies have invested heavily in new technology and this has reduced the number of employees needed to produce the products. Although the numbers employed in steel-making in the UK has declined, the value of steel produced has increased over the last decade.

- Multinational companies are now able to choose where they produce their products worldwide. They can move production to countries where labour costs are low or where productivity is high. In Europe car manufacturers like Volkswagen have expanded their production in eastern Europe to supply the western European market as unit costs are lower there.

- Service production – especially business and technological services – uses much less capital and offers much higher profit margins. It is much cheaper to set up a web site and a warehouse to sell clothing than to set up a factory to make the clothing.

TASK 1

Job losses at Luton

Griff Rhys Jones is not directly responsible for the recent announcement by Vauxhall that it was going to stop producing cars at Luton in Bedfordshire. He has been featuring in TV adverts as a limo-loving geek who has to make do with a Vauxhall. It is not the quality of the TV adverts that has led to the job losses. However, the growth of the advertising industry could be seen as a symbol of the changes to employment that are taking place.

General Motors management, which owns Vauxhall, made 2,200 manufacturing jobs disappear at Luton by making one phone call. However, think about the amount of non-manufacturing work that went into that decision. Management consultants would have been employed to decide which factories would close. Lawyers and human resource experts would have provided advice on redundancy packages for the workers. A public relations firm would be employed to handle the bad publicity from the decision. And General Motors spends a large amount on advertising. As well as the Griff Rhys Jones TV adverts, it uses Madonna's music to promote its cars and at the Birmingham Motor Show it put a car in a fish tank for publicity.

Source: Adapted from *The Observer*, 17 December 2000.

a Give four examples of business services which General Motors might have used when deciding to close the Luton plant.

b Why do you think General Motors made the decision to close the Luton factory?

c Why does the article suggest that the growth of advertising is a symbol of changes to employment that are taking place?

Women in the workforce

In addition to these structural changes to employment taking place there has been a major change in the number of women working over the past 30 years. In the late 1970s 38 per cent of people employed were female. By 1986, this had risen to 42 per cent and by 2000, to 44 per cent. Some 15 million jobs are now done by men and 13 million by women. However the increase in the numbers of women working has been almost totally in the service sector, and shows the same trend described in the last section.

This growth has been for a number of reasons:

- The Equal Pay Act of 1970 and the Sex Discrimination Act of 1975 (see Unit 31) have provided women with legal protection against unfair discrimination at work.

- Social changes, with more and better childcare facilities and nursery education, have allowed more women to return to work shortly after having children. Mothers and fathers now have better rights to take time off after a child is born or if the child is unwell.

- More women are gaining qualifications and degrees and are therefore able to compete better with men for jobs.

- Many of the new jobs created have wanted part-time or **flexible working** and this often suits women with younger families.

Although more women are working, they are still facing problems in gaining equal status with men at work:

- The average hourly wage for women is only 82 per cent of the average for men.

- Many women work only part time – 83 per cent of part-time workers are women – and this makes their earnings lag a long way behind their full-time, male colleagues.

- Many women are in low-skilled jobs with limited access to training.

- Some jobs, e.g. construction and engineering, are still mainly limited to men.

- There are almost twice as many male managers as female managers. Because women sometimes take time away from their employment to have children, they can lose opportunities for promotion.

TASK 2

Look at the table showing the percentage of employees by gender.

Employment category	Men		Women	
	1991	2000	1991	2000
Managers and administrators	16	19	8	11
Professional	10	12	8	10
Technical	8	9	10	11
Clerical and secretarial	8	8	29	25
Craft and related	21	17	4	2
Personal and protective services	7	8	14	17
Selling	6	6	12	12
Plant and machine operators	15	14	5	4
Other occupations	8	8	10	8
All employees (million)	11.8	12.8	10.1	11.0

a i Which are the two most important employment categories for men in 2000?

ii Which are the two most important categories for women in 2000?

iii Explain why there are differences in these categories for men and women.

b Have there been any major changes in employment patterns for men or women between 1991 and 2000?

c In groups, discuss the question: 'Should women be earning the same level of pay as men in the UK?' Decide your arguments for and against and present them to the class.

Flexible working

In 2000, 18 million people in the UK had full-time paid jobs and were employed by an organisation. This is still the main way that people work. However, a substantial and growing number of people work in a more flexible way.
In 2000:

- 5.7 million people worked part time.
- 2.9 million people were self-employed.
- 1.6 million people were temporary workers.
- 0.7 million people worked at home.

It is expected that changes in technology and communications will mean that more and more people will be working in a more flexible way in the future.

Part-time work is defined as working for less than 30 hours per week for an employer. Businesses have been taking on more part-time workers in recent years as they provide more flexibility than full-time workers. A supermarket opening for 24 hours may need shopworkers who can cover evening or nighttime shifts. A firm of accountants may want clerical assistance for five mornings a week. Because of domestic commitments individuals may prefer to work for less than 30 hours per week and would find flexible working times to their benefit. Recent legislation now gives part-time workers who have been with an organisation for a period of time the same legal rights as those in **full-time work**. However, they may not have the same access to training or the same promotion chances as full-time workers.

A variation of part-time work is a **job share**. This is where one job is done by two people. For example in a hospital, a ward manager might work for 18 hours per week and share the job with another ward manager who works for 18 hours. For the organisation this is one full-time job, but for the two sharing the job they are working part-time. Problems can occur if one of the job-share partners leaves – it may be difficult to find another person wanting to job share. The two people involved would also need to have a time when they can up-date each other on any work that is not complete.

Temporary work is when a business takes on workers for a short time to meet a sudden rush of work. They will be given a short-term contract for their work. The postal service at Christmas, farms during harvest, shops during sales, clerical 'temps' in offices have been a feature of the labour market for many years. But there are now more temporary workers in the professions, especially education, health, public administration and IT. For employers, temporary workers provide more flexibility; when demand for their product or service falls they can quickly reduce their wage bill. Businesses, however, sometimes find that temporary workers lack the skills or motivation that they need. Recent European legislation also gives temporary staff who have worked for a period of time in one organisation similar rights to holidays, equal pay, etc. as full-time employees.

Self-employment involves individuals who work for themselves. The numbers of self-employed people have grown slowly but steadily over the past 20 years. There has been considerable encouragement from governments in the form of grants, advice and support for people to set up their own business. Self-employment is most common in the craft occupations and professional services – from plumbers and electricians to IT consultants and school inspectors. It is often useful for larger businesses to be able to subcontract work to self-employed people. For example, a company which organises pop concerts might subcontract the design of posters to a self-employed person working independently. For the self-employed the advantages of 'being your own boss' have to outweigh the lack of a regular salary, the risks of not getting enough work and the costs of pension and National Insurance contributions they have to find.

Homeworkers may be self-employed or they may be employed by a company but able to carry out their work at home. The majority of homeworkers are women and they provide craft or professional services. A freelance journalist might work from home, as might a music teacher or a clothes maker.

Many homeworkers rely on the use of telephone, fax, e-mail and computer to work from home. These are known as **teleworkers**. There is also a substantial group of workers – 0.8 million in the UK – who work partly at home and partly in an office. Some companies which operate national call centres are now considering setting up individual teleworkers in their homes to receive customer enquiries. The table shows the advantages and disadvantages of homeworking.

Advantages	Disadvantages
Time and money spent travelling is saved.	You need a high level of personal motivation to avoid other distractions.
There is more control over when and how you work.	There is a lack of human contact.
It is easier to manage family commitments.	You need space to work in and the right technology.
There are no interruptions from a busy office.	There is less distinction between work and home.
	It is difficult for a business to monitor what homeworkers are doing.

TASK 3

Using your family and friends as contacts, try to find someone who is self-employed. There might be someone who has an office in your local high street. Arrange to carry out a short interview with that person (no more than 15 minutes). Devise your own questions before the interview, but try to find out the following information:

- how long they have been self-employed and what they did before
- why they became self-employed
- what benefits they see from being self-employed
- what disadvantages they see from being self-employed
- who their major customers are
- who their major competitors are
- what their future plans are, e.g. whether they are likely to continue to be self-employed.

Write up your research in the form of a short newspaper article about the person and his or her business.

KEY TERMS

Flexible working – offering the workforce opportunities to work at different times, in different ways and in different places.

Full-time work – working for more than 30 hours per week for an employer.

Homeworkers – people working from home either on a self-employed basis or employed by a company.

Job share – where one job is done by two people, usually through splitting the time at work.

Part-time work – working for less than 30 hours per week for an employer.

Teleworkers – those working at home who make use of telecommunications to do their job.

Temporary workers – where people are employed for a short period of time to meet an increased demand for work that the existing workforce can't cope with.

Office life is doomed

The teleworker's teleworker must be a German, **Volker Kreiger**. He works for a Swiss telecommunications company with customers all over Europe. 'I have three different offices. Twenty per cent of the time I am at home in Germany; 50 per cent of the time I am travelling and using my laptop computer hooked up to a mobile phone; 30 per cent of the time I am in one of the company's offices. About half of my work is 'virtual' and half face to face with customers. I think I can reduce this to 20 per cent. Today's school children will be natural teleworkers. To them using the tools of teleworking will be normal and not new.'

Anna Brady works from her flat in Dublin for a company with offices in California and New York. 'Only one or two people in the entire company actually work onsite', she says. 'The company runs newsgroups which gives you an idea of the history of different projects and of the personalities of other members of the virtual team. When I visited the US for the first time it was a surprise to see how some of these people looked in real life.'

Alan Denbigh, the director of the Teleworker Association, says, 'The conventional 9–5 workplace is actually unsuitable for work. The buildings are often unhealthy and there are constant interruptions.' He also criticises the fixed hours, the clothing and the office hierarchies. Teleworking will increase people's productivity.

'Moving a business from a high-tech office in London to a Kent cottage complete with hot and cold running children requires some degree of thought,' writes **John Graham-Hunt**, a TV producer. 'The theory seemed simple. You are working from home but you are not at home, you are at work and, ideally should not be disturbed ... That was how it was when you had a proper job and that's how it should work now ... Now I do it at home the myth is exploded ... I'm fair game for anything, from duck-feeding and DIY to shopping at Sainsbury's and the school run. And will somebody please tell me what fascinates children about a parent's office?'

Source: Adapted from The Times, 14 February 2000, and *The Observer*, 3 September 2000.

Q Questions

1 Three of the people talking above are in favour of teleworking. What reasons are given in the articles?

2 What problems with working at home are identified by John Graham-Hunt?

3 What advantages would there be for businesses if more of their employees worked at home?

4 Do you agree that today's school children will be natural teleworkers? In groups, develop your arguments for and against. Present your ideas to the class.

5 Are there any benefits to the community as a whole if more people work at home?

E Extension

1 What does Volker Kreiger mean when he says 'Half of my work is virtual and half is face to face with customers'?

2 How might more teleworking increase the profitability of companies who employ teleworkers?

INDEX

Acknowledgements

We are grateful to the following for permission to reproduce copyright photographs:

3i page 165; Ace Photo Agency pages 7 below (Berry Bingel), 64, 122 above right (Benelux Press), below left (Harry Lomax), 241 below left (Harry Lomax); Allen and Harris page 52; Art Directors & TRIP pages 6 centre right (H Rogers), 27 (J Okwesa), 82 (H Rogers), 154 (H Rogers), 162 (H Rogers), 179 (H Rogers), 213 (P Kwan), 231 (H Rogers); Auto Express Picture Library pages 12 below right, 146; Barclays page 25; Boots The Chemists page 19; Business Franchise Association page 39; Cadbury Schweppes page 19; Camera Press page 127; Corbis Stockmarket pages 1, 2 below, 73, 117, 153, 207; Dartington Crystal page 185; Dorling Kindersley Picture Library pages 7 centre, 11 right, 12 above, 12 below left, 36, 67 above; Eye Ubiquitous page 241 below right; Forest Life Picture Library page 6 above; David Hoffmann pages 15 above right, below left, below right; Katz Pictures pages 48 (Richard Smith), 65 (Erin Elder/Saba-Rea), 111 (Richard Baker); Leslie Garland Picture Library page 5 above; Life File page 245 above left (Frank Popely), above right (Mark Herbert), below left (Ray Ward); Littlewoods Stores Ltd page 41; McDonald's page 24; Marks & Spencer pages 21 right, 40; NatWest page 136; NEXT pages 40, 110; PA Photos pages 13 (EPA), 54, 84 (Paul Barker), 137, 250 (John Curtis); Parker page 136; Photofusion/David Monford page 20; Pictor International pages 11 left, 233; Popperfoto/Reuters pages 23, 33, 46 below, 76, 254; Powerstock page 241 left, centre right; Prontaprint page 114; Rex Features pages 6 below, 35 above (Adrian Sherratt), 35 below, 138 (Baumann Arnaud); Royal Bank of Scotland page 136; Sainsbury's pages 21 left, 96; Select page 5 centre; Shell LiveWire page 159; Telegraph Colour Library/V.C.L/Tipp Howell pages 5 below, 259; Topham Picturepoint pages 7 above, 46 above (Yurchenko), 67 below left, 115, 142 above left, 143, 169; Unilever plc for pages 92, 99.

We are grateful to the following for permission to reproduce copyright material:

Consumers' Association for extracts from the articles 'Take care with food claims' in *Which?* May 1993, 'Tariffic choices – competition for mobile phone customers' and 'The closure of C&A' in *Which?* September 2000; The Economist Newspaper Limited for table 'The most valuable global brands, 1998' in *The Economist* 12 June 1999; Financial Times Ltd for extracts from the articles 'UK house prices levelling' in *Financial Times* 27 June 2000, 'Wickes profits up 20%' in *Financial Times* 3 August 2000, 'Character shares fall 17%' in *Financial Times* 18 August 2000; Guardian News Services for extracts from articles 'Reorganisation at the BBC' in *The Observer* 30 January 2000, 'M&S banks on drastic new makeover' in *The Guardian* 30 March 2001; Independent Newspapers (UK) Ltd for extracts from the articles 'Where the money comes from' and 'Where the money goes to' in *The Independent* 22 March 2000, 'Hundreds of women share £12m bias payout' in *The Independent* 8 May 2000, 'The beer drinking baron from Belgium' in *The Independent* 28 June 2000 and 9 November 2000, 'Houses too pricey for "backbone of Britain"' in *The Independent* 3 August 2000, 'Mind the Gap' in *The Independent* 16 August 2000, 'Worse to come for clothing retailers' in *The Independent* 21 August 2000, 'Can the Olympics put the spring back in Nike's step?' in *The Independent* 13 September 2000, 'Smallest firms lag in using the Internet' in *The Independent* 30 October 2000; Manchester Evening News for extracts from the articles 'Superstores in search of new frontiers' and 'Pub battle set for showdown' in *Manchester Evening News* 20 October 1996, 'Japanese have no yen for euro-less Britain' in *Manchester Evening News* 4 July 2000; MBA Publishing (www.thetimes100.co.uk) for extracts from the articles 'The success of Pritt Stick', 'Jaguar's lean production', Waterstone's case study, 'Training in Autoglass'; News International for extract from the article 'Pop music centre hits low note' in *The Times* 4 February 2000; Telegraph Group Limited for extracts from the articles '75% of British voters say euro is a failure' in *The Daily Telegraph* 13 March 2000, '50 ways to give the customer better deal' in *The Daily Telegraph* 21 March 2000, 'Honda to create 1,000 UK jobs' in *The Daily Telegraph* 23 March 2000, 'Hold onto your Next trousers' in *The Daily Telegraph* 24 March 2000; www.bized.ac.uk for extracts from the articles 'Product development at British Aerospace', 'Quick Lamb', 'British Aerospace Company Facts'.

AQA (SEG) examination questions are reproduced by permission of the Assessment and Qualifications Alliance.

Crown copyright material is reproduced under Class Licence Number C01W0000039 with the permission of the Controller of HMSO and the Queen's Printer for Scotland.

In some instances we have been unable to trace the copyright owners of material and we would appreciate any information which would enable us to do so.